Caring for the Harvest Force
in the New Millennium

OTHER TITLES IN EMS SERIES:

#1 *SCRIPTURE AND STRATEGY: The Use of the Bible in Postmodern Church and Mission,* David J. Hesselgrave

#2 *CHRISTIANITY AND THE RELIGIONS: A Biblical Theology of World Religions,* Edward Rommen and Harold Netland, eds.

#3 *SPIRITUAL POWER AND MISSIONS: Raising the Issues,* Edward Rommen, ed. (out of print)

#4 *MISSIOLOGY AND THE SOCIAL SCIENCES: Contributions, Cautions and Conclusions,* Edward Rommen and Gary Corwin, eds.

#5 *THE HOLY SPIRIT AND MISSION DYNAMICS,* C. Douglas McConnell, ed.

#6 REACHING THE RESISTANT: Barriers and Bridges for Mission, J. Dudley Woodberry, ed.

#7 TEACHING THEM OBEDIENCE IN ALL THINGS: Equipping for the 21st Century, Edgar J. Ellison, ed.

#8 WORKING TOGETHER WITH GOD TO SHAPE THE NEW MILLENNIUM: Opportunities and Limitations, Kenneth Mulholland and Gary Corwin, eds.

Caring for the Harvest Force in the New Millennium

Tom A. Steffen
F. Douglas P. Pennoyer, eds.

Evangelical Missiological Society Series
Number 9

visit us at missionbooks.org

Caring for the Harvest Force in the New Millennium

Copyright 2000 by Evangelical Missiological Society
All Rights Reserved

No part of this book may be reproduced, stored in a retrieval system, or transmitted in any form or by any means—electronic, mechanical, photocopy, recording, or otherwise—without prior written permission from the publisher, except brief quotations used in connection with reviews in magazines or newspapers. For permission, email permissions@wclbooks.com. For corrections, email editor@wclbooks.com.

Published by William Carey Publishing (formerly William Carey Library)
10 W. Dry Creek Cir
Littleton, CO 80120 | www.missionbooks.org

William Carey Publishing is a ministry of Frontier Ventures
Pasadena, CA | www.frontierventures.org

ISBN: 978-1-64508-522-5 (paperback)

Printed Worldwide
27 26 25 24 23   2 3 4 5 6   IN

Library of Congress Cataloging-in-Publication Data on file with the publisher

CONTENTS

Author Profiles

Introduction *F. Douglas Pennoyer* 1

Theological Foundations of Care Giving

1 Spiritual Foundations of Care Giving *Will Norton* 11
2 The Pastoral Epistles on Care Giving *Charles Chaney* 29
3 A Theological Journey of Care *J. Julius Scott, Jr.* 43

Challenges of Care Giving

4 Caring for a Camcorder Culture *Paul Metzger* 69
5 Caring for a Coming Anarchy *Larry Poston* 89
6 Caring for Those in Crisis *Robert Klamser* 117

Contexts of Care Giving

7 Caring for Partnerships *Jehu Hanciles* 141
8 Caring for Indigenous Harvesters *Sue Russell* 163
9 Caring for Hungarians *Joi Van Deventer* 181
10 Caring for Members *Brent Lindquist* 199
11 Caring for GenXers *Tom Steffen* 213
12 Caring for the Children *Paul Cochrane* 231
13 Bibliography 243
14 Appendix 259

Author Profiles

Charles Chaney is professor of missions at Southwestern Baptist Seminary. E-mail: Chaschaney@Texas.net

Paul Cochrane serves with The Evangelical Alliance Mission (TEAM) as Regional Director for Southern Africa and South Asia. He is co-founder, along with Richard Edlin, of the Intermission MK Education Consultation. E-mail: pcochrane@teamworld.org

Jehu Hanciles is a Sierra Leonean by birth, and currently Associate Professor of Mission History and Globalization at the School of World Mission, Fuller Theological Seminary. E-mail: hanciles@fuller.edu

Robert Klamser is Executive Director of Crisis Consulting International, 9452 Telephone Road, No. 223, Ventura, CA 93004. Tel (805) 642-2549; Fax (805) 642-1748
E-mail: CrisisConsulting@xc.org Web: www.HostageRescue.org

Brent Lindquist is a clinical psychologist and President of Link Care Center in Fresno, California. E-mail: BrentLindquist@Compuserve.com

Paul Metzger is Assistant Professor of Christian Theology & Theology of Culture at Multnomah Biblical Seminary. E-mail: pmetzger@multnomah.edu

Will Norton, Sr. is professor of Missions at Reformed Theological Seminary in Charlotte, North Carolina. He was instrumental in the founding and development of the AEPM and EMS. (803)547-7011

F. Douglas Pennoyer is Dean of the School of Intercultural Studies, Biola University. E-mail: doug_pennoyer@peter.biola.edu

Larry Poston is professor of religion at Nyack College in Nyack, New York. He served from 1980 to 1984 with Greater Europe Mission at the Nordic Bible Institute and is the author of two books on Islam.
E-mail: Larry.Poston@nyack.edu

Sue Russell served 17 years with Wycliffe Bible Translators in Southeast Asia. She is an associate professor at the School of Intercultural Studies, Biola University. E-mail: sue_russell@peter.biola.edu

J. Julius Scott, Jr. is Emeritus Professor of Biblical and Historical Studies in Wheaton College Graduate School in Wheaton, Illinois.
E-mail: juliusscott@earthlink.net

Tom Steffen served 15 years in the Philippines and is associate Professor of Intercultural Studies at the School of Intercultural Studies at Biola University in La Mirada, California. E-mail: tom_steffen@peter.biola.edu

Joi Van Deventer is a missionary with Church Resource Ministries working in Hungary. E-mail: 74401.3014@compuserve.com

Introduction

"We can help your missionary," a brochure cover boldly proclaims in large print.[1] Inside the headlines emphasize that there's a vast need for Christian care and support for cross-cultural workers. Taking care of the needs of the hurting person and restoring the individual back to healthy functions, we are told, is both loving, and a sound economic policy. This "Mom and Pop" non-profit missions care firm features a dedicated couple with three Masters, a Ph.D, an M.D., a board certification in Preventive Medicine, 25 years of experience, and over 11,000 hours of counseling in cross-cultural environments. They cover everything from intensive care for couples, families, and individuals to educational workshops, organizational consulting, and applied research.

"Missionary Care: But we have this treasure in jars of clay (2 Cor. 4:7 NIV)" is a web page title for a group of member care colleagues who come together for consultations, counseling, training, and special projects.[2] They believe that world evangelization and plans to impact unreached people groups will fall short unless care is provided for missionaries. This group, like the agency above is not only providing short term counseling and seminar training but they are researching topics, analyzing data, and publishing articles on missionary care topics. They are not alone. An *International Guide for Member Care Resources* lists nearly a hundred agencies spread around the world on all

---

[1] Heartstream Resources, 101 Herman Lee Circle, Liverpool PA 17045. Heartstream@compuserve.com
[2] Member Care Associates, PO Box 4, High Wycombe HP14 3YX, England

continents.³ The 21ˢᵗ Century missions buzz word is "member care" and caring for missionaries has become a ministry industry.

Nearly half a century has past since the dramatic martyrdom of Jim Elliot and four others at the hands of the Auca Indians. The great waves of post World War II missionaries, and their children, discovered a harsh reality. At times it felt like it would have been easier to die a martyr than to suffer through a long, traumatic missionary career. Personal, familial, and ministry stresses and failures imposed a life sentence on some who felt imprisoned in the body's mental institution and strapped in a strait jacket of conflicting emotions and unresolved relationships.

We've come a long way since Clyde Narramore was the only Christian psychologist; the Narramore Christian Foundation began the first MK reentry seminars; and, the Rosemead School of Psychology was the only Christian institution offering a Doctorate in Psychology. Missiology, as the science of doing missions, has matured as an academic discipline with research studies as well as practical field applications. Cross-cultural training programs are becoming finely tuned to the actual needs of the worker, and area specific in terms of language and culture. The local church is learning to not only provide money but to encourage, mentor, and provide emotional support. Mission agencies are now aware of the complexities of selection, training, sending, and supporting missionary families. While there is room for improvement all around, the mission work force is better educated, trained, and finally, better cared for in the field. With

---

[3] See Kelly O'Donnell "An International Guide For Member Care Resources" in *Too Valuable to Lose: Exploring the Causes and Cures of Missionary Attrition,* William D. Taylor, ed. (Pasadena: William Carey Library, 1997), pp. 325-338.

years of foundational experience behind us, how do we care for the harvest force in the new millennium?

Caring for the Harvest Force in the New Millennium

The purpose of the Evangelical Missiological Society is to advance the cause of world evangelization through study and evaluation of mission concepts and strategies from a biblical perspective with a view to commending sound mission theory and practice to churches, mission agencies, and the schools of missionary training around the world. Publication of the papers presented at the annual gathering of society helps to fulfill this EMS purpose statement. This volume continues the EMS publication series by presenting an edited version of selected papers from the November, 2000 annual meeting in Nashville, Tennessee. The editors have also added several papers from the regional meetings held last year.

The 2000 theme was "Caring for the Harvest Force in the New Millennium" and this volume contains papers on various topics related to caring for the harvesters and the harvested. Member care is a broad subject encompassing many disciplines and sub fields of study and these papers are not intended to cover the entire gamut of such an expansive, evolving topic. We have chosen to arrange the selected papers into three divisions: Theological Foundations for Care Giving; Challenges for Care giving; and, Contexts for Care Giving.

Theological Foundations for Care Giving

Three papers contribute to our understanding of the Biblical underpinnings of member care. Will Norton's "Spiritual Foundations for Care Giving" takes us back to the first century for a look at the "Jesus Paradigm" of the first century to see if we have overlooked the obvious. Can we find spiritual foundations which are beneficial for the Harvest Force to complete the witness to His grace as the new millennium begins? His study reviews the disciples understanding (or lack thereof) after the crucifixion and resurrection of Jesus. Norton looks at the change that occurred in their lives, and observes the growth of their witness to the Lord as a response of their commitment bonding with Him as the ascended Care Giver. He also observes the result of their conduct as the Lord added numerically to the church and they continued their care giving to the first century Harvest Force.

Charles Chaney in "The Pastoral Epistles on Care Giving" reminds us that the "Pastoral Epistles" are three letters written by the leader of a missionary team to two veteran missionaries. He draws attention to Paul's care for two members of the harvest force, Titus and Timothy, and suggests that we can learn from Paul's missionary instructions, nurturing, and mentoring. Chaney raises a question that we must face as member care becomes a well-defined, systematic practice: "Are our approaches in caring for the harvest force informed more by the various social sciences of modernity or by biblical example and teaching?"

Juluis Scott's "A Theological Journey of Care" is a unique description of a personal odyssey of discovery. He discovers that Biblical, rather than systematic, theology is the best place to start "doing" theology in and for the non-Western, Two Thirds World. Those of us who cut our teeth on intercultural communications, grew up with Missiology, and have lived, ministered, and researched in cross-cultural settings with the Church around the world, will deeply appreciate Scott's journey. The world came to his theology classroom, the professor became the student, and the students guided him through an experiential learning exercise not covered in the syllabus. Scott takes us inside the paradigm shift without using "missiologicalese," the familiar language we all speak and write. But make no mistake about it, he understands the key principles. A concluding observation is a testimony to a complete conversion experience: "...the student of the Bible will seek to pierce to the very heart of its message to find its concepts and principles about God, the universe and their relationship and then apply that message in appropriate forms in the modern world."

Challenges of Care Giving

The challenges of care giving are addressed in three papers by Paul Metzger, Larry Poston, and Robert Klamser. In "Caring for a Camcorder Culture" Metzger tells us that fragmentation is a characteristic of the age of camcorder productions. He warns that when the Church uses doctrine to guard against discomfort, it deconstructs Christ. Metzgar calls the Church to embrace an apologetic so embodied with the empowering presence of Christ that it overcomes devolution and disintegration.

Poston's "Caring in the Coming Anarchy" asks us to consider planning and training now for possible deteriorating world situations that might lead to political and social anarchy. He suggests we manage persecution well, gear up for displaced peoples, rethink several family issues, avoid a dependency on technology, study the science of war, and prepare for underground Christian living. He suggests we need holistic, multi-disciplinary, spiritually based training regimens analogous to those of the Green Berets, the Navy Seals, or the Army Rangers. Christians, he warns, must be prepared to deal with chaotic political, economic, social and religious conditions around the world.

Robert Klamser's "Caring for Those in Crisis" paper created a stir at the Nashville meetings because Bob was nowhere to be found at the time of his presentation.[4] A fax arrived at the conference explaining that he had been called away to deal with a hostage situation somewhere in the world. It was an unequaled opportunity to underscore the importance of member care and the reality missionaries face in a troubled world. In this paper, Klamser emphasizes that external security factors, and the organization's competence and approach to handling security, are a major factor in the overall health of the missionary or Christian worker, and thus they are a major factor in the effectiveness of the ministry of the organization. He presents some common characteristics that mission organization leadership would do well to understand and consider as part of the overall program of care for their personnel. He discusses the elements of a foundational security management plan involving risk management, contingency planning and training. Klamser's paper sets forth several response models and provides a helpful outline of the key elements of crisis management.

Contexts of Care Giving

Six papers in this division deal with particular contexts of care giving: partnerships; local harvesters; a specific people group--Hungarians; member care in general; GenXers; and missionary children. Hanciles' "Caring for Partnerships" paper sounds a clarion call for a deliberate internationalization of structures, and leadership and ministries geared towards a global missions movement. He says it is time to reflect on what models or strategies Third World missionaries will/should adopt as they become the largest segment of the Protestant missionary force.

---

[4] See Kenneth Mulholland, "Caring for the Harvest Force in the New Millennium: Do new conditions call for new paradigms?" EMS Occasional Bulletin, (Winter 2001) Vol. 14, No.1, pp. 1-2.

Introduction 7

While there is much to learn from the earlier western missionary enterprise, the non-western movement does not have the educational, economic and technological advantages of the former nor the protection of strong economic and military powers that the West enjoyed. Yet, he points out, non-western Christianity has a certain vigor and vitality that can stimulate a healthy interdependence.

In "Caring for the Indigenous Harvesters" Sue Russell focuses on the indigenous harvest missions force, converts already on-site. She proposes that one of the most effective ways to care for the indigenous harvest force is through facilitating and enabling partnerships. Russell presents the theological foundation and a missiological framework for developing partnerships that would provide the support, training and care to enable the indigenous harvest force to effectively participate in missions. She discusses mission strategies and new technology that promote partnership and care of the indigenous harvest force. She suggests that training is needed for the expatriate to work in partnerships.

Joi Van Deventer turns our attention to a particular people group, the Hungarians of Eastern Europe. In "Caring for Hungarians" she uses tenets from educational anthropology to answer the cultural issues that inhibit learning in the Hungarian context as she teaches and trains teachers. She show how four tenets can inform curriculum design efforts and how they can reveal many of the hidden relationships concealed in the educational process. She demonstrates care for Hungarians by applying insights from educational anthropology which helps form a new approach to cross-cultural curriculum development. While acknowledging that it needs to be carefully tested for cross-cultural application in real contexts, it holds great promise for further activity in designing cross-cultural curriculum. Van

Deventer is hopeful that a further examination of additional elements of the training arena, will reveal more insights about the adult learning contexts in Hungary.

Brent Lundquist as a psychologist, and director of a behavioral health management service organization care providing agency, approaches the context of care giving by appealing for a balanced approach drawing from the wisdom of multiple disciplines. In "Caring for Members" he clearly states that the overarching goal of member care is not helping alone, but helping people to become effective. People should be assisted to move in an intentional direction which will make them more effective in their ministry sphere and become "closer" to the people they are called to serve. Lundquist will warm the hearts of linguists and language trainers for he advocates including the linguistic component in the member care equation. With more and more people coming into missions from "dysfunctional" backgrounds he wants us to think about the issues of how to manage these individuals through appropriate member care strategies, rather than exclude these people. And finally, he issues a plea for cooperation and help in the member care arena while offering six ways we can help each other.

Tom Steffen looks at the incoming population of missions personnel, the GenXers, and sees two preferences that will impact mission strategies in the new millennium: the need for connection, and the proclivity to piece-meal participation. He challenges mission leaders to think in terms of long-term ministry through short-term assignments because that's the GenXer's mentality. Instead of chastising GenXers a for lack of commitment and the need for strong connection, mission leaders must learn to guide them from short term to longer term commitiments. And to keep from overwhelming those who have a difficult time making a long-term commitment, wise mission leadership will lead GenXers to a comprehensive plan with a shared goal in mind delivered in piece-meal fashion. Steffen also believes that this generation has the potential to take missions to a higher level in strategic partnerships than possibly any previous mission generation.

Paul Cochrane's "Caring for the Children" takes us back to the roots of member care, the education of missionary children in mission agency sponsored schools, This was one of the first arenas for partnership and cooperation across denominational lines, and even some mission agencies who maintained strict boundaries and distinct lines of separation joined with others for the common goal of delivering a quality education in the field. Cochrane explores the pros and cons of that collaboration and considers suggestions for future deeper and more intentional cooperation. He sees future needs in these educational topics: international curriculum; wholistic education; urban location; internationalization of leadership; and, formal relationships with nationals. Cochrane compliments the 36 mission agencies doing MK education and thinks their track record is remarkable. He is encouraged by the involvement of the Association of Christian Schools International with both North American MK schools, as well as national Christian schools. The current activities in creating strategic partnerships in mission for church planting, he says, can only help achieve greater collaboration for MK education. He wants someone to take the initiative and set out a strategic plan for future MK education and suggests that organizations like the International Missionary Kid Educational Consultation can provide direction to the mission community in the developing the necessary strategic plans.

Conclusion

Two crisis events separated by nearly half a century involving missionary planes and tragic deaths show the progress of care for missionary workers and the growth of support systems in the member care business. When the Acua Indian incident of 1956 happened, there was no community of trained care givers to help with the aftermath of the martyrdom. The recent downing of a ABWE missionary plane in Peru because it was mistaken for a drug running plane, and the untimely death of a missionary woman and her baby, brought into action mission agency personnel, local church leaders, crisis counselors, and a host of people prepared to offer a variety of member care services to the affected family members. We have grown in this important missions arena, and these twelve papers provide the evidence that care has moved beyond a simplistic approach, beyond even just crisis counseling, to carefully constructed systems of loving, and sharing talents and gifts in a variety of professions and educational disciplines.

F. Douglas Pennoyer, Dean
School of Intercultural Studies
Biola University
La Mirada, CA

Theological Foundations of Care Giving

Chapter 1

Spiritual Foundations of Care Giving

Will Norton, Sr.

Missionary leaders such as A. T. Pierson and A. B. Simpson led the charge to close out the 19th century with a special missionary thrust. A sense of optimism prevailed as the great missionary conference convened in New York City in 1900. Not unlike the end of the 19th century, the leadership of the evangelical community at the close of the 20th century put forth a similar end-of-the-century thrust for world evangelization. Witness the great effort of AD2000 and Beyond, the Frontiers movement, the Adopt-A-People effort and the 10/40 Window.

Meanwhile the call goes out to reinvigorate missions in the new millennium. Studies such as *Transforming Mission* by David Bosch and, more recently, *Changing The Mind Of Missions; Where Have We Gone Wrong* by James Engel and William Dyrness challenge us through scholarly research in history and theology as well as the social sciences to re-evaluate the ways and means of modern evangelical global outreach.

In spite of such strong emphases on completing the biblical task of world evangelization, church planting and growth over a 100 year period, numerous study conferences, both evangelical and ecumenical, demographic studies and the development of sophisticated sociological data centered in evangelism and cross-cultural communication, not to overlook the phenomena of 70 years of linguistic triumph in reducing unwritten languages and translating the Scriptures for the forgotten peoples of the world, with missionary giving at an all time high, local congregations involved in short term missions in an unprecedented way, the Urbana Missionary Conventions still attracting thousands of students to study, pray for and commit to global evangelism and church outreach, and the involvement of non-western churches sending thousands of their members in cross-cultural witness, the task of Jesus' Harvest Force remains uncompleted. So new paradigms are suggested for the new millennium.

It might be more productive, however, to take a fresh look at the "Jesus Paradigm" of the first century — just in case we might have overlooked the obvious. Hebrews 13:8 reminds us cogently, "Jesus Christ is the same yesterday, today and forever." We might, perhaps, discover some abiding spiritual foundation, beneficial for the Harvest Force to complete the witness to His grace as the new millennium begins. The reader is exhorted in Hebrews 13:7 to, "Remember those who led you, who spoke the Word of God to you, and considering the result of their conduct, imitate their faith" (all quotes taken from KJV).

Let us return, therefore, to the first century once again and observe those who led us initially and spoke the word of God and consider the result of their conduct in order to imitate their faith. This study will review the understanding (or lack thereof) among the disciples after the crucifixion and resurrection of Jesus. We will observe the change occurring in their lives as Jesus reviewed His death and resurrection in light of the teaching of the Old Testament. We will observe the growth of the witness to the Lord as the disciples responded with their commitment, bonding with Him as the ascended Lord. We will also observe the result of their conduct as He added to the church and caring to the first century Harvest Force.

The Harvest Force is our *current* term for the disciples who "followed" Jesus and who "learned" of Him for three years (Mt 11:29). It is awesome to observe, however, that Jesus could claim *not one* Harvest Force worker on resurrection day! Immediately before His crucifixion Jesus quoted from Zechariah (Zech 13; Mt 26:31) that the Shepherd would be taken and the sheep scattered. Consequently on resurrection day He stood *alone* at the open tomb at the breaking of dawn. He had to start anew to assemble His Harvest Force.

Heading in the direction of Emmaus (Luke 24), their backs to the Lord, eyes glassy with dismay and straining for the security of home, two of Jesus' would-be Harvest Force tried to talk out their distress and devastation between themselves. Then Jesus caught up with them, the "heretics!" in denial of Jesus' resurrection. Their hopes had been shattered at the tomb where Jesus' body was placed. In fact, the Eleven in Jerusalem were in total denial, rejecting the words of the women who had seen and heard the angels' report. Luke states, "...these words appeared to them as nonsense and they would not believe them" (Luke 24:11, Mark 16:14; John 20:9).

Using non-directed counseling methods, Jesus drew out of their innermost beings their erroneous concepts and anxieties issuing from their misunderstanding of the nature of the Messiah, "...a Prophet, powerful in word and deed before God and all the people...sentenced to death...crucified...but we had hoped that He was the one who was going to redeem Israel...and what is more...some of our women...went to the tomb...but did not find His body...They told us they had seen a vision of angels, who said He was alive" (Luke 24:23). At that point Jesus shifted the therapeutic process with the expletive, "Fools!" (Luke 24:25, KJV) *anoetai,* "lacking in understanding, bordering on folly," and *bradeis,* "slow of heart to believe all the Prophets have spoken."

Jesus declared that Christ must first suffer and then enter His glory; this was the way it *had* to occur. The source/ base/

foundation of this reality was the Old Testament. "And beginning with Moses and all the Prophets He *(diermenousen)* interpreted for them all the things concerning Himself" (Luke 24:27). The *Living* Word lived His life by the *written* Word. For seven miles Jesus provided the Emmaus wayfarers a tutorial in Old Testament Christology. On arriving at Emmaus they urged Jesus to stay with them. He accepted their invitation.

As He was breaking the bread, giving thanks and handing it to them, "...their eyes were opened and they recognized Him..." (Luke 24:30-31). Then Jesus vanished. In their subsequent debriefing they testified to their burning hearts as He talked with them on the way. He "...completely opened up *(dianoigo)* the writings to us" (Luke 24: 32).

Jesus' role modeling on the Emmaus road is the first example of caring by His unbelieving, "heretical" disciples. Jesus, the Living Word, in love and grace went out of His way to open the Old Testament writings, "the written Word," to His Emmaus Harvest Force. They bonded with Him through His interpretation of the Old Testament. The authority of the written Word, as interpreted by Jesus, the Living Word, impelled them to spontaneous witnessing. Immediately upon Jesus' self-disclosure and disappearance they started out again on the seven-mile return trip to the Eleven in Jerusalem to announce to their colleagues, "The Lord has really risen!" (Luke 24:34). This was the second example of caring for the Harvest Force as the Emmaus disciples witnessed to their unbelieving "heretical" peers.

The witness of the Emmaus Harvest Force to the risen Lord testifies to the original paradigm shift in world evangelization. The spiritual bonding of the Harvest Force occurred with the risen Lord Himself. From the Old Testament He patterned His life, His death, and His triumph over the grave. Their new understanding of Jesus drove the Emmaus Harvest Force irrepressibly to witness to their new relationship with Him. This event must be the initial recorded experience of "two or three gathered" and Jesus in their midst (Mt 18:20).

As they were recounting the details of their tutorial journey, Jesus Himself stood among them and greeted them (Luke 24:36). He reminded them of His teaching, "These are my words which I spoke to you while I was still with you, that all things written about me in the Law of Moses, the Prophets and the Psalms must be fulfilled" (Luke 24:44). This was yet a third example of caring for the Harvest Force by His expanded teaching of the Old Testament prophesies. The Old Testament Scriptures were basic to understanding that Christ must suffer and rise again on the third day (Luke 24:36). "...and (in addition) repentance and forgiveness of sins will be preached in His name to all nations (ethnic groups, *panta ta ethne)* beginning from Jerusalem" (Luke 24:46).

He opened their minds fully to understand, *suniemi* ("get it all together") the Scriptures. The coherence implied in "getting it all together" was essential to their understanding and bonding with Christ the Lord, based on the totality of the message of Moses, the Prophets, and the Psalms.

Jesus concluded His second tutorial with the statement, "You *are* witnesses of these things" (Luke 24:48). Now the Harvest Force had been re-constituted as witnesses to Jesus' resurrection. Jesus' christological summary of the Old Testament Scriptures infused the first century Harvest Force with an insatiable desire to share the good news with their peers. In so doing they instituted the fulfillment of the third prophecy, "...repentance and forgiveness will be preached in His name to all nations" (Luke 24:46). No missionary command was given in Luke's report. Caring for all the ethnic groups globally was announced in the

Old Testament on the same level of importance as the prophecy of His death and resurrection.

Luke further expands the record of Jesus' post-resurrection instruction in Acts 1:3, summarizing the six weeks' seminar in Galilee by "...giving many convincing proofs that He was alive, over a period of over forty days, and spoke of the Kingdom of God." It would appear that the summary nature of these general statements led scholars to overlook the simple significance of the spiritual bonding of the Harvest Force with the risen Lord Some of the content of that seminar in Galilee is subsequently revealed in part through Peter's messages at Pentecost and at Solomon's Porch (Acts 2 & 3).

Stephen further enlarges on Jesus' teaching during His defense (Acts 7), as did Philip's preaching in Samaria and Gaza (Acts 8), and Peter evangelizing Cornelius (Acts 10). Saul's conversion was the fruit of Stephen's witness resulting in his subsequent evangelistic church planting and apostolic teaching in the epistles — all based on the Old Testament Word of God.

The spiritual foundation or the bonding of the Harvest Force of the first century church had been initiated by Jesus on the road to Emmaus, reinforced by His teaching the Eleven in Jerusalem and was finalized by His Old Testament seminar in Galilee. The apostolic examples of spiritual caring were continued as Peter commanded his audience at Pentecost to repent (Acts 2), and as he reached out in the healing of the lame man (Acts 3). These examples of spiritual caring included caring for their many physical needs of the believers, "...There was not a needy person among them" (Acts 4:34).

The identity of the risen Lord with His Harvest Force was as crucial for *witnessing* as the identification of the sinless Lord in His death was crucial *for the salvation of the sinner*. The paradigm shift from an erroneous messianism of orthodoxy to a living, throbbing witness to the crucified, risen and ascended Lord as High Priest interceding for the Harvest Force (Hebrews 4:7) bonded the early believers with their Lord and with one another (John 17:21) in a caring fellowship of servant-witnesses. (I John 1:3).

The ascension of Jesus further strengthened the identity of the Harvest Force with Him. The new meaning of the Old Testament Word is immediately evident in Acts 1 as Peter announces the need for a replacement of Judas, which he based on Psalm 69:23 and 109:8. His agreeing colleagues were "...of one mind...continually devoting themselves to prayer" (Acts 1:14). In this context Peter spoke, "It is therefore, necessary... that one of these should become a witness with us of His resurrection" (Acts 1:21-22). After they prayed they drew lots for Matthias. Using the Old Testament Scriptures as their guide and imploring the ascended Lord for guidance they accepted Mathias into the Harvest Force (Acts 1:20). The Harvest Force was now fully functioning on the same Old Testament Word that had directed Jesus and His ministry. The Harvest Force was now becoming effective through the new paradigm of their conscious oneness with the ascended High Priest directing the global witness. The Old Testament had personal as well as collective meaning for the daily decision-making by the Harvest Force. Peter, with deep concern for the well being of the apostolic Harvest Force, re-invigorated them to a conscious oneness in Christ as they anticipated Pentecost.

Ten days after the ascension of the Lord, the Holy Spirit "...as a violent rushing wind...filled the whole house where they were sitting" (Acts 2:2). Tongues of fire rested on each of them. "They were all filled with the Holy Spirit" (Acts 2:4).

In the context of the Emmaus road teaching by Jesus, His expanded teaching with the Eleven in Jerusalem and His subsequent extensive instruction on the Kingdom of God presented in Galilee, the Holy Spirit fell on the initial Harvest Force at Pentecost. The multitude of languages (Acts 2:8-11) of the Middle East at the time provided the media for the Holy Spirit to speak through the Harvest Force, fulfilling Jesus' promise in John 16:24, "He shall glorify me for He shall take of mine and disclose it to you."

Peter, with the Eleven, interpreted the phenomena to the crowd, speaking from the Prophets and the Psalms (Joel 2:28-32; Psalm 16, 132, 84, 10; Isaiah 44, 54, 57). He commanded the crowd to "...repent and each of you be baptized in the name of Jesus for the remission of sins...and you shall receive the gift of the Holy Spirit" (Acts 2:28). The 3,000 "...who had received the Word were *baptized* and...were continually devoting themselves to the *apostle's teaching* (of Jesus from the Old Testament) and to fellowship...breaking of bread...and to prayer" (Acts 2:41-42). The paradigm of the authority of the Old Testament interpreted by Jesus and prayer had bonded the Harvest Force in its spontaneous witness to Christ and in fellowship and communion with the ascended and invisible Lord as they were empowered by the Holy Spirit. The Harvest Force was imbued with a keen sense of biblical authority.

Peter's second message (Solomon's Porch) explained Jesus from the Pentateuch — Moses and Abraham, "and all the Prophets" as he declared the meaning of the healing of the lame man (Acts 3:13, Exodus 3:6). "The God of Abraham, Isaac, Jacob, the God of our fathers has glorified His *servant* Jesus..." (Isaiah 53:49). Peter also quoted Moses (Deut 18:15), "The Lord God shall raise up for you a Prophet like me from your brethren; to Him you shall give heed in everything He says to you." He also affirmed Abraham's seed as the source of blessing to all the families of the earth (Gen 22:18, Acts 3:25).

Peter's first and second recorded sermons, therefore, identify with the teaching of Jesus in Luke 24 where He states that His death and resurrection occurred exactly as Moses, the Prophets and the Psalms had prophesied. The message and the ministry of the first century Harvest Force was firmly founded on Jesus' post-resurrection teaching. In addition, Peter's defense before the Sanhedrin (Acts 4) presented Jesus from Psalm 18:22 as the "Stone" that was rejected but which became the Cornerstone (Acts 4:11). Consequently "...there is no other name under heaven given among men by which we must be saved" (Acts 4:12; Isaiah 33:10-13, 45:3-7).

The irrepressible urge of Peter and John to witness of the Lord Jesus Christ is clear in Acts 4:19-20. The prayers they offered in Acts 4:24 are filled with Old Testament references of worshipful praise from Psalm 2 as "...they lifted their voices to God with one accord..." and implored Him for boldness to speak the Word with all confidence (Acts 4:24-29). Consequently, "...there was not a needy person among them..." because of their commitment to one another based on their love of God and their neighbors (Acts 4:32-34).

Jesus initially had introduced His hermeneutic of the Messiah in Matthew 16 when Peter confessed, "...you are the Christ the Son of the living God." Jesus responded, "...On this rock I will build my church." Acts 2:47 informs us that the Lord was adding to the church daily. Acts 5:14 further indicates that the believers were constantly being added. The use of the passive in this case indicates that the addition was the result of an outside Force. It is very clear, therefore, that it is the Lord, as He promised in Matthew 16, through the witness of His Harvest Force.

After their second imprisonment (Acts 5), Peter and John are released by an angel of the Lord who tells them, "Go, stand and speak to the people in the temple the *whole message of this Life*"

(Acts 5:20). The authorities found them in the Temple the following dawn witnessing of the living Lord. Before the high priest and the Council they affirmed, "...We must obey God rather than men." The God of our fathers' raised up Jesus whom you had put to death by hanging Him on a tree. He is the one God exalted to the right hand as the Prince and Savior to grant repentance to Israel and forgiveness of sins. We are witnesses of these things and so is the Holy Spirit whom God has given to those who obey Him" (Acts 5:29-32).

Having been released through the counsel offered by Gamaliel, the Harvest Force counted themselves worthy, "...to suffer shame for His name" (Acts 5:41). "And daily in the temple and from house to house they kept on teaching and preaching Jesus as the Christ" (Acts 5:42). Meanwhile Stephen and the seven were appointed as members of the Harvest Force to minister to the Hellenistic widows. The record indicates, "...The Word of God kept on spreading and the number of the disciples continued to increase greatly in Jerusalem..." (Acts 6:7), as they proclaimed from the Old Testament that Jesus was the ascended Lord and Christ. This message created intense antagonism among the Jewish leadership.

Consequently, Stephen was placed before the authorities who questioned him about his incessant speaking against the Holy Place and the Law. Stephen responded in Acts 7 with no less than 120 references and allusions to the Old Testament, presenting Jesus from Moses, the Prophets, and the Psalms. Stephen confronted the Council with the actions of their fathers who had killed the Prophets. Now, they (the Council) had killed the "Righteous One" (Acts 7:52).

Stephen climaxed his defense by quoting from Isaiah 68:2, "'What kind of house will you build for me,' says the Lord, 'or what place is there for my repose. Was it not my hand that made all these things?' You men who are stiff-necked and uncircumcised and have hardened ears are always resisting the Holy Spirit; you are doing just as your fathers did. Which one of the Prophets did your fathers not persecute? And they killed those who previously announced the coming of the Righteous One whose betrayers and murderers you have become; you who received the Law as ordained by angels and did not keep it" (Acts 7:49-53).

Instead of repenting as the crowds at Pentecost and Solomon's Porch had done, the authorities rushed Stephen, dragged him out of the city and stoned him. His testimony was clear. Full of the Holy Spirit (Acts 7:55), he gazed intently into heaven beholding the glory of God, and Jesus, standing at the right hand of God. He said, "...Behold, I see the heavens opened up and the Son of Man standing at the right hand of God" (Acts 7:55-56).

Saul was guarding their clothes, as they kept on stoning Stephen calling on the Lord saying, "...Lord Jesus receive my Spirit" (Acts 7:59). A member of the first century Harvest Force, Stephen modeled at its best the witness to the ascended Lord, restating the hermeneutic of Jesus (Luke 24). He was full of the Holy Spirit, full of the Old Testament Word revealing Jesus whom he saw at the right hand of the Father. Stephen bonded with Him and was in full communication with his ascended Lord. His defense was the watershed of the witness of the Jerusalem Harvest Force. The new paradigm of the authority of the Old Testament revealing Jesus as the Savior and the High Priest interceding for him would indicate that Christ was coordinating Stephen's verbal witness and the witness of his body language. Stephen was calling on the Lord to forgive his enemies, not unlike Jesus in His dying moments on the cross.

Saul (Acts 8:1) indicates clearly that he "...was in hearty agreement in putting him to death."

Philip, meanwhile, preached Christ to the Samaritans in the wake of the persecution that followed the death of Stephen, "...preaching the good news about the Kingdom of God in the name of Christ..." (Acts 8:12). The great number of outcast Samaritans coming to faith in Christ impacted the apostles in Jerusalem, who "... heard that Samaria had received the Word of God..." and they sent Peter and John who prayed for them that they might receive the Holy Spirit. "Then they began laying their hands on them and they were receiving the Holy Spirit" (Acts 8:14-17). Peter and John returning to Jerusalem "...were preaching the gospel to many villages of the Samaritans" (Acts 8:25)

Meanwhile, Philip was ordered to change his venue "...and go south to the road that descends from Jerusalem to Gaza" (Acts 8:26). There he encountered the Ethiopian treasurer reading from the opened Scriptures the account of the servant of the Lord in Isaiah 53. Invited to interpret this portion of the Old Testament, Philip joined the Ethiopian in his chariot and "...beginning from this Scripture he preached Jesus to him" (Acts 8:3-5). The Ethiopian pointed to the water and asked what would prevent him from being baptized because he said, "'I believe that Jesus Christ is the Son of God'" (Acts 8:37). Philip continued to "...preach the gospel..." in all the cities on the way to Caesarea (Acts 8:40).

Meanwhile, as Saul approached the gates of Damascus, he was overcome by a light from heaven and a voice inquiring, "Saul, Saul why are you persecuting me?" (Acts 9:4).

To Saul's response, "Who are you, Lord?" the Lord replied, "I am Jesus whom you are persecuting" (Acts 9:5). It would appear that this encounter by Saul with the risen Lord is the direct consequence of the testimony of Stephen. In his later life Paul defended himself before the Jews in the Temple, stating, "When the blood of thy witness Stephen was being shed I was also standing by approving and watching out for the cloaks of those who were slaying him" (Acts 22:20). He had heard the "Word of Christ" from Stephen. Based on these accounts we conclude that the power of the Old Testament Word delivered by Stephen was so effective that the closer Saul came to Damascus to attack the Christians, the closer he came to his meeting with the Lord. He had heard Stephen recounting from the Old Testament the teaching about Christ through Moses, the Prophets, and the Psalms. The impact of Stephen's testifying and praying to the ascended Lord that He not hold these sins against them, led Saul to personal faith in Christ. The Holy Spirit began to make the things of Christ real to Paul (Jn 16:14).

Prayer loomed large as Ananias (Acts 9:11) is commanded by the Lord to go to the blind and "praying" Saul, residing on the street called Straight. The Lord instructed Ananias, "Go, for he is a chosen instrument of mine to bear my name before the Gentiles and kings and the sons of Israel, for I will show him how much he must suffer for my name's sake" (Acts 9:15-16). Obediently Ananias fulfilled his assignment, prayed and told "brother Saul" that he would regain his sight and be filled with the Holy Spirit! "...and immediately he (Saul) began to proclaim Jesus saying, 'He is the Son of God.'" (Acts 9:20). Thus began the ministry of the apostle Paul, the leader of the Gentile Harvest Force.

Ananias' sensitivity to the will of God in spiritually caring for Enemy #1 of the Harvest Force modeled yet another example of spiritual caring in the witness to Jesus.

Paul ultimately (at the close of his ministry) concluded his testimony before King Agrippa, some thirty years after Jesus met with the Eleven in Luke 24. Paul stated categorically, "And so, having obtained help from God, I stand this day testifying to small and great saying nothing but what the Prophets and Moses said would take place, that the Christ was to suffer and that by reason of His resurrection from the dead He should be the first to proclaim light both to the Jewish people and to the Gentiles" (Acts 26:22-23). Paul, who had first heard this message from Stephen, summarized his own life's ministry before King Agrippa using almost the identical words that Jesus used in Luke 24.

Peter, meanwhile, is confronted by the delegation from Cornelius imploring him to come and to speak to Cornelius (Acts 10). In responding to this invitation Peter stated, "The Word which He sent to the sons of Israel preaching peace through Jesus Christ (He is Lord of all) you yourselves know the thing which took place throughout all Judea starting from Galilee..." (Acts 10:36-37). Peter continued, "Of Him *all the Prophets* bear witness that through His name everyone who believes in Him receives forgiveness of sins" (Acts 10:43). While he was preaching the Holy Spirit fell on the Gentile believers who then were baptized in the name of Jesus Christ.

The full-blooded Jews at Pentecost received the Old Testament Word that revealed Jesus and were filled with the Spirit. Their Harvest Force colleagues on Solomon's Porch likewise heard that Jesus had come from Abraham's seed to bless the nations. Stephen proclaimed Jesus from the Old Testament pointing up in great detail from Moses, the Prophets and the Psalms how Jesus came into the world, died at the hands of unbelieving Jews, arose from the grave, and ascended into heaven and was standing to receive Stephen's spirit. Philip preached from the Old Testament in Samaria and led the Ethiopian to personal faith in Jesus as the Son of God on the basis of Isaiah 53. Saul came to faith in the wake of what he heard from Stephen verbally and saw from his body language as he cried out forgiving his murderous enemies. Consequently Paul later affirmed in Romans 10:17 "So faith comes by hearing and hearing by the word of Christ."

In summary, we observe that Jesus Christ is the underlying foundation-source of the spiritual caring of the first century Harvest Force. He provided the content (teaching/hermeneutic) in His post-resurrection instruction from Moses, the Prophets and the Psalms. He also provided the means, the promised Holy Spirit (Jn 16:14) who at Pentecost began to make the things of Christ real.

The written Word of the Old Testament was Jesus' authority for living, dying, and rising again from the grave and ascending into heaven. The same Old Testament Word written became the authority for the message and the witness of the first century Harvest Force.

The sustenance of the Harvest Force was their "in-Christness." They were beginning to discover their oneness (Jn 17) with the ascended Lord Jesus who had promised to "...be with them to the uttermost..." (Mt 28:20). He had affirmed, "I will build my church..." (Mt 16:18) and invited whoever would come along with Him to "...deny himself, take up his cross and follow Me" (Mt 16:24).

They were conscious of His presence, a oneness with the Lord that was leading them to pray and share their concerns with Him, "...Whatever you ask of the Father, He may give to you" (Jn 15:16). And "...ask, and you will receive, that your joy may be made full" (Jn 16:24).

The presence of the Lord and the reality of prayer characterized the early witness of the apostolic Harvest Force (Acts 1-15). Saul recognized His presence outside the gate of Damascus and inquired in his first prayer to the ascended Lord,

"Who are you, Lord?" (Acts 9:5). When Jesus confirmed the fact, Saul committed himself, "What do you want me to do, Lord?!" (Acts 22:10).

As the Lord pursued the dispirited Emmaus disciples, so He tracked Saul from Stephen's martyr prayer to the Damascus gate.

The extension of the witness to the ascended Lord proceeded as "...the Word of the Lord continued to grow and be multiplied..." (Acts 12:24). The church at Antioch prayed and laid hands on Barnabas and Saul as the Holy Spirit sent them away in unity and agreement "...to proclaim the Word of God..." (Acts 13:3-5). We are almost startled by Paul's message at Pisidian Antioch when he begins with Moses and continues through the Prophets and the Psalms as his message strikingly echoes that of Stephen in Acts 7. "And we preach to you the good news of the promise made to the fathers" (Acts 13:32). The Jews rejected the message. In "...turning to the Gentiles," (Acts 13:46), Paul quotes Isaiah, "For thus the Lord has commanded us, 'I have placed you as a light for the Gentiles that you should bring salvation to the end of the earth'" (Isaiah 49:6, 29:6). When the Gentiles heard this they began rejoicing and glorifying the Word of the Lord; and as many as had been appointed to eternal life believed" (Acts 13:46-38).

James, leading the Jerusalem Council, affirms the accepting of the Gentile believers by quoting from Amos 9, Deuteronomy 28, Isaiah 45, 52, 49, Jeremiah 14, and Daniel 9. A supporting letter accepting the Gentiles was carried by Judas and Barnabas because, "...it seemed good to the apostles and the elders, with the whole church to choose men from among them to send to Antioch with Paul and Barnabus..." (Acts 15:22). The subsequent Harvest Force ministry of Paul expands the significance of the oneness in Christ and the common denominator of the Old Testament Word as he speaks to the churches in his many epistles: 2 Cor 5:21; Gal 2:20; Ro 6, 8, 12:1-2; Ph 1:21, 2:5, 13; 2 Cor 2:14 and 9:8, among others.

At the close of the first century John, the last of the apostolic force, emphasizes oneness in Christ with the Father and the Son, stressing the commandment to "Love one another" (1 Jn 4:7-21).

The John 17 prayer for the oneness of the Harvest Force with the Father and the Son as they mutually are one in the love the Father has for the Son, as demonstrated by the risen Lord. Jesus pursued His ignorant and unbelieving disciples, leading them from error, misunderstanding and misjudgment, to a vibrant witness of His resurrection.

Stephen's overflowing love for his enemies, uttering his last gasping prayer to the risen, ascended Lord, cried out for their forgiveness. Saul, the church's enemy number one, ultimately prostrated himself to do the will of God in role-modeling service to his Master.

Peter overcame the biases and prejudices of his orthodox Judaism and reached out in saving love to Cornelius and his household. Ultimately he wrote to his suffering colleagues of the Dispersion, heralding the reality of believers partaking of the divine nature (2 Peter 1:4).

Paul affirmed his oneness with the ascended Christ, writing to the Galatian believers (Gal 2:20) that he was crucified with Him and that Christ was living within. So at the end of his ministry, incarcerated in Rome, he exulted in his testimony to the Philippian believers, "For to me to live is Christ and to die is gain" (Phil 1:21).

The love of the Father for the Son (John 17) was evident in the several exhortations to "fellowship" *(koinonia)* with the Father and the Son, in John's epistles, as the prisoner of Patmos witnessed to the love of God at the end of the first century.

The indwelling Christ, according to Paul, made His presence known by the fruit of the Spirit — Love (Gal 5:22). The Roman Christians learned from Paul that the love of God was poured out into their hearts by the Holy Spirit (Ro 5:5). And he taught the derisive Christians at Corinth the definition and meaning of love in 1 Corinthians 13, the inseparable (Ro 8:35), controlling element in Paul's ministry (2 Cor 5:14).

Peter also affirmed the love of the invisible God and the irrepressible joy and fullness of glory produced in the believers (1 Peter 1:8). At the close of the first century, John was preparing the Harvest Force of the second century by exhorting them, "...If anyone loves Me, he will keep My word; and My Father will love him, and We will come to him and make Our abode with him." (John 14:23). "...God is love, and the one who abides in love abides in God, and God abides in him" (I John 4:16). Paul had already written essentially the same message to the Philippian church when he told them "...it is God who is at work in you, both to will and to work for His good pleasure" (Phil 2:13).

Fredrik Franson, founder of TEAM and leader in the founding of fifteen other mission agencies and denominations at the turn of the 19th/20th centuries, summarizes our efforts in articulating the basis of spiritual caring for the Harvest force of the new millennium when he exhorted his missionaries 100 years ago to practice Constant Conscious Communion with Christ.

Chapter 2

The Pastoral Epistles on Care Giving

Charles Chaney

D. N. Berdot and Paul Anton did us no service in the early eighteenth century when they began to refer first to Titus and then to Titus and 1 and 2 Timothy as "Pastoral Epistles" (Wright 1992:3; Guthrie 1957:11). From that day forward, at least, the perception that Titus and Timothy were pastors on Crete and in Ephesus has misdirected our understanding of these epistles.

These three letters were written by the leader of a missionary team to two veteran missionaries. They are essentially missionary documents. Titus and Timothy had served with Paul at least 15 years. The bulk of their ministry had been in pursuit of a very focused missionary strategy in the Aegean Basin.

The perspective that Timothy and Titus were pastors, however, is pervasive in the exegetical and expository literature of today. A brief perusal of a few commentaries, Bible dictionaries, and handbooks will illustrate this extensive assumption. A look at one pre-eighteenth century commentary and an unscientific sampling of a few more recent works will make the point.

Calvin's commentary on Paul's letters to Timothy was dedicated to Edward Seymore, Duke of Somerset, the uncle and mentor of Edward VI, and is interpreted with an eye toward the reformation of the Church of England. Unfortunately, Somerset was beheaded before the commentary was published in English in 1556. Calvin's commentary on Titus, however, is a little more on target. He says that Paul had "commissioned Titus as an evangelist to carry on his (Paul's) work" (1964:349). However, it was dedicated to William Farel and Peter Viret, his predecessors and former colleagues in Geneva. They had since gone on to Neuchatel and Lausanne having been called by the churches in those cities to "rescue them from the papal tyranny." Calvin's role in Geneva was like that of Titus. Farel and Viret were like Paul. Calvin evidently saw himself as an evangelist, but the actual designation he gave to himself was "pastor" (1964:347).

Alfred Plummer, in a famous nineteenth century exposition, said the letters were written to Paul's delegates and "officers of the church." They were to be treated from the point of view of "that of the overseer or minister" (n.d.:3). A. T. Robertson agreed with this delegating role for Titus, but Timothy, according to Robertson, was left in charge of the great church in Ephesus (1979:155, 165). Charles A. Tretham says in a little book written for laymen, that in those letters "we have the wisdom of a great pastor whose work was to train pastors and provide leadership for the churches he had helped to establish" (1959:9). Many times Paul identified himself as a missionary (apostle)[1] and a deacon (servant), but not once did he identify himself as a pastor, elder, or overseer. John Stott has said that

---

[1] I have argued in other places: (1) that we need to distinguish between "the Twelve" and "apostles." (2) that while the Twelve were also apostles, there are at least twelve other people in the New Testament who are identified as apostles; (3) that the role of the Twelve was to be eyewitnesses to the ministry, teaching, death and resurrection of Christ and, as such, they can never be replaced; (4) that the Greek root for "apostle" has the same meaning as the Latin root for "missionary;" and that the primary role of "apostles" was to go to new areas or new people groups, make disciples, gather them into churches, and raise up leaders among them. See for example *Church Planting at the End of the Twentieth Century*. First edition (Wheaton, Ill.: Tyndale House Publishers, 1981), pp. 154-157.

Timothy was left in Ephesus as "a kind of embryonic bishop" (1973:19).

William Hendrickson, writing in 1957, about 400 years after Calvin, did not identify Titus and Timothy as pastors. He found multiple purposes for each letter. However, ecclesiastical organization and decorum were a primary purpose for all three epistles (1979:41-44). Ralph Earle wrote in 1978 that these letters were called "pastoral" because "they were addressed to pastors of churches to outline their pastoral duties" (1978:344). A. T. Hanson, in 1982, held that one of the three primary purposes of these three letters was "to provide a solid handbook for church leaders which would strengthen the authority of the ordained ministers" (1982:23). Gary Demerest says that these letters "stand alone...having been written to two men who were pastors" (1984:10-11). George Knight, III, in his prestigious recent commentary, says nothing about these letters being related to Paul's missionary vocation (1992:147). Thomas Lea, late dean of the School of Theology at Southwestern Baptist Theological Seminary, saw the purpose for writing each of these three letters as quite distinct: 1 Timothy, to combat error; Titus, to fully organize the Cretian church; and 2 Timothy, to express personal concern and encouragement to Timothy. However, there is no stated relationship to the Gentile mission (1992: 42-44).

A quick glance at some well-known Bible handbooks, dictionaries, and one volume commentaries will prove revealing as well. John Rutherford, writing in the classic *International Standard Biblical Encyclopedia*, avowed that the Pastoral Epistles are a distinct group of letters because

> they were addressed to two Christian ministers. When Timothy and Titus received these Pastoral Epistles they were not acting, as they had previously done, as missionaries or

itinerant evangelists, but had been left by Paul in charge of churches...The Pastoral Epistles were written to guide them in the discharge of the duties devolving on them as Christian pastors. (1939: 2258)

According to the *Holman Bible Dictionary*, these letters were written after the era of missionary work in the Aegean Basin, and in the time of well established churches. Timothy was sent to Ephesus where Paul urged him to remain as pastor. The letter contains instructions about the organization of the church (or churches) and "practical advice for the young pastor" (Butler 1991: 1077, 1350, 1353). The *Holman Bible Handbook* does recognize *the missionary role of* Timothy and Titus but says the letters "address the need for pastoral oversight" (Dockery 1992:736, 742).

Archibald Hunter, in his *Introduction to the New Testament*, says that these letters "consist mostly of advice to younger ministers" (1973:150). Donald Guthrie, in his classic *New Testament Introduction,* asserts both the missionary and pastoral role: "[T]he apostle means to give his two associates written instructions about methods of procedure in their respective churches for which they are temporarily responsible" (1973:622). Two one-volume commentaries published in 1983, while they do not identify Timothy and Titus as pastors, tend to interpret these letters from the pastor's perspective. The *Liberty Bible Commentary* says clearly that Timothy was not the pastor at Ephesus (Falwell 1983: 2493) and *The Bible Knowledge Commentary* insists that the letters were not "handbooks" on pastoral duties. Both volumes do give *instructions* about what Titus and Timothy are to do and teach as pastors in the churches (Walvoord and Zuck 1983: 727, 761).

Of various sources I have perused, only E. Glenn Hinson's work in 1971 takes the Gentile mission seriously. After a sterling defense of the Pauline authorship, Hinson insists that the "only credible [historical situation for the writing of the epistles] is Judaistic opposition to the Gentile mission." He goes on to insist that these letters "cast more light on the method of the early mission than any other New Testament writings save the book of Acts" (1971:304).

Hinson is surely on target. Most commentators on the Pastoral Epistles write from the viewpoint of a legally or culturally established Church, or from a role in an institution primarily committed to training pastors, not from the perspective of new congregations on a mission field. Therefore, they have failed to see the true purpose and intent of these three brief epistles. The letters do address doctrinal error and suggests steps to combat it in the young congregations. They do deal with character traits essential to the principle leadership in the churches, overseers or elders and deacons. They do give instructions about the behavior of Titus and Timothy and give them assignments. However, all of this is because these are letters of missionary instruction and nurture.

Titus is primarily focused on the thorough evangelization of Crete. It contains instructions about bringing existing (probably predominately Jewish) churches into gospel order, assuring that the churches are supplied with indigenous leaders and that congregations have been planted in every city and village.

1 Timothy contains instructions for a missionary team member who has been sent into a field of mission churches — all under 15 years of age — that have fallen into extensive error. Political and social tension among the young churches had existed in Ephesus and Roman Asia since the Ephesian riots (Acts 19). The historical era of this assignment was that of the

persecution under Nero, and the time of the burning of Rome. Terrible political tensions in Judea would soon lead to war. Radical, deviant, cultic doctrines had arisen much as they have in Uganda today.

In my judgment, 2 Timothy was written to a mission team member who had left the field in discouragement and defeat. It is essentially a call for Timothy to get back into the fray, to recommit himself to the Gentile mission and rejoin the depleted missionary band.

What I am suggesting in this paper is that we need to look at 1 & 2 Timothy and Titus through a different lens — as missionary epistles not as pastoral epistles. Therefore, I want to "underscore" a few highlights that illustrate this perspective, giving special attention to Paul's care for two members of the harvest force.

Titus

My assumption is that Paul was released from prison in late 63 A.D. or early 64 A.D. before the burning of Rome, and returned to visit the Aegean Basin mission field before attempting to go to Spain. Though we can not know this for sure, he probably went first to Crete, where a few early Jewish Christian congregations existed. Paul may well have visited Crete because it represented the southern rim of the Aegean Basin and was an area that Paul had not touched in his ministry. James and others had been put to death in 62 A.D. The hostility between Jews and Christians was extreme. The Jerusalem church was scattered, and the political unrest before the Jewish Wars and the destruction of Jerusalem throbbed throughout the eastern Mediterranean. The Jewish Christian churches were in doctrinal and organizational disorder. A number of assemblies may already have died. There were numerous towns that had not been penetrated with the gospel.

Paul left Titus in Crete with a clear assignment, reiterated in his letter: (1) Set in order those congregations still existing, and (2) appoint elders in every city [on Crete this should be read: towns or villages] (1:5).

He describes the character of those who are to be appointed leaders and instructs Titus to reprove severely those who flirt with unsound doctrine and Jewish myths (1:13-14).

He suggests aspects of ethical behavior that should be taught to various segments of those who make up the churches [old men, older women, younger women, young men, and bondslaves] (2:1-10). He describes the civil conduct that should characterize all Christians (3:1-3). Both sets of instructions are justified and grounded in a statement about the grace of God, the return of Christ, and eternal life (2:11-14; 3:4-7).

Factious men are to be separated from the congregations after a second warning in order to save the young churches from further divisions (3:10-11). Elders are to be appointed in the remaining towns. These elders may, in my opinion, have become the founding pastors of new assemblies of believers. Their roles might actually be seen as that of church planters.

Finally, Titus is summoned to Nicopolis where Paul will spend the winter before he, I assume, will take Titus with him to Spain. Titus is to come after replacement missionaries have arrived to relieve him. Meanwhile he is to expedite the itinerant evangelistic ministry of Zenas and Apollos throughout Crete (3:12-14).

All of this letter constitutes very clear missionary instructions about how to proceed with the thorough evangelization of the island.

1 Timothy

I assume that Paul's activities after his release from prison may have been something like the following:

1. Shortly after his release in late 63 A.D., he sent Timothy to Phillipi and Macedonia with the news of his release (Phil. 1:23-26; 2:19-24).
2. He began his journey by way of Crete (Titus 1:5) and, after some time there, left for Ephesus.
3. Titus was to complete the task of evangelism, evidently consisting of making and gathering disciples into congregations in every town and appointing leaders in each congregation.
4. Paul journeyed then to Ephesus, and eventually up to Colossi (Philemon 22), afterward returning to Ephesus.
5. Timothy joined him in Ephesus with the news from Macedonia.
6. After some time in Ephesus and Roman Asia, Paul departed for Macedonia. From here he probably wrote both 1 Timothy and Titus.

Like the letter to Titus, First Timothy has precise written instructions, advice, and encouragement about how to continue the reclamation and restoration of the churches in Ephesus and, to some degree, the entire mission field of Roman Asia. When Paul and Timothy arrived in Ephesus, they found that the assemblies had left, what the Risen Christ thirty years later called, their "first love" (Rev. 2:4). Before the riot that drove Paul from Ephesus, emissaries won and trained in Ephesus, like Epaphras in the Lycus Valley (Col. 1:7), had taken the Gospel to all who lived in Asia (Acts 19:10). By 64-65 A.D. the teachers in the congregation(s) were immersed in apocalyptic speculation and Jewish mysticism that left the churches lethargic, divided, and immobilized. The intense political and military pressure of the period had helped to lift these speculations to the level of priority in interest and effort. The whole network of mission churches in Roman Asia was in great danger.

This letter is intermixed with (1) instruction about what Timothy was to achieve among the congregations in Ephesus and how he was to go about it; (2) personal instruction for Timothy himself, not only warning him about the dangers inherent in combating heresy, but also about such things as mundane and sublime as the nurture of his own spiritual life and his physical health; and (3) instructions about both the leadership and the ministries of the churches.

Paul's instructions for Timothy about what he was to achieve were simple, but extremely difficult to bring about. He was to instruct certain teachers in right doctrine but in such a manner as to produce "love from a pure heart," a clear conscience and genuine faith (1:3-5). Timothy was to go about this by standing firm against the prevailing Judaistic legalism and budding Jewish gnostic heresies, by constantly prescribing and teaching sound doctrine and moral accountability, and by living in such a manner himself that people would respect his maturity and follow his example. He was to give attention to the public reading of Scripture, to exhortation, to teaching, and giving his full attention to the revitalization of the churches. All this was to be done with perseverance (4:11-16).

Carefully relating himself to the founding members of the churches, he was to listen to them as if they were wise parents (5:1-2). He was not to jump to judgment about the deviant doctrine or behavior of any leader, requiring two or three witnesses before acting. Everything was to be done without bias or partiality (5:19-21). If some persisted in their heresy, or if they with unbridled greed from their exotic and speculative teaching created havoc within the congregations, those individuals were to be considered arrogant and void of true understanding. He warned especially about inordinate love for money. Food and shelter was enough for true godly contentment (6:1-10).

Paul was obviously concerned about Timothy's doctrinal steadfastness in the face of strongly held and persuasively presented heresies. He encouraged him to wage a strong battle for the faith. Some of Paul's workers had failed in this battle and, consequently, had shipwrecked their ministries (1:18-20).

He encouraged Timothy to uphold leadership standards. Through faithfulness at this point, he would be "nourished" on the word of faith and sound doctrine (4:6-7). Timothy should discipline himself in godliness, which Paul insisted, holds promise in this life and the life to come. For true godliness, Paul insisted, he and his team labored with all their might (4:7b-8).

The consistent pursuit of godliness would create harmony and reestablish sound doctrine. To do this he must flee the inordinate attachment to money but pursue the fruit of the spirit in his life: righteousness, godliness, faith, love, perseverance, and gentleness (6:11-12).

In terms of physical health, Paul affirmed that Timothy should be careful about the water in Ephesus, and take a little wine for his many ailments (5:23).

Paul urged that prayer be central to the life of the church, especially in times of persecution (2:1-7). Men were to pray, not debate; women were to dress modestly and maintain a low profile in public worship (2:8-15). Contrary to the situation on Crete, men aspired for leadership in the congregations. As in the letter to Titus, Paul reminded Timothy of the character required for both "bishops," "deacons," and their wives (3:1-15). He gave careful instruction about charity and social concerns among the fellowship. Christian families were first to take care of their own (5:3-4, 16). Only older, genuinely dependent widows, should be given support from the church, and might become part of the "order" of widows devoted to prayer, hospitality, and good works. Younger widows should not be admitted to this group but should remarry (5:5-15).

Some elders, those who give stalwart leadership, have a good work ethic, especially in the tasks of preaching and teaching, should receive the monetary support of their congregations (5:17-18). Care is to be taken so that men are well proven before they are set aside for this ministry (5:22). He is also to instruct the rich to be generous and help meet the needs of struggling saints (6:17-19).

This letter could well be considered an example of first century mentoring. Without telegraph, telephone, radio, e-mail, and the World Wide Web, Paul had to depend upon "snail-mail" without opportunities to ask questions or hear responses. His first letter to Timothy, therefore, covers a multitude of anticipated problems.

2 Timothy

Paul's second letter to Timothy is of a much different nature. If, as I assume, Paul indeed made his trip to Spain he probably did so after his winter at Nicopolis. He probably took Titus with him. Tension between Christians and Jews was high and at the breaking point between Jews and the Roman government. Christians were considered a part of the Jewish complex. Sometime after his return from Spain, probably in late 67 A. D., Paul was imprisoned again. He may have made a hurried trip to the Aegean Basin churches shortly before his imprisonment in

Rome. Thus, his coats and books were with friends in Troas (4:13).

However it all happened, Paul discovered to his dismay and disappointment that Timothy had left the field in Ephesus, probably in failure and in the face of growing persecution. I believe he had returned to his ancestral home — to the comfort of his family.

This letter is an earnest impassioned plea for Timothy to come out of his recluse and get back into mission service again, even in the face of persecution and death.

This brief letter portrays a man who has withdrawn from his ministry. He had left Ephesus in fear and defeat (4:12) and gone home (1:1-5). He was in extreme burnout and deep depression (1:6-7). He had left the field and was living in abject fear (1:8-12). He had lost his sense of values (1:13-14).

It is interesting to see Paul's method of nurture and encouragement, calling Timothy back into the battle. His very first step was to express appreciation and affection. In 1:1-5 he expressed deep gratitude and concern, an almost unfathomable affection, and amazing confidence in Timothy.

In the second paragraph (1:6-14) Paul urged Timothy to rekindle the passionate missionary gift received through Paul. Paul asks Timothy to reflect on the fact that he had received the gift of the Holy Spirit. That indwelling Spirit who was not a spirit of cowardice, but of boldness, power, love, and discipline. He urged him to refuse to be intimidated by the threat of danger or ashamed of the Lord. He asked him to remember what God had done in Christ and that Paul (and by inference, he himself) had been appointed an evangelist, missionary and teacher for the Gentiles. Paul asserts his own confidence in the face of suffering and death. He urges Timothy to exhibit the same. Then, as if to drive in the last nail, he urges him to refuse to be like two missionary failures but to be encouraged by the bold ministry of Onisephorous (1:15-17).

In the second chapter Paul shifts gears suggesting ways Timothy might recover his lost boldness and spiritual impact. He should "be strong in the grace that is in Christ Jesus." "Be strong" is literally "be empowered" and the ministry of Holy Spirit is clearly implied (2:1).

Next, he suggests how one must conduct his ministry in hard times like the era in which they were then living. The only alternative when persecution is threatening and error is rampant is to reach and empower new believers who will reach and empower other new believers (2:2).

He then calls Timothy to a life of discipline, of physical labor, and of endurance. He uses three metaphors: the good soldier, the successful athlete, and the hardworking farmer. But his extended discussion deals with the life of a soldier. Paul calls on Timothy to be willing to undergo hardship, just as Paul had done and was doing (2:4-13).

After this stirring appeal, Paul seems to assume that Timothy will respond in a positive way. He offers instruction again about how to deal with established heresies and divisions (2:14-19), ending up with an appeal that Timothy will be a vessel for honoring God. Timothy can achieve this goal by keeping himself clean and constantly available to the Master (2:20-26).

In 2 Timothy 3, Paul returns to the turmoil of the present era and the struggle Timothy had in Ephesus. He explained the storm of controversy that engulfed Timothy in Ephesus in terms of the end times. He then reminded Timothy, however, that he had been true to sound doctrine. All, he said, who would be godly will suffer persecution. Timothy was to remember Paul's previous mentoring and to continue to equip himself in the Scripture for every opportunity for good work even in troubled times (3:1-17).

The fourth chapter is a series of charges that Paul gave, anew and afresh, to the reclaimed Timothy.

1. Preach the Word, always ready to...reprove, rebuke, and exhort with great patience and clear instruction (4:1-4). Some of these things were hard for Timothy.
2. Stay balanced and in control, willing to endure hardship (4:5a-b).
3. Be constant in making disciples (4:5c).
4. Discharge all the duties that servanthood requires (4:5d).

The remainder of the letter is about Paul's current situation, the deployment of the rest of his mission team, and personal instructions about what Timothy is to do on his way to Rome. What does all this mean? Let me give four responses:

1. Whether or not you concur with my construction of Paul's movements in the last months of his life, or my reading of Paul's instruction, we must agree that the three letters are addressed primarily to missional, not pastoral concerns, and are an expression of instructions for, and care of, a missionary team.
2. Looking at these three letters as missionary instructions and nurture puts these letters in an entirely new light.
3. We can learn much from Paul's methodology here as from other facets of his ministry.
4. I raise a question: Are our approaches in caring for the harvest force informed more by the various social sciences of modernity or by biblical example and teaching?

Chapter 3

A Theological Journey of Care[1]

J. Julius Scott, Jr.

During my 37 years of college and university teaching I have taught both Biblical and Systematic Theology. For more than the past quarter of a century my primary, but not exclusive, attention has been upon Biblical theology, especially that of the NT. I have no desire to debate here the relative merits of the two approaches. My thesis is that at this time in history Biblical, rather than systematic, theology is probably the best place to start "doing" theology in and for the non-Western, Two Thirds World. The scope of this thesis also intends to include many groups out of the mainstream of technical, academic theology in the Western world, such as ethnic and cultural minorities and those living in small town and rural settings.

Many aspects of the essence of this thesis have been considered extensively by missiologists and by scholars of the Two Thirds World. They have produced an impressive body of literature dealing with both corporate and individual attempts to address the need for and possible structures for theological statements appropriate to their many geographical and cultural

---

[1] Presented at the Mid-West Regional Meeting of *The Evangelical Theological Society,* Florissant, MO, April, 2000. Revised edition presented at the National Meeting of the Evangelical Missiological Society, Nashville, TN, November, 2000.

areas.[2] My concern is with inter-theology methodological approaches.

Personal Experiences in Cross-Cultural Settings

Three experiences have been significant in bringing me to think about issues inherent in the title of this paper. A conversation with a just graduated student centered around the work he would soon be taking up in his native East Africa. At the close I asked what were some of the important issues theology should address there that were not a part of the focus of his education at the Wheaton College Graduate School. The content and quickness of his answer shocked me and I realized just how provincial we can be both in our views of international political-social issues and in choice of curriculum. His list included (1) attitudes toward ancestors; (2) circumcision, (3) polygamy, (4) issues related to charismatic theology and experience, (5) diviners, spiritualists, and demonism, (6) the nature of the Christian family, (7) poverty, (8) development in such areas as economics and education, (9) tribalism, (10) Islam, (11) traditional African religions, and (12) AIDS. I could have added

---

[2] See John Gration, "Willowbank to Zaire: The Doing of Theology," *Missiology* 12/3 (July, 1984), 227-309; K. Gordon Molyneux, *Africa Christian Theology: The Quest for Selfhood* (San Francisco: Mellen Research University Press, 1993) and "The Contribution to African Theology of the Faculty Faculté de Théologie Catholique in Kinshasa, Zaire," *African Journal of Evangelical Theology* 11/2 (1992),58-89; and Bong Rin Ro and Ruth Eshenaur, eds. *The Bible and Theology in Asian Contexts* (Taichung, Taiwan: Asia Theological Association, 1984). See also review of Molyneux, *African Christian Theology* by A. Scott Moreau, *Evangelical Missions Quarterly* 36/1 (January 2000), 109-112. Insight into another area is provided in the series of essays edited by Cain Hope Felder, *Stony the Road We Trod. African American Biblical Interpretation*. (Minneapolis: Fortress, 1991).

more, but this was his list. Another student, from another part of the world, listed (1) how to present the Gospel in an area that has three other main religions and government will not permit proselytizing, (2) what should be the Christian response in a society in which bribery is the only way to get things done, (3) the dilemma faced by a Christian running a business in a country in which, by law, 10% of all employs must be Muslims and every corporation must have at least one Muslim on its board of directors, (4) what is a Christian to do when there are national-cultural festivals located in a temple, (5) worship of ancestors, and (6) the problems inherent in a society in which all marriages are "arranged marriages" and the family determines that a Christian woman must marry someone of another religion. Second, as students were leaving the final examination of a course dealing with the Biblical theology of a particular NT book, a minority student said, to the effect, that this approach (Biblical theological) would "preach" in his churches but systematic theology would not. Finally, the evening of the day in which I had concluded a three week course in Nigeria on "The Jewish Backgrounds of the NT" a delegation of students came to see me. After the traditional expressions of gratitude the leader said, "We do not believe you understand what you have done for us. Before this class our study of the NT required our going from the African world to the Western to that of the Bible and then, again back through the Western world to ours. As a result of our study in this course we are now able to go directly to the Biblical world." Another added, "You know, our world is much closer to that of the NT than is yours."

Describing Biblical and Systematic Theology

Both the definition and function of Biblical and systematic theologies are controversial. Most contemporary Systematicians want to distinguish between "Biblical Doctrines" and "Constructive Systematic Theology." The former involves arranging Biblical teachings under some such topical outline as Prolegomena, Revelation God, Human Persons, Christ, Salvation, The Christian Life, the Church, and Eschatology. The primary structure and methodology for this enterprise usually begin with the study of the Bible, and often includes gathering proof-texts for each category. Biblical doctrines also draw from philosophy.

Constructive theology attempts to apply religious truth to the contemporary historical-cultural situation by translating its message into the conceptual world-view and framework of the modern world. Its objective includes both extending and applying the content and intent of religious teachings meaningfully in the target society. This requires careful analysis of all religious issues involving human persons and those cultures in which the message is stated. In making these analyses the theologian draws from Biblical studies, history (both world history in general and that of Christian theology and experience), philosophy, literature, the social sciences, the arts, natural sciences, and any other areas that are helpful in understanding human nature and the environment of the society and/or the individual being addressed. The organization and presentation of this form of systematic theology is then heavily influenced by one or more of the areas used in making the analysis. Thus method and structure of both the study and presentation are different from that of the Bible itself.

In *Biblical theology* all statements about God, human beings, Christ, righteousness, and salvation derive their meaning and connotation in terms of their function within the plan and on the plane of the history of the Bible and its times. It seeks to understand Biblical truth within the conceptual world-view and historical-cultural framework of the *Biblical* world. Biblical theology derives its content by steadily focusing attention upon the Bible in its original setting. It employs the (critical) tools of linguistic, historical-cultural, and literary investigation.

In addition to ideological ones (such as liberal versus traditional viewpoints) numerous controversies surround virtually every feature of Biblical theology. We will mention only two, those involving its organization and its objective.

One has only to look at the table of contents of a number of different books on Biblical theology to realize how diverse are the organizational structures employed by the authors. In general they are usually organized along the lines of either an analytic or thematic (synthetic) approach.[3] The former investigates the various units (such as the Pentateuch, prophets, writings, synoptic gospels, the writings of John, those of Paul, and other divisions) to determine the teachings and emphases of each. Synthetic structures look for common themes and the distinct ways they are dealt with throughout the Bible or in the particular testament under consideration. At times a writer may combine

---

[3] The thematic or synthetic approach is less often used than the analytic structure. Donald Guthrie, in his massive study *New Testament Theology* (Downers Grove, IL: InterVarsity Press, 1981) uses a more-or-less synthetic approach. George Ladd, *A Theology of the New Testament* (Grand Rapids: Eerdmans, 1974) uses an analytic approach. A. M. Hunter, *The Message of the New Testament* (1944), expressed the hope that all future textbooks in New Testament theology be written from the synthetic point of view. This is a largely unfulfilled desire.

one of these approaches with some of the divisions usually found in systematic theology (Guthrie 1981). Other approaches include investigations which seek the implications of the New Testament writers' use of the Old[4] or the so-called word-study method.[5]

Disagreements involving the objective of Biblical theology focus upon whether it is a legitimate study in itself or a step in a greater enterprise; that is, is Biblical theology merely descriptive or can it be normative as well? G. E. Ladd is quite clear, "Biblical theology is primarily a descriptive discipline. It is not initially concerned with the final meaning of the teachings of the Bible or their relevance for today. This is the task of systematic theology"(1974:25).

On the other hand Donald Guthrie (1981:32-34) eloquently sets forth the case for Biblical theology as normative. This, he says, is so because of the sinful nature of all human beings whose need of a favorable relationship with God does not change, regardless of time and place. He also argues that the

---

[4] See C. H. Dodd, *According to the Scriptures: The Sub-Structure of New Testament Theology* (1952); *The Old Testament in the New* (1952; reprinted 1963). F. F. Bruce, *The New Testament Development of Old Testament Themes* [British title: *This is That: The New Testament Development of Some Old Testament Themes* (1968) and *The Time is Fulfilled: Five Aspects of the Fulfillment of the Old Testament in the New* (1978).

[5] See G. Johannes Botterweck, and Helmer Ringgren, eds. *Theological Dictionary of the Old Testament*. John T. Williams trans (Grand Rapids: Eerdmans, 1974 ff); Colin Brown, ed. *New International Dictionary of New Testament Theology* (Grand Rapids: Zondervan, 1967-1985) 3 vols, plus Index.; G. Kittel and Gerhard Friedreich, eds. *Theological Dictionary of the New Testament*. G. Bromley, trans (Grand Rapids: Eerdmans); Ernst Jenni, and K. Westermann, eds. *Theological Lexicon of the Old Testament*.. Mark E. Biddle, trans (1971; E.T., Peabody, MAS: Henderickson, 1997) 3 vols.; W. Van Gameren, ed. *New International Dictionary of Old Testament and Exegesis* (Grand Rapids: Zondervan, 1997), 5 vols.

Bible must speak to each generation on its own terms. Guthrie sees the NT theologians as more than a "museum keeper" or "mere antiquarian" but someone who has found meaning, views it as relevant, and responds to the message. He places emphasis on the "changelessness of man's basic need for God" as the foundation for the normative character of NT theology and lays the responsibility on people in every age to discover the relevance of theology to their present needs.

The distinction between Biblical and Systematic Theology is not always easy to grasp. Not infrequently students come to me a year or more after taking a class with me and say, "I'm finally understanding the difference between Biblical and Systematic theology." Once when I was trying to explain the difference to an engineer friend, he commented that Biblical theology also has its systematic elements. He was, of course, correct. The line between the two is not sharply defined. The major differences between Biblical and Systematic theology, I believe, lie in their starting points, methodologies, and organizational models. The points addressed and emphases placed upon them may also be diverse.

The Traditional Gateway to Theology

The beginning point for formal theological training of those who will become pastors, teachers, missionaries, and informed laypersons is frequently through the study of Biblical Doctrines or some other form of systematic theology. This has the advantage of quickly and neatly presenting the essential teachings of the Christian faith. It is a strategy I sometimes employ myself when working with new Christians or beginning students. Nevertheless, I have several questions and disagreements associated with this method.

One question is which orientation and organization (or structural outline) will be used — Eastern Orthodox, Roman Catholic, Lutheran, Reformed-Calvinistic, Anglican, Anabaptist, Wesleyan, Charismatic, or some other? Which philosophical, sociological, or other grid will determine the methodology, assumptions, and structure for the study? Into which cultural framework will the presentation of Christian doctrines be placed?

One of my concerns include that Biblical and theological study must always begin with the Biblical text in its own context. If other settings and methodologies are permitted to drive the study there is the danger, possibly an inevitable one, that it will be founded upon and continue without a real Biblical base — external elements may become the controlling influences. To say it another way, failure to begin with and continue to investigate the Biblical text in its own world as the setting for studying the Christian faith leaves us without much needed "control." Consequently, the contemporary cultural or intellectual scheme chosen may become tyrannical and impose extra-Biblical influences and criteria upon understanding the Biblical message rather than the framework simply being a tool for making applications for the modern writer's audience.

This leads to a major potential problem that occurs if in her/his training the potential leader has met only one form of systematic theology, especially if it has been learned in an "indoctrination" environment. The person then takes up work in another culture, either in her or his homeland or abroad. She or he has no option but to teach or preach what has been taught without help in understanding the need or means for adaptation without compromising "the faith revealed once and for all" in Jesus Christ. More than likely the two cultures will not "fit." The structure used will be "foreign."

Some Often Overlooked Factors Which Influence the Biblical Student

Internal-Subjective Factors which Influence the Student

Less obvious than the type of theology with which to begin are differences stemming from subjective factors within the individual student/theologian. All of us come to our studies with personal preferences, commitments, experiences, and presuppositions. Complete objectivity in the theological enterprise is unobtainable.[6] We must acknowledge our presuppositions and note their influence upon the way we work and the results that come from it. We must learn to deal with our presuppositions lest they become "blinders"[7] which narrow our field of vision and force us to go straight ahead without even considering other options, methods, or needs.

Furthermore, individuals respond in various ways to intellectual-academic approaches to a subject. The same philosophical, or historical, or social scientific, or aesthetic handlings will not appeal equally to all. Such matters are deeply involved in complex matrixes including psychological, intellectual, societal, cultural, and many other factors.

Biblical theology is also influenced by the personality, cultural-economic situation, the intellectual environment of the student, and more. A survey of the history of the discipline is sufficient to demonstrate the strong influence upon Biblical and

---

[6] In a well-known essay Rudolf Bultmann asked, "Is Exegesis Without Presuppositions Possible?" and then demonstrated how influential were his own in his work.

[7] I fear many readers may be too urban and/or young to understand this allusion. Pieces of leather were sometimes sewn to the bridle of a horse or mule in such a position as to obscure vision to either side. These pieces of leather were called "blinders."

theological studies of the dominant philosophy and methodologies of any given historical period.

Societal-Cultural Factors which Influence "Doing" Theology

In addition to individual, personality, philosophical, and environmental differences, diverse cultural factors have a major influence on the way people think and learn. A missionary physician, a veteran of work in a number of locations, and I were discussing different educational styles. She observed, "Half the world memorizes, the other half learns to think."

Even more significant is the fact that although all humans share a store of commonalities, individuals and people groups have different thought patterns, ways of evaluating evidence, and means of problem solving. Bernie Harder, teacher of linguistics, medieval literature, and international literature at the University of Windsor, Ontario, Canada, offers a perceptive study of the effect of culture on thought processes, social customs, beliefs and rituals, language, and especially upon the learning of a language other than one's mother-tongue.[8] Even sentence structure and syntax can be affected. In some cases a statement or question made to a speaker of English as a second language may be misunderstood and taken in a way exactly the opposite than that intended by the speaker.

Harder, also cites observations, confirmed by others (Lakoff 1987), of Robert B. Kaplan of the University of Southern California. He describes several different patterns of logic employed in the English essays written by foreign students in his courses. He explains that the English structure is a straight line because of its linear development. The Semitic structure is a

---

[8] "Weaving Cultural Values on the Loom of Language," *Media Development* 3/1989, 25-28.

series of parallel arrows connected with a broken line, the Oriental pattern is like a spiral moving inward, and the Romance pattern is a zig-zagged arrow. The Slavic, or Russian, is more difficult to explain (Kaplan 1966:4-14). He diagrams five thought patterns as follows (Kaplan 1966:15):

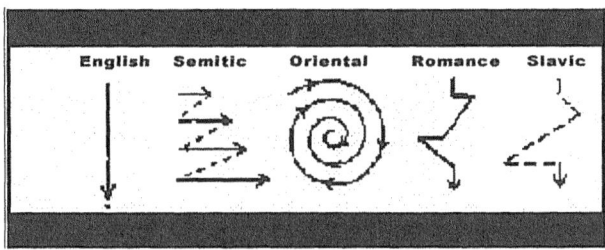

Kaplan (1966) states, "Logic (in the popular, rather than the logician's sense of the word) which is the basis of rhetoric, is evolved out of a culture; it is not universal...but varies from culture to culture and even then from time to time within a given culture (p.2)."

Many of these conclusions from the field of linguistics have their corollary in theology in a cross-cultural setting. They show that people-groups think differently. Therefore we must not assume that the forms of theologies which appeal to, and are relevant to, one group will necessarily be so for another.

Even more to the point are some issues raised by Orlando Costas (1986). Although he is not directly concerned with our topic, Costas makes a direct, positive contribution to our study by his insistence that Western theology, even among Evangelical Christians, is "too obsessed with the Enlightenment" and that preoccupations with "the reasonableness of faith" is not necessarily a primary concern in the Two Thirds World.

Furthermore, he insists, that Western and other parts of the world have different primary agendas. The West seems predisposed to address "the skeptic, atheist, rationalistic-heathen — the nonreligious person" (Costas 1986:320). In the Two Thirds World major concerns are more likely to be poverty, powerlessness, oppression, and religious pluralism (Costas 1986:321).

Potential Problems of Western Systematic Theology in the Two Thirds World

Most systematic theologies are Western constructions using Western methodologies, systems, and logic. They produce answers for Western peoples, and are often directed toward the academically oriented. What happens too often is that the methods, tools, conclusions and even the controversies of Western systematic theology are simply transported into locations and cultures foreign to it. Issues raised in one environment frequently will be of little or no significance in the new setting. Concerns important in the target society may not even be recognized by the Western import. Even if they are, they may not receive proper consideration because to "outsiders" they seem of little significance. Proposed solutions from outside the culture, without full awareness of what is at stake, may be superficial, legalistic, or unworkable. The question of what should be done about polygamy by Christians spurred a vigorous discussion in a class session of one of my courses. American students proposed relatively simplistic answers. Eventually a Two-Thirds World student arose to say he was the youngest child of his fathers fourth and youngest wife. If his father had followed most of the advice given in the discussion, he said, either he and his mother would have starved to death or she would have been forced to become a prostitute. Externally proposed solutions are also likely to be patchwork at best and dangerous at worst. Irving Hexham, in response to a plenary session paper, "The Role of Evangelicals in American Society," by Martin E. Marty, read before the 1984 Chicago National Meeting of ETS, demonstrated that Christians, either led to Christ or renewed by the revivals in South Africa in which Andrew Murray played a dominant role, divided into two distinct groups after Murray's death. One self-destructed into radical self-centered religious subjectivism, the other, with no native expression of Christian theology, transported Dutch Calvinism and tried to force it to fit that culture. This latter group became the forefathers of the later apartheid society that reaped bitter and shameful fruits for decades.

There are some theological statements, interpretations, or demands that are strictly Western in their origin and implementation. Some of us have either read about or encountered personally some of these being vigorously contested or made tests of orthodoxy in countries or cultures where combatants neither know nor understand the background, history, or what was really at stake. Need I go on? The problem to which I allude is well documented by most contemporary studies in missiology.

One fact already raised illustrates an important issue that runs deep. Western theologians usually assume the validity of logic as an unassailable methodological tool. But Enlightenment-style logic, which considers sacrosanct such principles as that of non-contradiction, is not necessarily appropriate in all societies. Remember Kaplan's distinction of different thought patterns (1966) and Costas' complaint about the West's obsession with reason and reasonableness (1986).[9] Yet, we must stress that although the logical process in non-Western societies may be different from ours, they work for and make sense to them.

Let me dare to go a step further. Familiarity with some of the literature from the same locales and time of Biblical books suggests that we are probably making a major mistake in attempting to fit Biblical thought into such schemes as those available in Aristotelan or other Western forms of logic. Semitic thought forms did not and often still do not operate that way. Can the Western mind really adequately describe and give the rationale for the chronological or logical scheme of the Book of Jeremiah?

Two Thirds World systematic theologies should reflect familiarity with and sensitivity to the religious customs and traditions and the cultural and social issues of the target areas. The writers should be those with first hand knowledge of the group, preferably nationals, not writers with mainly a Western point of view. They should reflect the ways of thinking and expression indigenous to the area being addressed. At best Western systematic theologies might be studied merely as examples, but even then with a careful effort to explain the kinds of societies, cultures, and issues of the environments within which they arose and the types of and reasons for the methods used.

Biblical Theology and the Two Thirds World

We have already sought to demonstrate that all Biblical theologies are not of the same kind. Contemporary Biblical theological studies are influenced by the same types of prior

---

[9] Note also Lakoff (1987).

commitments and agendas as are systematics. Nevertheless, we are concerned here with context and methods of approach, not with the final results of various practitioners of a method. Biblical theology, at least initially, is not concerned with Western, or any other contemporary structures. Biblical theology starts with the Bible in its own historical-cultural environment and this is its distinct advantage. It begins, and at its best, stays very close to the setting from which Two Thirds World scholars, like those in the West, can work directly in seeking to state theology for their communities.

The Inherent Nature of Biblical Theology

Biblical theology begins by seeking to determine the message of the Biblical writers in their culture. These cultures are not subject to change for they are now "frozen" in time and place. Biblical cultures are "foreign" to all modern peoples and cultures. Thus theological work, which begins by seeking Biblical truth as it came in its original context, places all participants on a level playing field since it is foreign and neutral to all members of all contemporary societies.

Even an elementary awareness of the situations within which the Bible was written and the world-views of its characters challenges interpreters in subsequent ages to ask the question, "What did it mean to its original writers and hearer/readers?" before asking, "What does it mean in our very different time and setting?" It forces all Christians to come together in the house of the interpreter, each from multi-cultural viewpoints, to seek the meaning of the message initially revealed in another time and place, before proclaiming its words of salvation, life, and hope in the diverse settings of our world.

Secondly, with a Biblical theological approach those from cultures of the Two Thirds world may actually be better equipped to see issues in the text in its original context. Western approaches, especially systematic theology, may be heavily influenced by the outlook and interests of the educated, privileged classes, from which much academic theology comes. The Western view of the text may be too easily glossed over by familiarity with traditional exegesis and theological formularies. Starting from the Biblical context also makes it much easier for us to hear our non-First World sisters and brothers when they raise as a part of the Bible's own agendas such issues as truth and justice, slavery and oppression, poverty and wealth, religious pluralism and idolatry, nationalism and tribalism, sexism, classism, exploitation, governmental and business ethics, and many more. Scholars from the Two Thirds World are also able to help us see the blotches on our own societies, attitudes, and personal lives to which we have become blind or desensitized but which are exposed by the text.

Is Biblical Theology Normative Theology

The essence of the Christian faith is not primarily assent to doctrine, shared religious experiences or feelings, or the quest for authentic existence. It is a personal relationship with God. This relationship is made available through Jesus Christ, and continued through the presence and work of the Holy Spirit. The facts about this relationship and their implications are the major concern of the Bible.

With the possible exception of two or three books, the Bible is not even close to any particular type or system of theology. It reveals God by showing His person and His will, by recounting His words and works, His actions and reactions over a long period of time, in numerous places and cultures. It relates how many human persons and groups have acted and reacted as God so revealed Himself.

The Biblical accounts of the past can be immediately relevant to the present because they are not primarily concerned with presenting knowledge in and of itself, not laws nor liturgy, not human ideals, nor any other kind of "program." Rather, the Bible presents a person, one who "is the same yesterday, today, and forever" (Heb 13:8).

How was the message applied by the original writer and reader? By revealing, not a theology nor concepts, but the person of whom they spoke and the nature and implications of the relationship with him. The problem arises when persons and groups living after the Biblical period are unable or unwilling to see and hear the message in its original setting before seeking to move it into theirs. The abstract, technical language of philosophy or other modern disciplines is not sufficient for presenting and bringing one into a relationship with another person, let alone the ultimate One.

The prophet Micah asserts that it is through remembering events of God at work in the past that one "may know the saving acts of the Lord" (6:5). Throughout Scripture it is assumed that its narrative is normative revelation. True, there are also the messages of prophets and apostles, words of worship and wisdom, and more, but all these are within or cognate to the narrative. I maintain that Biblical theology at its best focuses upon the person and will of God and upon the flow and lessons of that narrative within which he works. Interestingly enough a narrative framework is one within which much of the Two-Thirds World is most comfortable. The same is true of many, especially the less erudite, in the First World.

All forms of Biblical interpretations, including theologies, are concerned with understanding and applying revelation in ways that are useful for faith and practice in our worlds. However, it seems to me, to be at least an open question of just how far the Biblical message must be removed from its original form and setting to see its relevance. This becomes evident when we recognize that the Biblical message has a subjective aspect which must affect the inner, the spiritual, emotional, and volitional components of persons as well as an objective, cognitive one.

The Biblical writers themselves considered their message as more than description and delivered it in a variety of times and cultures. God seemed to think the type of presentation we find in the Bible was both understandable and normative. A form of theology which stays as close as possible to that method will not stray too far afield.

"There and Back Again," A Paradigm for Beginning Theology

My Nigerian friends, probably subconsciously, put their finger on a series of issues about preparing students and actually "doing" theology in a variety of cultural settings. The sentiments they expressed beneath trees overlooking the African savannah echo the task of the Biblical interpreter once described by Professor C. H. Dodd:

> The ideal interpreter would be one who has entered into that strange first-century world, has felt its whole strangeness, has sojourned in it until he has lived himself into it, thinking and feeling as one of those to whom the Gospel first came, and who will then return into our world, and give to the truth he

has discerned a body out of the stuff of our own thought. (Dodd 1936:40-41)

Recent decades have witnessed a growing realization of the close connection between all forms of theological studies and hermeneutics — the study of interpretation theory and procedures. A major part of hermeneutics, at least in the world of traditional Biblical and theological studies, is the attempt to bridge what is called the "gap" which separates our time and culture from the world of the Bible,[10] how to go "there" and "back again."[11]

The journey is essential because Biblical theology must begin with the assumption that (with the possible exception of predictive prophecy) no interpretation is likely to be correct which could not have been intended by the original author nor understood by the original recipients. Thus interpretation begins by seeking the intent of the authors.

This authorial intent is the revelation of the person, will, and acts of the eternal, unchangeable God. It also demonstrates that there are spiritual and moral principles which are rooted in and gain authority because they reflect the nature and will of God

---

[10] Such differences as (1) time, (2) culture, (3) language, (4) geography, (5) literature, (6) institutions, including political, social, etc., (7) philosophy (8) world-and-life view, and the like.

[11] Note Karl Barth's description of John Calvin's interpretative method. It might be called "going there and back again." "See how energetically Calvin, having first established what stands in the text, sets himself to re-think the whole material and to wrestle with it, till the walls which separate the sixteenth century [Calvin's day] from the first becomes transparent." See also *Epistle to the Romans* (Eng. trans; London: Oxford University Press, 1933), 7. The title of C. H. Dodd's book of childrens' stories is *There and Back Again* (London: Hodder and Stoughton Ltd, 1932).

himself; our living in harmony with them pleases God.[12] Sometimes these principles are presented abstractly and in absolute form. More often they are revealed as they are applied specifically to culturally controlled situations and over many centuries. Both of these modes are valid and relevant although they must be interpreted and applied in different, appropriate ways.

The presentation of these basic moral and spiritual principles in the absolute form has a trans-historical, trans-cultural character. The other form of presentation is closely wedded to specific circumstances, those arising out of cultural, social, and historical situations. Both the books of the OT prophets and the NT epistles are "problem centered." The writers were frequently applying basic theological principles to specific problems faced by those to whom they were originally writing. In such cases the Biblical text must be examined carefully to recognize the problem and to identify the general principles which lie behind the application made by the prophet or apostle. The methods with which the principles for life and conduct were applied to the situations faced by the first readers are also important. The interpreter must be aware of these methods for they will provide guidelines for applying the same principles in different times and places. Each piece of this Biblical data, each in its own way, is a part of the total which is normative and relevant for that teaching, reproof, correction, and training in righteousness designed to bring the people of God to maturity and equip them for every good work (cf, 2 Tim 3:16-17).

We journey into the Biblical world to learn of God, the reflections of his nature in the principles of which we have spoken, and to see how they were applied in the Biblical world.

---

[12] See John 8:29; 1 Cor 7:32; Col 1:10; 1 Thes 4:1; 2 Tim 2:4; Heb 11:4.

One of our main concerns in this study is to insist that regardless of which country or culture from which one begins the journey, the destination is the same, the Biblical world. God, the spiritual and moral principles, and the guidelines for employing them are the same. Differences come when we apply them in our diverse situations after we have come "back again."

Such is the purpose and goal of the interpreter's journey. But is it really possible to go to, what Professor Dodd called that "strange world of the Bible?" (1936). The answer, first of all, is that of course it is impossible to completely enter some other time and place. Yet, through seeking evidences of situations, including events, personalities, social institutions, cultural phenomena, and the rest, historians do, with some success, enter past places and societies all the time. They focus upon the study of documents, both primary and secondary, and archaeological evidence. Historians work forward from the past and backwards from the present. Their primary objectives include offering reconstructions of ancient societies, determining what caused their distinctive characters, and seeking to identify the intermediate developmental steps between then and now.

The vehicles to bear us to the Biblical world are, in one form or another, the elements of Biblical studies. Textual work begins with the evaluation of manuscripts now available. Whenever possible it involves working in the original Biblical languages and an understanding of the genre and other literary and rhetorical features within the texts. It was learning about the Biblical world that my African friends found so helpful. The study of the historical-cultural situation can begin by asking what seems to be the nature of the times, daily life, customs, attitudes, and aspirations assumed in the text. But then one may go to cognate literature contemporary with the Biblical period and other remains for additional historical-cultural evidence. There is also a growing recognition of the importance of archaeology, not only for apologetics, but also as a major contributor to rediscovering the ancient context.[13]

The more often one enters that other world in order to become acquainted with the context of the Bible, the more he or she becomes familiar with the main ways of getting into it. In addition there are also secondary "roads" and byways which go there. These less traveled ways pass through different terrain, hamlets, and scenery. By occasionally taking one of these we see the Biblical world from other angles. The distinctive view offered by alternative "approaches" provides a fuller understanding of the nature of the goal of our trip once we are "there." For example, A study of and traveling along the approaches to Jerusalem from various directions vastly helped my understanding of the city and its history. Likewise, we sometimes gain insights into the Biblical text in surprising ways and places when we look at its context from different vantage points.[14] (One misses a lot by traveling only by air or on the interstate highways!)

---

[13] See John Gray, "Toward A Theology of the Old Testament: The Contribution of Archaeology," *Expository Times* 74/11 (August 1963), 847-351.

[14] My understanding of the content and setting of the Book of Jeremiah was enhanced by the novel, *Harken to the Voice* by Franz Werfel. There is much to be gained with familiarity with the methods and interpretations of the Bible by the so-called "Church Fathers," writers from the Reformation and earlier periods, e.g., the series, *Ancient Christian Commentary on Scripture*, Thomas C. Oden and Christopher A. Hall, eds. (Downers Grove: InterVarsity., 1998 ff).
See also Leland Ryken, *How to Read the Bible as Literature and Get more Out of It* (Grand Rapids: Zondervan, 1984). Reading the Bible just as literature (which is not what Ryken proposes) has its limitations, see Krister

Of course it helps to have companions along on such a journey. Without the company of fellow students-travelers who have gone before, especially those who have left the records of their "journeys" (i.e., their research), each generation of theologians would have to start from scratch. And from contemporary travelers we can benefit from expertise they may possess — theologians travel in pilgrim bands, they must not be "lone rangers"!

Now, all this is "old hat" to most of us. It is relevant precisely because the various elements involved in Biblical studies are at least one valid starting point for those who would found their theology upon the Bible, regardless of their ethnic or cultural origin.[15] These are the time-tested elements of making an exegesis of specific parts or passages of the Bible which must be fitted into the over-arching whole of the Biblical panorama.

To those who object that such a journey is too rigorous, I reply only that the theological discipline requires discipline. Too often I see students from this as well as other countries gravitate toward what appears to be more simple, more practical, the more immediately applicable courses of study. They then leave the formal phase of their education without a sound Biblical and theological foundation upon which to build. They have little of that kind of maturity which the writer of the Epistle to the

---

Stendahl, "The Bible as A Classic and the Bible as Holy Scripture," *Journal of Biblical Literature*, 103/1 (1984), 3-10.

[15] For summaries of traditional interpretative procedures from a Western point of view see Gordon D. Fee and Douglas Stuart. *How to Read the Bible for all its Worth* (Grand Rapids: Zondervan, 1982); Dan McCartney and Charles Clayton, *Let the Reader Understand (Grand Rapids: Baker,* 1994); H. A. Virkler. *Hermeneutics: Principles and Process of Biblical Interpretation* (Grand Rapids: Baker, 1981).

Hebrews says is "for those who have their faculties trained by practice to distinguish good from evil" (Heb 5:14).

I am haunted by a report given me by a colleague who had been a long time missionary. He told of a bright young student from another continent who earned a Master's degree in a "practically oriented" area. He avoided taking all but the absolutely required minimum courses in Bible and theology. He then returned to his homeland and, because he did not know the difference, led a denomination of three million into liberalism.

I have implied foundational steps from a Western a perspective. That is my cultural orientation. Those who can identify better equipment and way-stations for the trip into the Biblical world in ways more appropriate to other cultures should do so.

Such is the equipment to bear the Biblical student-theologian "there." The requirements for coming "back again" are not so easily identified. They vary from culture to culture and from time to time. But then, in this return leg of the journey the student is coming home, to his or her world, the place and culture she or he knows best. But here the Biblical student needs to learn from the systematic theologian, that there is more to our culture than meets the eye; careful analysis to see what is beyond the surface is a requirement if we are to be most helpful and relevant.

Sometimes the "body out of the stuff of our own thought" given "to the truth...discerned" after our return "into our world" may take the form of systematic theology, at other times, story. Personally I have found helpful the process of seeking to identify the broad questions, either stated or implied, which were in the minds of the writers. The form must be determined by the culture; the content must never be compromised.

Some Concluding Observations

The task of the Biblical theologian in any culture is first to assert the existence and nature of the One sought in virtually every culture, through whom "the world was created...[so that]...that what is seen was made of things which do not appear" (cf, Heb 11:3). Then she or he must move to identify both the questions implied in the text itself, the divine principles, and their implications as they were worked out in the Biblical world. This means that the student of the Bible will seek to pierce to the very heart of its message to find its concepts and principles about God, the universe and their relationship and then apply that message in appropriate forms in the modern world.

The very nature of systems frequently makes the transportation of their methods and statements from one culture to another potentially inappropriate, dangerous, and tyrannical. On the other hand, Biblical theology, when properly done, should be the foundational discipline as various peoples and cultures seek statements of their own Biblically based theologies. It will assure that such formularies will be wedded to the message of Scripture in its own day and that applications in all modern settings will be relevant.

Perhaps it may appear that I have strayed from my announced topic, "Some Observations on The Contribution of Biblical Theology for Christianity in the So-Called 'Two Thirds World." I think not. These observations assume that "from all peoples, nations and languages" (cf. Dan 7:14) Christians who stand within the traditional spectrum of the faith regard the Bible as God's authoritative word for faith and life. The fact that it was given at specific times and places must be taken seriously. Of equal import is its eternal, unchanging message.

These observations also come from a conviction on my part that, although I appreciate the value of systematic theology, all systems are created by human beings, are temporal, culturally bound, and become obsolete. They are always incomplete, for God is greater than any system. And, ultimately, all theology must seek not about God, but God himself, his person and will. As Alfred Lord Tennyson said,

> Our little systems have their day;
> They have their day and cease to be.
> They are but broken lights of Thee;
> And thou, O Lord, art more than they.
> — "In Memoriam"

Challenges of Care Giving

Chapter 4

Caring for a Camcorder Culture

Paul Metzer

In "The Vacation," the poet Wendell Berry writes of a man who spends his entire holiday capturing it on video so as to preserve it forever on film. The irony of the situation, however, is that although he went *on* vacation and captured the vacation *on* video, he was never *in* his vacation. "With a flick of a switch, there it would be. But he would not be in it. He would never be in it."[1]

The poem bears significance for the purposes of this paper in several ways. For one, the immoderate appeal of camcorder or video productions symbolizes the *growing* problem of the *absence* of *real* presence in our society. The virtual or artificial is *replacing* actual reality. It is not only Wendell Berry who speaks to this concern. Bill Joy of *Sun Microsystems* sounds like a modern-day Nostradamus when he warns that the hour may soon draw near when artificial intelligence, specifically, those forms with self-replicating capabilities, may not need us, making humanity "an endangered species."[2]

Morpheus of the movie, *The Matrix*, would lead us to believe that artificial intelligence will indeed take over, after which time no one will know that it has. Is this not already the case? For society has not noticed the emergence of the camcorder as a

---

[1] Wendell Berry, "The Vacation," in *The Selected Poems of Wendell Berry* (Washington: HarperCollins, 1999), 157.
[2] Bill Joy, "Why the Future Doesn't Need Us," *Wired*, April 2000, 1, 3.

modern day mutation protruding from the head, or its counterpart — the cell phone.

Such mutations, although subtle, are by no means harmless, and not simply by means of posing potential threats as carcinogenic devices. For as Ken Myers of *Mars Hill* maintains, the use of the cell phone in public "pointedly ignores the presence of others."[3] Myers argues that the Church must address the real problem of the subtle invasion of trends that promote dehumanization and disembodied existence in our culture.[4] Whether one ignores the presence of others with a cell phone or one's own presence through the use of the camcorder as in the case of Berry's "Vacation," the same problem surfaces in each — disembodiment, that is, the absence of embodied presence.[5]

---

[3]Ken Myers, "Dehumanizing Tendencies Should Be Put on Hold," in *The Dallas Morning News* (Dallas), 1 April 2000.

[4]Ibid.

[5]In *The Postmodern God*, Graham Ward makes use of cyberspace "as a cultural metaphor for postmodernism." In cyberspace, "nothing is produced, though everything is marketed. Cyberspace *is* now the marketplace, though its reality is virtual, for such is the nature of the real." The metaphor of cyberspace suggests that Postmodernity's critique of Modernity entails a radically different conception of bodies, time, and space; access to the God of Postmodernity can only come by way of this shift in perspective. Graham Ward, "Introduction, or, A Guide to Theological Thinking in Cyberspace," in *The Postmodern God: A Theological Reader*, ed. Graham Ward (Malden: Blackwell Publishers Ltd., 1997), xvii. In addition to the metaphorical use made of camcorders, cell phones, and cyberspace for depicting Postmodernity, Stanley Grenz commandeers *Star Trek* and its sequel, *The Next Generation*, to portray the differences between Modernity and Postmodernity respectively. See Stanley J. Grenz, *A Primer on Postmodernism* (Grand Rapids: William B. Eerdmans Publishing Company, 1996), 5-10. See also Tom Beaudoin, *Virtual Faith: the Irreverent Spiritual Quest of Generation X*, with a foreword by Harvey Cox (San Francisco: Jossey-Bass Publishers, 1998). Note especially his point on

Berry's poem bears significance for the purposes of this paper in another way. For the *absence* of real presence is a hallmark of certain sectors of Postmodern thought.[6] For example, the author of the text, whether the author's name is Paul or God, or Wendell Berry, for that matter, is dead. There is no presence or meaning. The meaning one finds there is nothing but the projection of one's own desired intention. Thus, it is not simply that the virtual is replacing the actual, but also that the virtual is *all* there really is, was, and will be.

Not only is this true of Eiffel tower academic analyses of texts, but also it is true of news shows, Presidential scandals, even Bible studies, all of which demonstrate that Postmodernity is everywhere present — not simply in the Gen-X world of punk hair and body piercing. Dan Rather, the anchor for the CBS Evening News, once suggestively and provocatively stated: "We don't give you the news. We make it" — a point that the movie *Wag the Dog* so vividly portrays.[7] During questioning over the

---

Generation X as a movement given to irreverence and reverence, the virtual and actual in chapter eight, pages 145-158.

[6] For an exposition of the theme of absence in Postmodern thought, see Jacques Derrida, *Of Grammatology*, trans. Gayatri Chakravorty Spivak (Baltimore: Johns Hopkins University Press, 1991). George Steiner offers a critique of deconstruction and its apology for absence in *Real Presences* (Chicago: University of Chicago Press, 1989). Karl Barth has been hailed as a theologian who serves as a precursor and prophet of Postmodern theology. For a discussion on the tension between presence and absence in his theology, see the following works: William Stacy Johnson's work, *The Mystery of God: Karl Barth and the Postmodern Foundations of Theology*, Columbia Series in Reformed Theology (Louisville: Westminster John Knox Press, 1997); Graham Ward, *Barth, Derrida, and the Language of Theology* (Cambridge: Cambridge University Press, 1995).

[7] In *Toxic Sludge Is Good For You!*, the authors claim that reporters and news agencies receive much of their information from public relations firms committed to special interest groups. Thus, in many instances, it is not the

Monica Lewinski affair, President Clinton responded at one instance in the typical parlance of the "Lawyerese" language by stating something to the effect of, "It all depends on what the meaning of the word 'is' is." And finally, in Sunday Schools across the land, the central question is no longer, "What does the text say?" but "What does the text say to you?" or better, "How does the text make you feel?" The projected or virtual is all there *really* is, was, and will be. The thing in itself or actual reality is *actually* fiction — an illusion. This is the second item of importance.

Lastly, the poem bears significance for this paper in that if one were to use a broad stroke brush, Postmodernity represents the era of the poet or artist. Premodernity and Modernity, on the other hand, constitute the age of the priest and physicist respectively. The logic behind this sketch is that whereas Postmodernity celebrates the fiction of artistic rendition Premodernity champions faith and revelation. In contrast to each, Modernity sets forth facts of physics and pure, unadulterated reason.[8]

However, science has fallen prey to suspicion. The utopia it promised is but the afterglow of nuclear radiation. Truth itself, from whatever quarter, is suspect; many view it as an urge for mastery, the politically correct opinion of those wielding power.

---

news anchors and their entourage who control the news, but rather, the special interest groups. See John Stauber and Sheldon Rampton, *Toxic Sludge Is Good For You! Lies, Damn Lies & The Public Relations Industry* (Monroe: Common Courage Press, 1995). I wish to thank Rev. Derek Chinn for bringing this work to my attention.

[8]Initial inspiration for the three categories here is to be attributed to Robert W. Funk, *Jesus as Precursor* (Philadelphia: Fortress Press, 1975) and Kevin Vanhoozer, "A Lamp in the Labyrinth: the Hermeneutics of 'Aesthetic' Theology," *Trinity Journal* 8 (Spring 1987): 25-56.

On this account, knowledge is not power, but power is knowledge.[9] Power corrupts, and absolute power (and knowledge) corrupts absolutely.

It is the poet, the artist, who looms large as the prince of these Premodern times, and the collective works of Friedrich Nietzsche, though he himself is long dead, serve as its living, prophetic voice. For Nietzsche denounced Immanuel Kant's halfway house attempts whereby he relativized art yet safeguarded the relative absoluteness of science and ethics.[10] Nietzsche, on the other hand, claimed that truth and values are themselves matters of *taste*.[11] Thus, Nietzsche extended Kant's dictum that beauty is in the eye of the beholder to include in its grasp truth and morality as well. Everything is projection, the result of which is fragmentation.

In *Thus Spoke Zarathustra*, Nietzsche's prophet Zarathustra speaks of having "reached *my* truth."[12] He adds that inquiries regarding "the way" have "always offended my taste." For his own part, he prefers "to question and try out the *ways* themselves."[13] His approach, namely, wrestling through the various ways, is a matter of "taste," neither "good" nor "bad." One must choose a way, which again is a matter of taste. There is no such thing as "the way." For *the* way — that does not

---

[9]On knowledge as power, see the following: Michael Foucault, "Truth and Power," in *Power/Knowledge: Selected Interviews and Other Writings*, 1972-1977, ed. Colin Gordon (New York: Pantheon Books, 1980), 133.
[10]Refer to the selections of Immanuel Kant's critiques of pure and practical reason as well as aesthetic judgment in the following work: Lewis White Beck, ed. *Kant Selections*, The Great Philosophers, ed. Paul Edwards (New York: Macmillan Publishing Company, 1988).
[11]Friedrich Nietzsche, *Thus Spoke Zarathustra*, in *The Portable Nietzsche*, ed. Walter Kaufmann (New York: The Viking Press, 1968), 307.
[12]Ibid. (italics added)
[13]Ibid. (italics added)

exist."[14] In fact, for Nietzsche, "truths are illusions." They are like "coins which have lost their pictures and now matter only as metal, no longer as coins." Truth is a dead metaphor — "worn out and without sensuous power."[15] Thus, it is not simply for ornamental reasons that the paper begins with a poem. Consideration now turns *from comparing* the poem with Postmodern culture *to contrasting* Nietzsche's famous critique of truth as dead metaphor with the fact of Christian faith *and* the living Christ with the dead Church, namely, Christendom and culture.

The Contrast Between the Virtuous Christ and the Virtual Church and Culture

Contra Nietzsche, truth is not a dead but living metaphor. For in the incarnation of the divine Word of God, the central truth of Christian faith, poetry meets prose. The incarnation is not a mythical form,[16] nor an ornament of language. In Christ, the poetic Word, the language of the gods, becomes historical prose. As C. S. Lewis argues, "if ever a myth had become fact, had been incarnated, it would be just like this."[17] *In it*, one finds

---

[14]Ibid.

[15]Friedrich Nietzsche, "On Truth and Lie in an Extra-Moral Sense," in *The Portable Nietzsche*, ed. Walter Kaufmann (New York: The Viking Press, 1968), 46-47.

[16]The position set forth here stands in marked contrast to John Hick's work, *The Metaphor of God Incarnate: Christology in a Pluralistic Age* (Louisville: Westminster/John Knox Press, 1993).

[17]C. S. Lewis, *Surprised By Joy: the Shape of My Early Life* (London: Geoffrey Bles, 1955), 222.

the transcendent presence of God. The transcendent presence of God is embodied presence — poetic prose.[18]

In Christ, fiction has become fact and God's presence is embodied presence. Christ turns fiction into fact and heals the fragmentation of culture. The paradigm for the Christian's response to the current age centers, as it always has, in the incarnation of Jesus Christ.[19] The virtuous Christ is the basis for the Christian's critique and constructive dialogue with Postmodern culture.

Too often though, the virtuous Christ stands in marked contrast to Christendom — the virtual Church. For Christendom rests content, projecting a Gnostic or Docetic conception of Christ — disembodied presence, whereby the divine Christ only appears to be the human Jesus (See 1 Jn 4). Christendom mistakenly substitutes the vicarious death of Christ for vicarious living — Christ lived for us so that we would not have to live.

The Word became *flesh*. The reality of Jesus Christ stands in stark contrast to the Modern Project of detached speculation, the result of which is fragmentation — so evident in Postmodern thought and life. However, when the Church of Jesus Christ itself fails to flesh out the Gospel, for example, by falling prey to the

---

[18]George Steiner maintains that art uniquely reflects the fact that there is such a thing as transcendent presence (Steiner, 226-232). Questions of "aesthetic creation" and hermeneutical considerations are ultimately theological in nature (227, 231). Take away such presence and one abandons a full-orbed appropriation and appreciation of the aesthetic dimensions of reality to an early grave (229). Christian Scripture is the presentation of God in human history through the lens of literary reproduction. The artistic rendition of God in Scripture represents well the fact that we are not alone (226-232).

[19]Myers calls for "cell phone etiquette" whereby they give special regard for the embodied presence of others around them. Such etiquette "could demonstrate the high value that Christians place on embodiment, expressed in our doctrines of Creation, Incarnation, and Resurrection" (Myers).

great migration known as the white (and other colors) flight to the suburbs or by divorcing the soulish from the somatic concerns of the Gospel, it promotes further fragmentation. The eradication of enfleshment, of historical fact, gives rise to fiction — the fragmentation of fact. In such instances, the Church of Jesus Christ denies His incarnation by living a lie.

In "The Attack Upon 'Christendom,'" the Danish philosopher, Søren Kierkegaard, writes of the polarity between authentic Christianity and bourgeois religion or Christendom and the negative impact the latter has on the truth claims of Christian faith,

> Here then is the proof and disproof at the same time! The proof of the truth of Christianity from the fact that one has ventured everything for it, is disproved, or rendered suspect, by the fact that the priest who advances this proof does exactly the opposite. By seeing the glorious ones, the witnesses to the truth, venture everything for Christianity, one is led to the conclusion: Christianity must be truth. By considering the priest one is led to the conclusion: Christianity is hardly the truth, but profit is the truth.
>
> No, the proof that something is truth from the willingness to suffer for it can only be advanced by one who himself is willing to suffer for it. The priest's proof — proving the truth of Christianity by the fact that he takes money for it, profits by, lives off of, being steadily promoted, with a family, lives off of the fact that others have suffered — is a self-contradiction; Christianity regarded, it is fraud.[20]

---

[20] Søren Kierkegaard, *The Attack Upon "Christendom,"* in *A Kierkegaard Anthology*, ed. Robert Bretali (Princeton: Princeton University Press, 1951), 464-465.

To contextualize Kierkegaard's hyperbolic outrage,[21] one must view one's ministry, not as a profession (professionalism is the death knell of the Church), but as a prophetic call to service, even to the point of suffering. Otherwise, one makes a mockery of Christ's own suffering.

Although the incarnation of God reveals the fact that truth is not dead, the disengaged and disembodied Church deconstructs God's presence in that it is absent from the travail of culture, though not its treasures, thereby bringing death. As such, it is both a by-product and partial cause of the very fragmentation toward virtual reality facing the Postmodern culture it so readily confronts. As by-product and partial cause, the Church is "*of* the world but not *in* it."[22]

It is Christendom's dead creed, not the living Christ, which ultimately bears the brunt, if not of Nietzsche's ridicule, then at least, of Kierkegaard's critique. According to the great Dane, in Christendom, one detaches oneself from the insecurity and "discomforts" of engaging the world while securing "worldly goods" and "comforts." One confesses Christ with one's lips while denying Him with one's life. Orthodoxy may flourish

---

[21]See the editorial comments introducing the Kierkegaard essay where Bretali indicates that Kierkegaard later stated that his critique was exaggerated for the sake of "restoring the general balance" instead of resting in the status quo state of affairs (Bretali, 435).

[22]The statement is taken and adapted from Donald C. Posterski's work, *Reinventing Evangelism: New Strategies for Presenting Christ in Today's World* (Downers Grove: InterVarsity Press, 1989), 28. See also George Hunsberger's discussion of Posterski's insight in, "Acquiring the Posture of a Missionary Church," in *The Church Between Gospel and Culture: the Emerging Mission in North America*, ed. Geroge R. Hunsberger and Craig Van Gelder (Grand Rapids: William B. Eerdmans Publishing Company, 1996), 292.

throughout the land, but it is a meaningless orthodoxy whereby one simply plays the game of Christianity.[23] One thereby turns the Nicene Creed of the living Church into Nintendo cartridges and Sony Play Station CD's — virtual reality.

The problem, however, goes beyond the absence of real presence and the need for enfleshment to the abuse of power and the need for empowerment. Unlike that form of empowerment that patronizes, that condescends, refusing to see the other as an equal, biblical empowerment involves unleashing the people's own power, redirecting and redeeming the creative energies and talents God their Creator gave them. Biblical empowerment affirms the inherent dignity of all people as bearers of the image of God — the *imago Dei*. The lordship of Jesus Christ involves empowering people as He did — lifting up those who bear His image by living *among* the people as one of them rather than lording *over* them.[24]

Whereas Christ comes to serve and empower, Christendom often comes to be served and broker power. When the Church displaces Christ, exchanging empowerment for power, it renders the fact of Christ a fiction — virtual reality. Instead of using truth to enable, some use it as an instrument to enslave, as

---

[23]Kierkegaard, 437.

[24]Throughout the course of the paper, the use of the term "empowerment" involves connotations of unleashing the power of the people, releasing, redirecting, and redeeming the energy and creativity God their Creator gave them. The author is indebted to John Perkins for his insights into this matter. The Christian Community Development Association, which Dr. Perkins founded, involves the principle of redistribution. One should not understand redistribution as *taking* from the rich and giving to the poor, which would demean both parties. Instead, redistribution refers to the *sharing* of natural and spiritual gifts, talents, and abilities for the sake of enabling people to become all that God designed them to be, affirming their inherent self-worth and dignity.

Dostoyevsky so ably demonstrates in *The Grand Inquisitor*. According to the story, during the time of the Inquisition, the Pope exclaimed to a "reincarnated" Christ that the Church will kill Him again; for He fails to fathom that humanity wants to be ruled by Christendom's iron fist for food rather than be freed by Christ's forgiveness to love and live.[25]

Certainly, at this point, Christendom bears the brunt of Nietzsche's and Foucault's critique when they speak of "truth" being a form of the will to power, an urge arising from the desire for mastery over one's environment. If true, should we not focus a critical eye on what transpires in evangelism and apologetics? Should one not beware of those forms of apologetics, which involve setting forth evidence that demands a verdict that one's target victim is guilty so as to enslave?[26] In contrast to power ploy evangelism and power apologetics, forms of evangelism and apologetics *that empower* are required. Nietzsche's critique proves beneficial in that it sheds the light of suspicion on our motives. Sometimes the Church's worst enemies function as its best friends.

Another place where Nietzsche's critical gaze proves insightful is when he highlights the central thrust of Christianity. Whereas Christendom and so many of its critics have failed to

---

[25] Fyodor Dostoyevksy, "The Grand Inquisitor," in *The Brothers Karamazov: a Novel in Four Parts with Epilogue* (New York: Vintage Books, 1991), 252-260.

[26] The use of Josh McDowell's categories here (*Evidence that Demands a Verdict*) are simply for rhetorical purposes so as to combat the faulty use of Christian evidences. There is no intention here to disparage Josh McDowell's apologetic. See his work, *Evidence that Demands a Verdict: Historical Evidences for the Christian Faith*, rev. ed. (San Bernardino: Here's Life Publishers, 1979). However, from a different standpoint, one could say that many people today no longer find that particular approach to apologetics effective.

understand what Christianity is all about — an ethic — the ethic of the Crucified God, who is one's Good Neighbor, Nietzsche understood well the true Christian claim and mandate, even while rejecting it.[27] Nietzsche rejected Paul's religion of the Crucified God, claiming it to be the most harmful teaching ever taught by man. As Nietzsche saw it, Paul's religion kept man from rising to new heights to become more than human (Übermensch), for Paul esteemed the weak and despised.[28]

Although Nietzsche was wrong to debunk Paul's creed of the Crucified God, who is the Good Neighbor, he was right to see that Paul's creed esteemed embracing and empowering the weak and despised. In fact, Paul maintained that those who, like Christ, lower themselves to lift up the lowly (and there is a very real sense in which we are all lowly) actually ascend through such descent to new heights (See Phil. 2:5-11).

As Nietzsche's critique, and round about commendation of Christianity suggests, one's worst enemies may at times turn out to be one's best friends in that their critiques often expose blind spots and problems in need of attention and redress. Yet Nietzsche is actually Christendom's alter ego (Christendom as decoded from the creed of the Crusaders to the cry of Manifest Destiny),[29] when he rejects the Crucified God as Neighbor, who

---

[27]See my doctoral dissertation for a discussion of Nietzsche on this theme. Paul L. Metzger, *The Word of Christ and the World of Culture in and through the Theology of Karl Barth* (London: King's College London, 1999), 148-150.

[28]See note 77 on pages 148-149 of my dissertation *The Word of Christ and the World of Culture* for Walter Kaufmann's defense of Nietzsche and my accompanying critique.

[29]The Crusaders crushed the skulls of Muslims while declaring the creed, "Jesus is Lord!" during the Holy War. Mad with visions of destiny, those claiming to be the new children of Israel in America looked upon the First Nations peoples as Caananites, impostors on their promised land, crying, "Kill the Indian and save the soul!" Regarding the latter, see Richard Twiss' work,

empowers, replacing it with the empowerment of oneself, the self-sufficient super-human, the lone individual in isolation.[30] For whereas the alter ego Nietzsche, with all his egoism, rejects the ethic of Paul, Christendom willfully ignores it.

As stated above, Christendom itself is partly to blame for certain negative tendencies often associated with Postmodernity in that like Postmodernity it is a fractured organism of disfunction. For its existence, too, is virtual, and, as in the case of Nietzsche's superhuman, void of service to empower hurting people to be what they are created and called to be — truly human — living out the image of God. As stated above, so often, we have mistaken the vicarious death of Christ for vicarious living. He lived so that we would not have to. The Word became flesh and deed. But the Church so often exists as a deedless word, a word void of real *presence* and *empowerment*.

What happens when such enfleshment and empowerment are lacking? A void emerges — a longing in the lives of the lost. When culture and Christendom within it are void of Christ, a vacuum or black hole is left in its wake. What does this vacuum look like? Is there a window through which to view the void?

The Contours of the Vacuum

Many today are seeking after *authenticity, community, and mystery*. The question concerns whether or not they find them. Are they out there? The Broadway musical *Rent* offers us a window through which to gaze in order to glimpse precious portraits of a sub-culture made up of the homeless and

---

Five Hundred Years of Bad Haircuts now entitled, *One Church, Many Tribes: Following Jesus the Way God Made You*, with a foreword by John Dawson (Ventura: Regal Books, 2000) and the PBS documentary, *How the West Was Lost*.
[30]See Barth, CD III/2.

homosexual, which though despised in certain sectors of the larger society (of which Christendom is a part), reflects that society as its alter ego.[31] For it reflects the ubiquitous *loss of* and *longing for* authentic community rooted and enveloped in mystery.[32]

The play is rightly called *Rent*, for everything is ephemeral, inconstant, passing away: "Everything is rent." Everything is for rent, even love. Who or what can you trust? For as one of the songs screams out, "How can you connect in an age where strangers, landlords, lovers," even "your own blood cells betray?"[33]

Rent's song "Over the Moon" expresses expectation mixed with lamentation as well as offers a proposed solution to the crisis of the "rent" syndrome. The character who performs the song, Maureen, laments the emergence and dominance of cyberland and commercialism. The virtual devalues authenticity and community. She longs for authenticity, and wishes to express it in the context of a loving community. Her song suggests that the solution to the crisis rests in a communal leap of faith into the mysterious unknown.[34]

---

[31] I wish to express my thanks to Mr. Tony Kriz for first drawing my attention to this Broadway musical, and for numerous insightful conversations regarding Postmodern culture. Quite independently, Beaudoin argues that *Rent* is the "quintessential GenX musical." (*Virtual Faith*, xiii). He goes so far as to compare the orchestration of *Rent* to the enactment of religious pageantry and liturgy (xiii). Such a statement and perspective symbolizes the tension found in the Gen X cultural movement between "impropriety and irreverence" on the one hand and authentic religiosity on the other (See xiii).

[32] Jonathan Larson, *Rent* (Finster & Lucky Music, Ltd., 1996).

[33] Jonathan Larson, "Rent," in *Rent* (Finster & Lucky Music, Ltd., 1996).

[34] Jonathan Larson, "Over the Moon," in *Rent* (Finster & Lucky Music, Ltd., 1996).

But how can Maureen's proposed solution of hope and love prove sure given such a shattered society with no firm anchor for her faith? For the community itself, made up of those around her, is itself suspect and insecure. One must look elsewhere for that mystery which can sustain authentic communities. What will fill the void? Is there a door through which to pass — a means by which to build bridges and make contact?

Contacting in View of the Verdict that Demands Evidence

God calls the Church to be an authentic community inspired by and indwelled with the mystery of God revealed and experienced in Jesus Christ. Christ Himself was empowered with the Spirit to empower others with His presence. As in the case of the Lord it confesses, *the Church must overcome the projection of reality in cyberland and the camcorder world and seek after incarnation.* Christ's incarnation serves as the model for ministry, not the protagonist in Berry's poem, who films his world, but does not "enflesh" it, nor Nietzsche's superhuman who prevails over humanity rather than empowers it.

What is required is a hermeneutic of holism and responsible engagement, of live presence unto empowerment, itself empowered by the mysterious presence of God, which overcomes the hermeneutic of suspicion.[35] The reality of our reading of Scripture and the significance of what we mean by our

---

[35] Whereas Derrida speaks of suspicion in terms of the suspension of meaning in a text, we maintain that one suspends meaning by not enacting the word, giving rise to suspicion concerning the authenticity of one's Christianity, not Christ or the Christian Scriptures as such. From a different angle of combining ethics and hermeneutical concerns, see the following work. Roger Lundin, Anthony C. Thiselton, Clarence Walhout, *The Responsibility of Hermeneutics* (Grand Rapids: William B. Eerdmans Publishing Company, 1985).

speaking is shown forth in our living, embodying and empowering through God's empowering presence, solving the problem of suspicion and the suspension of meaning.[36]

The verdict that Jesus is the answer demands evidence — evidence of embodied presence, which empowers rather than seeks after power. There must be evidence that demonstrates the verdict that Jesus is Lord, that Jesus is God. Otherwise, the result is that truth is viewed simply as the will to power, as an urge for mastery over one's surroundings and others. In the end, such denial on the part of the Church, such an absence of evidence for the verdict, gives rise to the denial of Christ's deity.

Not rent, not one's nightstands, but ownership of a community from within the community, not fly-by nights of teddy bears and toothbrushes, and once a year Santa's helpers posing for photo-ops, but presence — the embodied presence of Christ in culture. Not a presence for self-promotion at the expense of the poor, but a presence, which empowers the poor to redirect and release their own God-given power through the empowerment of God's mysterious presence of Christ in the life of the Church. Religion may in fact be the opiate of the masses, as Marx maintained.[37] But the fact of the incarnation of Jesus Christ, the Pauper's King, is the basis for the awakening of the

---

[36] Wittgentsein argued that the meaning of a word is dependent upon the use made of it in a given community. See, for example, the following: Ludwig Wittgenstein, *Philosophical Investigations*, 3rd ed. (Old Tappan: Macmillan Collier, 1973). For the purposes of the present discussion, it is not only the meaningfulness but also the truthfulness of a term that is dependent on its use, indeed, whether it is used or not. For example, someone once remarked that love is a verb. The failure to "enverberate" a term renders it useless, meaningless, and untrue.

[37] Those rightfully or wrongfully suspicious of the Church may look at praise songs and hymns as tranquilizers and painkillers for the oppressed and as steroids and muscle stimulants for their oppressors.

Evangelical Church to overcome poverty, profiling, and their counterpart — racial (not simply urban) planning,[38] albeit from the inside out. The model for authentic human community inspired by and anchored in the divine mystery of God is set forth in Scripture, and centered in Jesus Christ. As in everything, the Church of the Lord Jesus Christ must look to Him.

Our God is a community of Persons, existing in eternal and blessed communion.[39] This God created humanity *in* its image (Gen. 1:26ff). Christ, however, *is* the image of God, though not in isolation. For He shares this image with His Church, whom He serves as its Head (Col. 1:15-18),[40] thereby signifying the participation in and reflection of the inner-Trinitarian life of eternity in human history. Thus, humanity, namely, the Church, the body of Christ, who is the Head, is called to image the Trinity, that unbroken communion of Persons, given its inclusion in the God-Man as His body and bride. Communion, the bond of faith, hope, and love in the Spirit, is what serves to unite us to Him and to one another.

Such communion and community engender safety, which in turn creates space for the expression of authenticity. The Apostle

---

[38]Following on from Marx's critique, what should one make of the matter of repentance for removing ourselves from taking responsibility for the sins of our ancestors? For sin is not simply individual. Sin is also structural — as in the case of racial planning, even in the context of urban planning. Too often, Evangelicals see sin as individual to the exclusion of sin as social and structural. Do we turn a deaf ear and blind eye to the structural juggernauts on the jugular vein, which keeps God from healing our land?

[39]Note the Trinitarian dynamic disclosed in chapters 14 to 17 of John's Gospel.

[40]See Karl Barth, *Church Dogmatics*, vol. III/1, *The Doctrine of Creation*, ed. G. W. Bromiley and T. F. Torrance (Edinburgh: T. & T. Clark, 1958), 205 for his insight into the relation of Gen. 1:26f. and Col. 1:15-18 concerning the image of God as set forth in relational terms.

Paul calls on us to bear one another's burdens (Gal. 6:2). Is this not what Christ has done and continues to do for us (See 1 Pet. 5:7)? Paul also encourages us to accept one another just as Christ accepted us in order to bring praise to God (Rom 15:7).

Community and authenticity require one another. Authentic community is rooted in compassionate service to one another and to those who are outside. But they also require anchorage in the personal reality of Jesus Christ, who is the revealed mystery of God (Col. 1:25-29). Otherwise, the communal leap of faith is simply a matter of the blind leading the blind. For apart from Him, the Church and its mission dissolve into a social agenda of self-worship and communal relativism.[41]

As the Church experiences the authenticity of Christ's communion, a communion that was realized at great risk and at great cost to its Lord, the Church will sense safety and seek after authenticity, and risk, even to the point of following its Lord *up* the path (toward Jerusalem) of incarnation to crucifixion. This involves promoting the fostering once again of the *parish* concept rather than allowing the community around one's church to *perish*. It also involves promoting humility in engagement rather than haughtiness, whereby one shoulders and shares, instead of shoves, where one is broken and binds up rather than breaks.

Let us proclaim and embrace Christ, God incarnate, laboring with all His energy, which has so powerfully worked in the life of the Church in days gone by (See Col. 1:28-29). His presence

---

[41]Recent trends in theology express potential to move in this direction of communal relativism. See the provocative though problematic study by George A. Lindbeck: *The Nature of Doctrine: Religion and Theology in a Postliberal Age* (Philadelphia: The Westminster Press, 1984). There Lindbeck sets forth a theological model for ecumenical dialogue based on a cultural linguistic analysis of doctrine.

will empower us to be present and to live lives of authenticity in community in the city of the world to empower and redeem it so that it might be transformed into the city of our God.

God in Christ is our Neighbor. Christ is the Good Neighbor, the one who reaches out and raises up. The incarnation, His making Himself nothing (Phil. 2:5ff.), was *not a denial* of His deity, *but a demonstration* of it. The verdict that Jesus is Lord is demonstrated by His life of service. The incarnation is the demonstration of Christ's deity. On the other hand, Christendom's failure to become incarnate is the denial of His deity and the partial inspiration for the emergence of a camcorder world — virtual reality. Today, God call us to be broken ministers who empower, rooted in the majestic presence of the empowering Christ, not power brokering messiahs, stymied in the mire of a mundane orthodoxy void of orthopraxis.

Fragmentation marks the age of camcorder productions. And when the Church plays the game of doctrine to guard against discomfort, it deconstructs Christ. The only way to overcome such devolution and disintegration is through embracing an apologetic of embodied presence that empowers, as inspired and empowered by Jesus Christ.

Rex Green, a Christian ministering in the inner city of Portland, has argued that it is easy to reach Postmoderns. But he adds that it will cost us everything, namely, incarnation in their lives.[42] Given the contours of the Postmodern cultural void, and the resources available to the Church (including community, authenticity, and mystery) to fill the void, there is real potential

---

[42] As in the case of Tony Kriz, I am extremely grateful to Rex Green for numerous insightful discussions regarding the plight of society given the current cultural malaise and the immense opportunities for ministry present to the Church.

for the Church to reach Postmoderns, leading them into the fullness of Christ's incarnate life of authentic community enveloped in mystery. But such potential does not come without a price tag. For true incarnation, which involves presence and empowerment, always leads to crucifixion — especially in a camcorder world.

Chapter 5

Caring for the Coming Anarchy

Larry Poston

Parallel to the Spirit-inspired prophets who appear regularly throughout the Bible — and who are still part of the current experience of some denominations — is a secular "equivalent:" a group of men and women who are attempting to interpret present-day trends and predict the future direction of humankind. In the 1970s and 1980s, names such as Alvin Toffler (*The Third Wave*) and John Naisbett (*Megatrends*) were mentioned regularly in such connections. In the 1990s, Samuel Huntington and Robert Kaplan became noted for their much more dire predictions of the world to come.

Huntington, for instance, in his work entitled *The Clash of Civilizations*, describes four possible scenarios for the future. These include the establishment of a single, unified and global governing structure ("Euphoria and Harmony"); a division into two drastically opposed socio-economic groups (with a majority of poor and a minority of rich, or an "Us and Them" configuration); a continuation of the status quo, with an ever-changing set of alliances and co-operative efforts between the various nation-states that currently exist or will come into being ("184 states, More or Less"); and a deteriorating situation leading increasingly to political and social anarchy ("Sheer Chaos"). Huntington believes that each of these scenarios contains both accurate and erroneous aspects. He prefers instead to adopt what he calls a "civilizational approach," viewing the world in terms of eight significant civilizational blocs, namely the Sinic (Chinese), Islamic, Hindu, Western, Latin American, African, Orthodox, and Japanese. Re-alignments of, and dynamic interactions between these entities, will comprise the future of life on our planet and will involve certain drastic changes for those who have been accustomed to the relationships that have existed between nation-states since the seventeenth century.

While in basic agreement with Huntington's paradigm, Robert Kaplan is decidedly more pessimistic in his own take on the future. The title of what has become his most well-known work—*The Coming Anarchy*—is indicative of his convictions. He adopts the position that Huntington calls "Sheer Chaos" and builds a strong case for its usage as an accurate reflection of "things to come."

At least some Christian missiologists are cognizant of the predictions of such writers. For instance, the July 2000 issue of *Missiology* contains an article by Wilbert R. Shenk on "Christian Mission and the Coming 'Clash of Civilizations.'" Shenk describes Huntington's paradigm and discusses some of its implications for the missionary enterprise. I believe, however, that Huntington's work is too broad to be of much use to "street level" missionaries. Although I do not agree with all of Kaplan's conclusions and predictions, I find his work to have much more practical value overall, and it is for this reason that I am using his thinking as the starting point for my essay. I appreciate Kaplan's "grassroots" approach — his willingness to travel independently, carrying only a rucksack — and his emphasis on ascertaining the opinions of the common people. His works *The Arabists, Balkan Ghosts, To the Ends of the Earth, An Empire Wilderness*, and *Eastward to Tartary* explore trends in, respectively, the Middle East, Eastern Europe, Central Asia, the "10-40 Window" in general, the United States, and the new states which formerly comprised the southern tier of the Soviet Union. *The Coming*

Anarchy, however, has earned him the most repute. Beginning as an article in the February 1994 edition of *Atlantic Monthly*, it was recently combined with several other articles written by Kaplan and published in book form by Random House. The thesis of the title article is found in the following description of the state of affairs in present-day Africa:

> West Africa is becoming *the* symbol of worldwide demographic, environmental, and societal stress, in which criminal anarchy emerges as the real "strategic" danger. Disease, overpopulation, unprovoked crime, scarcity of resources, refugee migrations, the increasing erosion of nation-states and international borders, and the empowerment of private armies, security firms, and international drug cartels are now most tellingly demonstrated through a West African prism. West Africa provides an appropriate introduction to the issues, often extremely unpleasant to discuss, that will soon confront our civilization. (Kaplan 2000:7)

Kaplan amplifies each of the facets listed above, offering historical commentary, true-life anecdotes experienced in the course of his travels, and predictions regarding the future. For instance, with regard to the breakdown of internal order and the empowerment of private armies and security firms, he tells of bodyguards in Abidjan who must accompany a person from a restaurant to his or her car — even if the car is only fifteen feet away.

Kaplan predicts that nation states — arbitrarily created as the result of colonialism and the World Wars — will eventually be replaced by "a jagged-glass pattern of city-states, shanty-states, nebulous and anarchic regionalisms..." (Kaplan 2000:44). While the "downtown" sections of these metropolises may be somewhat stable, the residential "interiors" will deteriorate over time. Lagos, Nigeria, is a case in point. Already this city's crime, pollution, and overcrowding make it "the cliché par excellence of Third World urban dysfunction" (Kaplan 2000:15) and its population will most likely double in the next twenty years.

He warns of the proliferation of diseases that make Africa an even deadlier place to live in the 21st Century than it was during the previous one. The HIV virus and tuberculosis are said to be "fast-forwarding each other," and already "virtually everyone in the West African interior has some form of malaria" (Kaplan 2000:9). New strains of the latter disease are resistant to the standard drug regimens, and so "defending oneself against malaria is becoming more and more like defending oneself against violent crime" (Kaplan 2000:17).

Kaplan describes the humiliation and sense of inferiority that many Africans and Asians feel at having been raised and educated by "colonialists" and their heirs, and relates the story of a young African who killed the couple who had been his benefactors in an attempt to assuage the humiliation of their patronage. This inner rage, he believes, is widespread.

He tells of the greed-driven destruction of natural resources by persons who take no thought for the future. Sixty-one percent of Sierra Leone, for instance, was primary rain forest in 1961. Now only six percent is left. Deforestation has led to soil erosion, which in turn has led to flooding and an increase in the mosquito population, which in turn increases the likelihood of contracting disease. In Kaplan's view, the environment is "*the national security issue of the 21st century*," (Kaplan 2000:19) for "future wars and civil violence will arise from scarcities of…water, cropland, forests and fish" rather than the current ideological causes (Kaplan 2000:21).

Whether in the country or in the city, volatility and instability will be the order of the day, as unemployed young men find meaning and purpose to life through military endeavors. For such persons "war and a barracks existence is a step up rather than a step down" (Kaplan 2000:44). Kaplan observes that "physical aggression is a part of being human, and only when people attain a certain economic, educational, and cultural standard is this trait tranquilized" (Kaplan 2000:45). He predicts that humans will become "re-primitivized" and form "warrior societies operating at a time of unprecedented resource scarcity and planetary overcrowding" (Kaplan 2000:48). State armies will shrink and be replaced by private security agents and urban mafias, such as those already operating in Russia.

Even in the "quiet zones" of Africa, says Kaplan, none of the governments except that of the Ivory Coast maintains the schools, roads, and police necessary for a viable civilization to exist. He predicts that as political and social conditions worsen, foreign embassies will be shut down one by one and "contact with the outside world will take place through dangerous, disease-ridden coastal trading posts" (Kaplan 2000:18). [1]

In contrast, many parts of the Muslim world are poised to progress, thrive, and dominate. Of Turkey he writes that "a culture this strong has the potential to dominate the Middle East once again" (Kaplan 2000:32). As in Africa, however, it is Islam's militancy that makes it so attractive to the poor and disenfranchised. Consequently, the word "dominate" must be understood as indicating not only strong cultural and religious influences, but military and political ones as well. The fact that Islam is the world's fastest growing religion has important

---

[1] Already in 1994, twenty-one U.S foreign-aid missions were scheduled to be closed, nine of these in Africa.

implications for the future of Christianity, not just in the Middle East but in the world at large.

While Kaplan has been criticized on occasion for excessive negativity, there is no one who believes that his analyses are entirely erroneous. And even if only some of his predictions materialize, the implications for the missionary enterprise are profound. Following are some attempts to analyze his thinking and to make use of it from the standpoint of evangelical missions. Five distinct suggestions are offered for discussion and consideration. The first suggestion may be seen as offering two macro-perspectives on the overall issue, while the following four may be considered micro-perspectives.

Capitalize on Advantages

Rather than simply writing off "The Coming Anarchy" as an overly pessimistic scenario, we should look more objectively at Kaplan's predictions and view them in light of the two thousand year history of Christianity. I would suggest that at least two large-scale recommendations may be made as a result.

Re-learn the art of managing persecution well. Throughout church history there have been those who have made a case for celebrating the persecutions experienced by the members of the early church while denigrating periods of peace and ease. According to this interpretation of historical events, the Church maintains a purity during times of stress that rapidly disappears whenever it and the world are on good terms.

I believe that it is wrong to glorify human suffering in and of itself. While the Bible speaks of its necessity in the process of sanctification (for instance, 1 Peter 4:1), it is biblically unsound to take delight in pain experienced by other human beings. Thus we are left with a curious paradox. On the one hand, we are called to do all that we can to ease the pain and suffering of others. Jesus modeled this through His healing ministry, in which is seen His enormous compassion regarding the afflictions of His creatures. On the other hand, suffering is to be viewed as an essential component of spiritual growth: "If we suffer, we shall also reign with Him" (2 Timothy 2:12).

Living in the midst of anarchic, insecure situations can have the effect of paring away the layers of "security" in which the modern world enfolds us. As Kaplan notes, "people find liberation in violence...worrying about mines and ambushes frees you from worrying about mundane details of daily existence" (Kaplan 2000:45).

Thus while the Christian is not to deliberately *seek* experiences or contexts which lead to suffering, he is to recognize that "in this life we will have tribulation," and when it comes will allow it to have the sanctifying effect that God in His sovereignty intends.

All of this is to say that present day apostles should not deliberately attempt to avoid conditions of political, social, or economic chaos in the hope of escaping suffering. Missionary candidates should instead be instilled with a "survivalist" mentality which will acknowledge the very real possibility of physical and mental suffering in the midst of missionary ministry and be prepared to deal with it on a day by day — even hour by hour — basis.

Gear missions training and strategy increasingly toward displaced peoples. If Kaplan's predictions regarding "the coming anarchy" are valid, we can expect a steady increase in the number of "displaced persons." These are individuals who have undergone traumatic circumstances through which they have lost their homes, families, and/or possessions and they have become so psychologically insecure that they are open to obtaining a new form of security such as that offered by biblical Christian faith.[2]

We will find most of such individuals in four locations. First, in "shantytowns" usually located on the outskirts of major cities. In this category would be the slum districts of Abidjan known as "Chicago" and "Washington," and described in detail by Kaplan. Every major city in the Third World has such districts, and the populations of these areas swell by tens of thousands every day.

Second, we will find displaced people in countries contiguous to those in which anarchic conditions exist. If we look at the various "hot spots" in our world today, we will see that Rwandans have fled to the Congo, Kosovars to Macedonia and Albania, Afghans to Pakistan, Palestinians to Lebanon and Jordan, and so on.

Third, not all refugees in the situations described previously are allowed to move freely within a foreign country. Many are gathered into refugee camps and are subjected to various forms of treatment. In some of these, conditions are such that "displacement" becomes a more or less permanent characteristic, since there can never be a sense of "settledness" on the part of those living in such camps.

Finally, many refugees from the Third World eventually make their way to the major cities of the First World: New York, Paris, London, Chicago, Los Angeles. Like those who came before them, they often take up residence in distinct "quarters," and continue — as far as possible — many of their cultural customs and practices.

---

[2] See, for instance, Donald Mc Garvan, *Understanding Church Growth* (Grand Rapids, MI:Eerdmans Publ. Co., 1970), chapter 12.

In light of these observations, our missionary training programs should be increasingly oriented toward meeting the physical, mental, and spiritual needs of displaced peoples. To develop a curriculum we must first ask ourselves what we would need to know to be able to minister to such persons. Here we could take a page from the training program developed by Ignatius of Loyola for his Society of Jesus, a program that required the attainment of knowledge in the fields of medicine, economics, and a trade or craft in addition to Theology and the Liberal Arts. Courses taught in our own training institutions might include the following:

- Philosophies and Methodologies of Relief and Development,
- Introduction to Social Work,
- Introduction to Urban Ministries,
- Principles and Methods of First Aid, along with CPR training, Red Cross Lifesaving, etc.,
- Introduction to Tropical Diseases, including extensive treatment of Malaria, Typhoid, Yellow Fever, and AIDS,
- Principles of Personal Finance and Economics,
- Methods of TESOL or TESL,
- Transferable and useful job skills (i.e., basic agriculture, carpentry, masonry, plumbing, electricity, auto mechanics, etc. in certain situations; computer software training and principles of accounting, bookkeeping, etc. in others),
- Apprenticeship in a specific trade or craft.

Some might contend that this range of courses is far too broad for any one person. They would advocate the assembly of teams that combine "specialists" in the areas mentioned above.

Such an approach is certainly acceptable, although I would argue for a more holistic education of individuals, each of whom would be "fully equipped for every good work." But in either case, I would recommend that three and four year undergraduate and graduate missions programs be carefully examined to see whether many of the "essential" courses we have traditionally included in our missions or ministry curricula are really so essential. I believe that many could be dropped in favor of some of those I have listed above.

2. Rethink Family Issues

It cannot be overemphasized that "the coming anarchy" is not a new phenomenon at all. The events Kaplan describes actually represent a *return* to previous conditions; indeed, it could even be said that they are a return to *normalcy* after a long hiatus characterized by a relative calm. Thus "missions in the coming anarchy" will actually be a resumption of "missions in the past," conducted in the midst of insecure, unpredictable and hostile environments.

For a very brief period of time most missionaries in our world have operated with a large measure of security when compared with their colleagues of the past. One of the advantages of colonialism was that when "the cross followed the flag," the flag usually afforded protection against indigenous peoples who might otherwise have expressed their resentment of the Gospel in much more drastic — and deadly — ways. In the aftermath of World War II a majority of young missionary couples have been able to complete a Bible College education, raise their support, reach their field of service, participate in language study, and take up evangelistic, church planting, educational or service-oriented ministries with only a modicum of discomfort. There have been, of course, the inconveniences of cross-cultural adjustments and family separations. There were tragic failures, unnecessary casualties, and personal losses, but in a large number of cases, languages have been learned, houses purchased and furnished, motor vehicles acquired, children born, raised and educated, ministries performed and retirement age reached in circumstances of comparative ease. Consequently, perhaps a majority of missionary candidates exude an air of excitement and of adventure that rarely includes a sober awareness that one's ministry could be brought to a shattering halt through a torturous experience or brutal death.

To be prepared for "the coming anarchy," then, missionary training must prepare candidates to face this sober possibility. This is not to say that we should seek to inculcate a sense of negativism or pessimism in our missionary candidates, but rather a sense of realism that forces them to heed Jesus' warnings to "count the cost." If one is not ready to give up everything he has, he cannot be a disciple of Christ (Luke 14: 33). Practical implications of these verses might include the following.

Re-examining the concept of marriage. Is the married state really the "ultimate" that it has been portrayed to be in recent years by evangelical advocates of "family values"? Or might it not be better to recommend for some the pursuit of a life of undivided commitment to apostolic ministry that would include what could be called a "neo-monasticism?" In its efforts to divorce itself from its Roman Catholic origins, Protestantism has neglected and deprecated a lifestyle celebrated and recommended by the Bible itself (see 1 Corinthians 7 and other passages). From the standpoint of emotional entanglements, it is certain that single missionaries would be better able to deal with the insecurities afforded by increasingly unstable political and social conditions than would married couples.

Re-evaluating the desire for large families. Jesus made it clear that not everyone can receive his teaching regarding the benefits of celibacy (Matthew 19:11). Despite the advantages of a single ministry, given the sexual temptations of the current day, natural cultural expectations, and the social pressures of certain Christian institutions, most missionary candidates will likely marry. And, biblically speaking, nothing can be said against such a choice. The bearing of children, however, necessitates further decisions, and such decisions should be made only after a sober analysis of one's ministry contexts. While it is beyond the authority of any Christian organization or individual to dictate such a thing as family size, it is not beyond the realm of propriety to pose serious questions regarding the advisability of having large families — or any family at all — while in missionary situations. Conservative Christians scoff at the reasoning behind the reluctance of humanists to "bring a child into a world such as the one we live in." But such sentiments should not be so hastily written off by those who anticipate ministries in some of the more unstable parts of the present-day world. Might there not be something irresponsible in bringing a large number of children into a missionary situation comprised of "criminal anarchy, disease, overpopulation, scarcity of resources, refugee migrations, erosion of nation-states and international borders, empowerment of private armies and international drug cartels?" Might it not be the way of wisdom to advise our missionary candidates — particularly those who are already married — to think through these issues and to recommend a family size of no children, or, at most, one or two?

Cultivating a proper sense of "apostolicity." Aspiring missionaries must be sent on their assignments with the knowledge that even the most career-oriented situation might end up being a very "short-term assignment." Rather than adopting what might in other circumstances be called an immigrant status, involving a mentality of *rootedness*, of houses, vehicles, and other "creature comforts," our missionaries should be advised instead to seek to cultivate the attitude evinced by Ignatius of Loyola: "Workers in the vineyard of the Lord should learn to stand upon only one foot. The other should always be lifted, ready to go."

Here I am speaking first and foremost of an inner *mentality* rather than of externalities. There is nothing intrinsically wrong with buying a house or a car in a foreign country. One must certainly live somewhere, and one must have some means of transportation. And we have been left with the apostolic example of "becoming all things to all people," that we might "by all possible means save some" (1 Corinthians 9:22). Such adaptations may well include (some would say *must* include) locating oneself in the midst of an urban or suburban neighborhood. But each missionary agent must be trained to constantly ask himself/herself the question: have I slipped over the line between "apostolicity" and "immigrancy?" And we must teach them the difference. The apostle is in a specific location for the purpose of *ministry*, first and foremost, day in and day out. The immigrant is in a place to live, raise a family, be at home. The apostle is never "at home" — he or she always has "a foot raised," so to speak; always sees himself or herself as a "temporary," a "stranger or pilgrim," and views himself/herself as "other" than those among whom he or she ministers.

Avoid Technological Dependency

The world in general — but the West in particular — has become inordinately dependent upon technological gadgetry. One could even claim that Western populations have been "bewitched" into thinking that the "technological revolution" will enable us to "save the world" — or at least fulfill the Great Commission. But this is no more than an illusion.

The above statement is not meant to be taken as a Luddite pronouncement. I do not intend to demean the accomplishments of, for instance, the Jesus Film Project, which has reportedly reached at least 3.3 billion people with the story of Jesus (Bush 2000:16), or Billy Graham's 1996 World Television Special, through which the evangelist was able to reach more people in a single day than in all of the forty-five previous years of his ministry combined (Bush 2000:15). Nor would one want to take away from the benefits that the computer revolution has produced, from databases of statistics regarding unreached people groups to increased rapidity of Bible translation projects to Internet chatrooms with apologetical content. Satellite programming and cellular telephones have drastically changed the way we live, but they have also created what may be considered a dangerous dependency upon electrical devices.

There are at least two problems with such a dependency. The first involves the kind of situation that Kaplan discusses in which inter-ethnic or inter-tribal strife brings about an unstable political situation. In such circumstances, the electrical network of a town, village, or mission station becomes an extremely vulnerable item, subject to attack and easily sabotaged. Such sabotage would bring about the cessation of light, heat, hot water, cooking, computer services — anything that requires electrical power. Communications are just as easily sabotaged, with the possible exception of telephone systems which use digital satellite technology, and these are useful only as long as their cell phone batteries last.

Persons above the age of thirty are perhaps not so utterly dependent upon electricity, particularly the aspects connected with computer services. It is thus difficult for them to comprehend how large a role electronic devices play in the lives of the young people now preparing for missionary service. Are these candidates prepared to live under emergency conditions without electricity? If they are not, how can we prepare them for such an eventuality?

A second problem is even more daunting, and it is the way that technology has effected the educational process. Sesame Street television programming, Internet services, word processing spelling and grammar checks, Powerpoint presentations, and distance learning have all impacted and changed the learning process. Many warnings have been issued about the possible long-term effects of such electronic wizardry upon rational thought and creativity,[3] but these have gone unheeded by all but a few.

I propose two measures to deal with these problems. The first involves the creation of a program of cross-cultural adjustment that includes a module in which individuals would be weaned from dependence upon electronic technology. I have actually taught such a course, breaking the semester into two-week periods during which various assignments were given that would expose students to radically different living situations from their accustomed patterns. Students were to write essays regarding each of these two-week modules, analyzing and evaluating their thoughts and attitudes prior to, during, and after each assignment. During one of these periods the participants were forbidden to use electrical devices of any kind. No television, no stereo (including portable, battery-operated stereo systems), no electric

---

[3] See, for instance, Neil Postman, *Amusing Ourselves to Death* (Viking Press, 1986), Jerry Mander, *Four Arguments for the Elimination of Television* (William Morrow, 1978); and Jacques Ellul, *The Technological Society* (Random House, 1967).

alarm clocks, no microwave ovens, no popcorn poppers, no computer games. In every semester that I taught the course, this section was considered to be the most difficult of the seven assignments. Students were invariably amazed to discover how ubiquitous electrical devices are and how dependent they as individuals had become upon such devices. Most gained an appreciation for ancestors who had lived without electricity and an awareness of the paradox involved in the knowledge that life without electrical gadgets was, in one respect, much simpler and slower-paced than today's society, but at the same time, much harsher and more difficult. The assignment created a confidence that life may indeed be lived without electrical appliances — an important aid to self-confidence for a missionary in "the coming anarchy."[4]

A second measure to address the problems inherent in a technological society would involve the adoption of an educational philosophy and teaching style that would be precisely counter to the prevailing trends. We are currently moving in our schools towards an ever-*increasing* usage of electronic media, be these computerized distance-learning courses, Powerpoint presentations, overhead projectors or copious amounts of photocopied materials.

Do these technological devices really enhance the educational process? Or are they merely part of a current trend or "fad" created by Western market economies? After all, people were educated — both formally and informally — for centuries without benefit of such devices. Are we certain that abandoned

---

[4] The textbook used for this part of the course in cross-cultural adjustment was a novel: Pat Frank, Alas, Babylon (New York: Bantam Books, 1959). It is heartily recommended for all missionary candidates, particularly those going to Third World countries.

techniques — such as rote learning and memorization — were jettisoned with good reason? And if — contrary to available evidence — we assume that these electronic devices produce as well or better educated students, is it wise to assume that such devices will always be readily available? If we cannot assume such availability, would it then be wise to develop a teaching philosophy and style that depend so completely upon electronic media? For we have already determined that electricity may be one of the first things to be threatened or lost in crisis situations. Might it not be better to devise educational techniques that are more easily transferable to any and all situations?

I would like to propose that teachers and trainers of missionaries consider returning to forms of education developed during the high Renaissance and Enlightenment periods of history. These forms, of course, made no use of electrical gadgetry at all. As mentioned earlier, Ignatius of Loyola's training program as documented in the Society of Jesus' *Constitutions* could be used as an excellent starting point for the development of a system for the present day. Some of the more outstanding characteristics of Jesuit education were (and in many cases remain) the following:

- An emphasis upon holistic education, with studies in Grammar, Poetics, History, Rhetoric, Latin, Greek, Hebrew, Arabic, and the writings of Cicero, Quintilian, Virgil, Cyprian, Caesar, Sallust, Livy, and Curtius. These were followed by three years of the Natural Sciences, Aristotelian Logic, Physics, Metaphysics, Moral Philosophy and Mathematics, followed by four years of Scholastic Theology, Positive Theology, Canon Law, and Sacred Scripture. Included throughout these years were directives regarding care of the physical body (calisthenics, diet, sleep and clothing). Loyola and his followers constantly emphasized the idea of *ne quid nimis* — "nothing in excess." While the writers and languages may need to be adjusted, surely the breadth aimed at here is exemplary.

- Pre-eminence given to Biblical and Theological subjects, these being placed *after* the studies in liberal arts fields. Literature, philosophy and ethics were all to be filtered through the sieve of Theology and what remained, said Loyola, "could be used by the Society like the spoils of Egypt" (*Constitutions* IV, ch. 5, clarification E).
- Emphasis upon individual mentoring, for "in the Jesuit school, the chief responsibility for moral as well as for intellectual formation rests finally not upon any procedure or curricular or extra-curricular item but upon the teacher, under God" (Donohue 1963:179).
- Emphasis upon a life-long commitment to activism. Each member of the Society of Jesus was to learn a trade so that in situations where self-support was necessary, he would be able "not only to live as a Christian gentleman but also to earn his living in a way satisfying to himself and beneficial to society" (Donohue 1963:176). Loyola was convinced that "when the merchants and moneylenders realize that you are as well informed as they are as regards the affairs of daily life, then they will admire and confide in you. Otherwise the admonitions of a priest are only greeted with laughter."

The entire training program was conducted, of course, without benefit of overhead projectors, photocopiers, or computerized presentations. Instead, the Jesuit instructors used lecture and discussion, sprinkled liberally with staged rhetorical debates, drama presentations, and stringent requirements for reading, writing, and rote memorization. These pedagogical techniques can be used in any culture and under any circumstances, a claim that certainly cannot be made by the advocates of electronic media.

Study the Science of War

The Bible is at its most paradoxical when it comes to the subject of war. On the one hand, Jesus is given the title "Prince of Peace," he exhorted followers to not resist evil and "turn the other cheek," and his dialogue with Pilate included a statement to the effect that if His Kingdom was of this world, only then would his followers involve themselves in warfare. Based on these and similar passages, many — perhaps most — members of the Church through the centuries have avoided military service. Indeed, entire denominations have been established with pacifism as a central emphasis.

On the other hand, God directed the ancient Israelites in the conquest of Canaan and other similar endeavors, is said to be "a man of war" (Exodus 15:3), trained David to be a warrior (Psalm 18:34), will in Christ battle against the foes arrayed against Him at Armageddon and in the battle of Gog and Magog (Revelation 19-20), and inspired Bible writers to use military metaphors in describing the expected lifestyle of the people of God (Ephesians 6:11-17 and 2 Timothy 2:3-4). How well are contemporary Christians equipped to deal with these paradoxical elements of biblical revelation? How much do we know about war?

Kaplan discusses in detail changes in warfare techniques that are already being seen and which will be increasingly evident in the future. Borrowing from writings by Thomas Homer-Dixon and Martin van Creveld, he predicts that future wars will arise from scarcities of resources such as water, cropland, forests and fish rather than ideological conflicts.[5] Despite the interest in pacifism and world peace which has characterized Western society since the 1960s, it is wrong to suppose that men do not like to fight. "People find liberation in violence," says Kaplan, whether it be in Serbia, Afghanistan, Somalia, Haiti, or Sierra Leone. Physical aggression is simply part of being human, and the sooner that we acknowledge that fact, the better prepared we will all be to deal with it. Urban crime, according to Kaplan's reading of van Creveld, "may develop into low intensity conflict by coalescing along racial, religious, social, and political lines." State armies will shrink while private security personnel will multiply enormously.

Michael Ignatieff's work *The Warrior's Honour* complements Kaplan's thinking. Ignatieff observes that war used to be fought by soldiers, but is now fought by irregulars. Warriors — professional soldiers — usually act in accordance with "rules of war," which specify limitations and penalties for harm done to civilians and non-military property in the midst of skirmishes. Contemporary and future conflicts, however, are and will be fought by "irregulars," for whom such rules are irrelevant. The problem today, says Ignatieff, is our psychological inability to accept and deal with the ugliness of "war without rules."

I propose that the study of warfare become a permanent part of our missionary candidate training, field personnel meetings and annual conferences. I believe that we as Christians must come to grips with the issue of war in a new way. I realize that there are many Christian groups that are known for their

---

[5] See Thomas Fraser Homer-Dixon, "On the Threshold: Environmental Changes as Causes of Acute Conflict." Cited in *The Coming Anarchy*, p. 21. Also, Martin van Creveld, *The Transformation of War* (Free Press, 1991).

pacifistic or non-resistance convictions. Some of these groups are actively involved in peacemaking, peacekeeping and reconciliation efforts throughout the world. I am not proposing that these efforts be abandoned, for as *supplements* to the command to "preach the Gospel to every creature," they are highly commendable ministries. But they are doomed to failure at any other than the individual and local levels of society, and even at those levels success will be limited and temporary.

Our discipling will have to include at least three different aspects regarding this subject. First, we must educate and train Christians to live at peace among themselves and their neighbors. We must make every effort to attain a *true* peace, not a grudging tolerance of people different from ourselves for the sake of an appearance or a "testimony."

Second, we must continue to do what we can on the peacemaking, peacekeeping and reconciliation fronts, harboring no illusions that we will accomplish lasting peacefulness between human beings still in the grip of their sinful natures. As Westerners we must strive to avoid two things that Ignatieff warns us concerning. These are *moral disgust*, involving an attitude of "let the brutes exterminate themselves," and *compassion fatigue*, meaning an active repugnance at the inability of societies that receive aid to do anything to cure themselves. Either of these attitudes can be deadly to missionary ministries, and being aware of their dangers is the first step in avoiding them. College and seminary courses as well as missionary candidate school programs should have specific modules dealing with these subjects. Field directors and other mission leaders must be constantly on the lookout for the appearance of these attitudes on the part of the missionary personnel they are responsible for.

Third, we must teach our disciples to view war as the "default mode" of human social relationships. We must inculcate in them the knowledge that what happened in World War II's Europe, in the Cold War's China, and more recently in Rwanda, Chechnya and Bosnia-Herzegovina could conceivably happen anywhere on earth, given the proper conditions. What would this mean practically? For some it might mean the preparation of a backpack or rucksack with elemental "survival" gear, accessible at a moment's notice. For others it could mean the development of a pre-planned "escape route" so that in emergency situations there would be no hesitation regarding procedure or direction.

The idea of "running" may not be palatable for a number of modern day apostles, just as it was not for Christians living during the first two centuries of Church history. Great controversies arose concerning those who fled during times of persecution (study, for instance, the Novatianist controversy). Voluntary martyrdom was a "test for spirituality" and was preferable to "running." But Jesus was clear on this point: "when you see Jerusalem surrounded by armies, flee to the mountains," he said (Luke 21:20-21). And he was morosely practical about such situations. "How dreadful it will be for pregnant women and nursing mothers in those days," he warns — it is difficult to be running for your life while carrying a dependent infant. "And pray that your flight be not in winter" (Matthew 24:19-21) — for the cold and difficulty of procuring food may put your survival in doubt.

Engaging in intensive studies of warfare could also have profound spiritual implications beyond a renewed appreciation for Jesus' eschatological teachings. It may also shed new illumination upon the military metaphors used through the Pauline epistles, and could make the idea of "a Christian soldier" take on entirely new meaning. Adoption of the biblical ideal of

"Christian soldierhood" might lead to any or all of the following applications.

1. A soldier is disciplined, with a commitment to physical and mental fitness.
2. A soldier is subject to a set of daily training routines, which contribute to his overall fitness.
3. A soldier is skilled, with a commitment to proficient use of his weaponry.
4. A soldier has all of his (real) needs supplied by the army that employs him.
5. A soldier is focused on his mission, with no entanglement in "civilian affairs."
6. A soldier has a strong sense of duty, and fulfills his commitments in accordance with that duty.
7. A soldier expects to receive orders, and obeys them without questioning his commanding officer.
8. A soldier is deliberately placed in dangerous situations, with high levels of tension and stress.
9. A soldier is intent upon engaging the enemy.
10. A soldier fights in such a way so as to still be standing at the end of the day, after the last battle has been fought.
11. A soldier is surrounded by a community or fellowship of soldiers equally trained, competent, and accountable.

It is entirely probable that due to its peace-oriented convictions, contemporary Christianity has lost something that Abraham, Joshua, Caleb, David, and Nehemiah would recognize instantly as missing.

Revive Christianity's Heritage as an "Underground Elite"

I have argued elsewhere that biblical Christianity is in reality a minority religion — it always has been and always will be.[6] Christians have at times reflected this reality in their interactions with the non-Christian adherents of the various cultures of the world; witness their dealings with the Roman Empire prior to Constantine's reign and the experiences of the fledgling churches established throughout Asia and Africa during the Great Century of missionary expansion. But often a *majoritarian* viewpoint has been adopted, as was the case in Constantine's Roman Empire, Charlemagne's Europe, the world of Manifest Destiny and Divine Right of Kings, and "The Moral Majority" of more recent days.

Missionaries and missiologists are no less prone to such a majoritarian view, as James Engel pointed out in a recent article in *Christianity Today*. He observes that "far too many claims of numerical success are based on partial or misleading indicators" and warns that "such actions can be motivated by many things apart from interest in the Gospel" (Engel 2000:57).[7] Luis Bush shares the same concern, believing that growth is being promoted at the expense of depth. He reports that the First International Consultation on Discipleship held in 1999 in Eastbourne, England issued a statement acknowledging that the Church's "zeal to go wider has not been matched by a commitment to go deeper"(Bush 2000:14). In our desire to "preach the Gospel to every creature" we have often neglected the command to "make

---

[6] See Larry Poston, "Christianity as a Minority Religion," in Edward Rommen, *Christianity and the World Religions* (Pasadena, CA: William Carey Library Press, 1975).

[7] James F. Engel, "Getting Beyond the Numbers Game," *Christianity Today* (August 7, 2000): 57.

disciples in all nations...teaching them to obey everything [Jesus] commanded."

Granted, we cannot lay aside all evangelistic efforts in order to concentrate on discipling believers. We should rather think in terms of a shift in emphasis. For many — perhaps most — missionary agencies, priority has been given to pre-evangelistic, evangelistic and support activities. And often, even those activities which could be considered "discipling ministries" — such as Christian higher education — are conducted according to a Western model, imposing the same distance between teacher and student that is found in American and European institutions. This may, of course, be considered "discipling" in some sense — but is it what Jesus meant? Does it imitate the paradigm he demonstrated for us?

It is possible that some Christians resist the close relationship that the biblical model of discipling involves because of the disdain that most Protestants have for anything even distantly approaching autocratic leadership. This is perhaps a holdover from the revolt against the perceived spiritual imperialism of Catholicism. Such wariness is commendable, for the Bible warns against "savage wolves" who will be unsparing of the flock (Acts 20:29). But an excess of such caution prevents us from submitting ourselves to duly constituted authority — which the Bible commands us to obey in both the spiritual and temporal realms (Romans 13:1-5 and Hebrews 13:17) — and from exercising proper authority over others in discipling relationships.

It is also possible that there has been no commitment to "go deeper" because many are unsure as to what this "depth" consists of, or, if known, how to impart it to a follower. This problem is exacerbated by the fact that if one has never been educated or trained in the deeper aspects of the Christian life oneself, one will be unable to educate or train anyone else in them. The trait of "shallowness" is almost always intergenerational.

For "the coming anarchy," we will need spiritually-based programs analogous to the training regimens of the Green Berets, the Navy SEALs, or the Army Rangers. These programs will need to be holistic and multi-disciplinary, covering every aspect of human life. We must inculcate a *mystique,* including both a sense of *eliteness* and a sense of *mission.*

The conditions of "the coming anarchy" will require a certain toughness — even ruthlessness — which can only be the result of the Christian's conception of him/herself as a member of a thoroughly trained, highly competent, elitist "fighting force." Ezekiel, for instance, received the following promise from God: *"But I will make you as unyielding and hardened as they are. I will make your forehead like the hardest stone, harder than flint ... "* (Ezekiel 3:8-9). "Hardness" and "ruthlessness" are not the standard fare in missionary training programs; we emphasize instead the qualities of humility, meekness, compassion and the like. I am certainly not advocating that these latter traits be abandoned. Rather, I am recommending that the "softer" traits be complemented by "tougher" qualities so that missionaries will be able to cope both physically and mentally with the harsh realities of increasingly chaotic conditions. To inculcate such mental and physical toughness, missionary agencies should seriously consider adding to their candidate schools a program modeled along the lines of the survivalist "Outward Bound" program, which even major business corporations have utilized to increase their employees' "sense of self."

The sense of "mission" must consist of two parts. The first is an *organizational* aspect. Each missionary agency must enunciate clearly and concisely what its *mission* involves. Every member of the "team" should then individually adopt this mission for him/herself, perhaps in a special ceremony through which his/her commitment is publicly expressed. The second aspect is an *individual* aspect, forged by an individual as an expression of the gifts and training he/she has received. The two "missions" must be able to be co-ordinated in the candidate's mind and life, for in the long run, one cannot operate as a member of a mission organization without an awareness and commitment to "mission" in both of these senses. Chaotic conditions require an ability to work with others in a close-knit team environment while being able at the same time to function with full confidence in one's own individuality and uniqueness. Consequently, aspiring missionaries must be guided carefully in their search for a missionary "team" and should be dissuaded from *automatically* following a family or denominational tradition. In most cases, due to the environment of one's upbringing, the missionary candidate *will* be compatible with an organization with which he/she grew up, but it may well be that in certain cases, participation with a different organization should be advised and pursued. Personal counsel — in the form of specific suggestions — can be invaluable in ensuring that a proper "fit" is found.

Conclusion

Chaotic political, economic, social, and religious conditions have more often than not been the experience of Christian missionaries abroad in the world. While the recent past has contained brief periods of comparative peace, it should not be expected that in a world intent upon reverting to a "Sodom and Gomorrah" mindset, such relatively calm conditions will endure for any substantial length of time.

Those of us who have been entrusted with the task of preparing the missionaries of the future must take special care in our educational endeavors. We must unashamedly admit that many of us have never experienced what our students may eventually experience, and consequently our training will be lacking in a number of areas unless we take specific steps to anticipate and make up for those deficiencies. We may find it necessary to visit some of the anarchic areas of our world during summers or sabbaticals. We may need to review the testimonies and writings of those who have lived — and died — in such conditions, in order to be able to gain at least a sense of what our students may expect. We must do all that is necessary to avoid becoming too "comfortable" in our academic environments. The anarchy of the street is a different environment altogether, and our calling demands that the core of our lives remain at that level so that we can prepare missionaries for *their* future. And while doing so we must remain ever mindful that in *our* future awaits the special judgment for teachers mentioned by James the brother of Jesus.

Chapter 6

Caring for Those in Crisis

Robert Klamser

Then he said to his disciples, "The harvest is plentiful but the workers are few" (Matt. 9:37).

I am sending you out like sheep among wolves. Therefore be as shrewd as snakes and as innocent as doves (Matt. 10:16).

I have worked much harder, been in prison more frequently, been flogged more severely, and been exposed to death again and again ... I have been in danger from rivers, in danger from bandits, in danger from my own countrymen, in danger from Gentiles; in danger in the city, in danger in the country, in danger at sea; and in danger from false brothers (II Cor. 11:23-26).[1]

With these words, we are served notice of three truths regarding the harvest force: First, that the harvest force is small; second, that the work, the act of harvesting, can be arduous and dangerous; and third, that the workers, in this case missionaries, are vulnerable to the dangers that do exist.

The author has been involved in a support ministry to evangelical missionary and Christian relief and development organizations since 1983. Although the primary work of that ministry involves security and crisis management, there exists an inevitable and inescapable overlap between the external factor of security and the overall health of the Christian workers who

---

[1] Unless otherwise noted, all Scripture references are from the New International Version, The Zondervan Corporation (Grand Rapids, MI, 1985).

make up the harvest force. It is the author's conviction, and the thesis of this paper, that external security factors, and more specifically, the organization's competence and approach to handling security, are a major factor in the overall health of the missionary or Christian worker, and thus a major factor in the effectiveness of the ministry of the organization.

Consider three examples of the impact of security challenges, leadership response, and missionary reaction: In the first situation, a violent insurgent group that exercised dominance over a significant portion of the country had kidnapped a missionary. Ransom and other demands were pending, as were threats to kill the hostage. Many of the remaining missionaries from the organization still lived at the location where the kidnapping occurred, a location that was within only a few kilometers of rebel-controlled territory. During a consultation called to assess the ongoing danger to the rest of the missionaries, one made the statement "***Except for the kidnapping***, there has been less rebel activity around here than for the past several years" (emphasis added).

In the second example, field leaders of a missionary organization requested outside assistance in determining whether or not they should evacuate from their assigned location. They were living and working in an area where two violent extremist groups were increasing their terrorist activities against the population at large, and also specifically against the Christian community. In seeking assistance from an outside consultant, the field leadership described the security situation as follows:

- Terrorist activity was both increasing in frequency and expanding into the city where the missionaries were located — the most recent bombing in the city happened within two blocks of the mission's offices.

- The day before the inquiry to the consultant was made, the military increased its threat assessment to the highest possible level, skipping several intermediate ratings. At least a part of the reason for the military's upgrading of the threat level was a major Christian holiday upcoming within a few days and the history of terrorist threats against Christians.
- One of the two extremist groups had just successfully kidnapped a number of foreigners and continued to hold them pending ransom demands.
- The field leader of the mission organization told his regional director that it was his evaluation that at that time, the missionaries were in "grave danger."

Based on the information received from the field leadership as cited above, and responding to the requirement of the mission that an evacuation decision be made immediately (before the consultant could travel to the scene to conduct an on-site assessment), an evacuation was recommended, almost immediately ordered, and rapidly completed. Within a very few days, however, the evacuated missionaries, including the leader who reported the "grave danger," were arguing to return and faulting the decision to evacuate.

In the third situation, a missionary organization received an extortion demand (of the "revolutionary tax" type) from an insurgent group. The demand was consistent in form and content to those delivered to a number of organizations in the region. Although the tone was firm, it was courteous. Significantly, the organization had received a near-identical demand from the same group less than three years before, and following a personal meeting with leaders of the insurgent group at that time, the organization received an exemption from the demand and an endorsement of its work in the region. Assessment and evaluation of this new demand by field and headquarters leadership of the organization, assisted by outside experts, concluded that there was a high probability of negotiating an acceptable resolution to the new demand. It was also concluded that should the situation not be negotiable, there would be adequate time for an orderly evacuation and very little danger to any of the missionary personnel. Plans were made accordingly. However, part of the missionary group on-site rejected these conclusions, appealed to headquarters to restructure the crisis management team handling this situation, and some of the group unilaterally evacuated the area on their own.[2]

In the first situation some of the missionaries felt that leadership was over-reacting to danger. In the third situation some of the missionaries felt that leadership was under-reacting to danger. In the second situation, some of the missionaries at first indicated a strong fear and appeared to be seeking "permission" to evacuate, but as soon as that happened, leadership was criticized for the decision and the group determined to return within a very few days. Based on the author's involvement in these cases, and with monitoring of these situations over time, there appear to be some common characteristics that mission organization leadership would do well to understand and consider as part of the overall program of care for their personnel:

1. Missionaries often tend to accept danger, and especially steadily increasing danger, as a normal part of the environment until a "critical mass" is reached.

---

[2] The author has first hand experience in all three scenarios but is withholding the specifics to protect the identity of the organizations and personnel.

2. Unless that critical mass has been pre-determined or pre-defined, the most common action is for individual missionaries to "tough it out" and accept levels of danger they are personally uncomfortable with in the absence of leadership guidelines to the contrary. In such a situation, however, when the individual missionary finally determines that the danger level is unacceptable, the reaction is often hasty and ill-considered.
3. In the absence of contingency plans and pre-determined action points, when danger does impact a missionary team, one of the almost inevitable consequences is a crisis of confidence in leadership. This often results in long-term organizational concerns that are more significant, in terms of ministry disruption, than the original danger.
4. In each of these profiled situations the author is convinced that the organizational consequences could have been significantly reduced, and the overall health of the affected missionaries significantly protected, with more effective and more proactive crisis management capabilities by the organization's leadership.

The Linkage Between Security and Member Care

It seems intuitively accurate to link security to the emotional well-being of people. It seems self-evident to presume that people who feel physically safe will avoid some of the stress, tension and related problems of people who are constantly exposed to danger. Those would seem to be normal reactions. But are missionaries "normal"? After all, missionaries are the only population who were known to travel overseas using caskets as luggage, anticipating their death in the line of duty.

Missionaries are certainly a population with a higher percentage of people motivated by faith in God than secular expatriate populations such businessmen, diplomats or military personnel. But does this affect how they react and respond to danger?

John Fawcett serves as the Stress and Trauma Support Services Coordinator for World Vision International, and has considerable experience dealing with the impact of danger on Christian workers in the field. He observes that

> (Christian) workers, along with all those with strong spiritual beliefs, may be significantly affected by exposure to such events (i.e., significantly traumatic events). Rigidly held belief structures may not hold up under exposure to complexity and ambiguity. The 'ambiguity factor' appears to be critical here. The more black and white the belief structure held, the more strain it is under in contact with new and unusual conditions ... For those who have a predominately positive world view – for instance, that God is a God of love and healing – the evidence of their own eyes can create internal conflicts of a profoundly traumatic nature. The need to resolve these apparent contradictions and the amount of psychological and spiritual energy required to manage the confusion can lead to some workers needing to leave the field. For a few, the choice has been suicide. (Fawcett 2000: 96)

Fawcett goes on to say, "One aspect of stress and trauma that asks for more examination is religious or spiritual belief. Traumatized staff display, along with the recognized psychological symptoms, profound spiritual trauma" (2000: 114).

Fawcett (2000) observes that Christian workers — missionaries — are not only susceptible to the impact of danger-induced stress, but even suggests that their faith can contribute to the stress and trauma they suffer when it is in stark juxtaposition with some of the graphic horrors of the world. His observation is very much consistent with the author's experiences in the field over the years.

In 1986, while conducting an assessment tour of a Latin American country besieged by terrorist acts, the author was asked to present a workshop on sexual assault to a missionary audience one evening. At the conclusion of the workshop, as most everyone was leaving the room, a woman approached, asking for a private meeting. During that meeting, which stretched through most of the night, the woman and her husband told of her being raped by a man in her home church, shortly before she left for the mission field. Although the rape had been reported, the man had denied it and the woman had not felt supported (or even believed) by her church leadership. Feeling rebuffed by the church, she had not sought any professional support or assistance to deal with the emotional trauma associated with the rape. She brought the emotional aftermath of the rape, and the unsatisfactory experience of reporting it, with her to the mission field. As this situation was discussed that evening, some very important things became apparent:

- By the woman's own confession, the emotional aftermath of this violent incident was dominating her life.
- It had made her, in her own words, completely ineffective as a missionary.
- It had also significantly affected the quality of her relationship with her husband.

- The husband reported that this had also affected his own effectiveness on the mission field.

When this woman was asked to describe the emotions she was feeling, and how she was reacting to those feelings, the dominant response was that she felt guilty about how she felt. Asked to explain, she described feelings such as shame, humiliation, anger, rage and a desire for revenge (against the rapist). She articulated her belief that feeling such things was un-Christian, and that she believed that experiencing those emotions and feelings was an indication that her faith, her relationship with God, was somehow flawed (otherwise, she would have more "Christian" feelings about what happened). This case study graphically, albeit tragically, supports Fawcett's observations.

Although the above case study deals with the aftermath of a single traumatic event, experience indicates living in a dangerous environment, or otherwise being exposed to danger on a more or less continuous basis, creates the same kind of stress and potential trauma. In the three examples described earlier in this paper, at least a part of the emotional trauma that came into play during and after these events appeared clearly to be the result of longer-term exposure to a dangerous environment. Others, such as Gill Eagle, have noted the same:

> Resilience literature is beginning to hint that prolonged continuous exposure to multiple, significantly traumatic events may not increase general resilience, as was previously thought, but rather lead to people becoming more vulnerable to the development of intransigent trauma symptoms.[3]

---

[3] Gill Eagle, workshop presentation, European Conference on Traumatic Stress (Istanbul, Turkey, June, 1999)

What is the Organization's Reasonable Responsibility?

If it is accepted, as both experience and the literature indicate, that security factors affect missionary health, and by extension, their effectiveness in conducting ministry, then the question becomes what should the organization do? How responsible can the organization be for the safety and security of personnel? And, what is reasonable for the organization to do?

It seems that first, we should be guided by Biblical principles. Christ gave overwhelming evidence of being personally concerned with the lives and the well-being of his disciples. Modern-day Christian organizations should do no less. As Fawcett says "Any (organization) that presents itself as an entity valuing people will wish to demonstrate that same quality inside as well as outside (the organization)" (2000: 93). Unfortunately, the issue of emotional trauma carries some stigmatization in the Christian community. Some in the church, including some in missionary service and missionary leadership, have a genuine (but in the author's judgment mistaken) belief that all psychology, and the disciplines that flow from psychology, is inconsistent with the basics of Christian faith. It is beyond both the scope of this paper and the author's competence to refute such a belief, but it may be helpful to consider contrary opinions from two different Christian perspectives.

John Testrake was the Captain of TWA flight 847, hijacked in the Middle East in 1985.[4] A strong and committed Christian, John participated in the production of a videotaped account of his 17-day ordeal that is used to train missionaries for surviving in

---

[4] His book, *Triumph Over Terror on Flight 847* (Fleming H. Revell Co., 1987) is compelling reading.

hostile captivity. When asked about the broad issue of man's actions, decisions and tactics perhaps being somehow contradictory to acceptance of God's sovereign will and leading in human circumstances, John's response was:

> I feel that God gave me an intellect and a mind, and He gave other people with whom I work intellects and minds, and collectively we come up with better ways of doing things. I just have to give God the credit for maneuvering the situation around and improving on man's efforts to make this thing work out successfully.
>
> I like to look upon God as perhaps the manipulator of a giant lever. If I'm capable of exerting one pound with that big lever, then He magnifies that with that big lever and He turns it into a thousand pounds of effort. BUT IF I DON'T APPLY THE ONE POUND, THE THOUSAND POUNDS IS NEVER EXERTED (emphasis added).[5]

Testrake describes a partnership in which God gives us certain tools and resources, and then expects us to use them to the best of our ability. At the same time, God stands ready to step in with His sovereign will and power when it is the proper time for that to happen.

Another Christian professional offers this view:

> In health, as in all things, we should combine our faith in His ability to save and protect us with our own efforts to walk in the knowledge and understanding He has given us. We can truly claim God's protection only when we have done all

---

[5] John Testrake, videotaped interview with the author, 1987

within our power to follow the guidance He gives to prevent or alleviate our suffering.[6]

A missionary organization's response to this issue can, and should, be divided into two components: First, there are proactive or preventative steps that can and should be taken. Second, a prepared and adequate response system and protocol should be in place before a member suffers emotional trauma that requires access to that system and protocol.

Proactive Steps
"If adequate field support is not provided in the project infrastructure from the beginning, programs will fail and lives could be lost" (Fawcett 2000: 92). "Preventing traumatic injury is far cheaper than treating the impact of trauma...professional field staff are an increasingly rare commodity, and no (organization) can afford to lose essential staff through preventable causes" (Fawcett 2000: 93). Dr. Richard Farley, a Christian and a clinical psychologist specializing in Post-Traumatic Stress Disorder, says, "In 1974 the U.S. Congress acknowledged the emotional needs of disaster victims. Legislation was established that mandated funds be given to disaster-struck communities to establish community mental health programs. The emotional needs of disaster survivors were to be cared for. Can mission boards do less for their trauma victims? Can we do less than the government does for its casualties?" (Farley 1992:142).

The author's experience in nearly twenty years of missionary work dealing with safety and security issues, and the findings of

---

[6] Dr. Christine Aroney-Sine, Survival of the Fittest (MARC, Monrovia, CA, 1994), pg. 12

professionals such as Farley, Fawcett and others all point to the inescapable conclusion that an organization that is proactive in dealing with security issues will receive the additional benefit of having and keeping workers with better mental and emotional health. A foundational security management plan for a missionary organization will include the following components:

1. Risk assessment – A structured and considered plan for evaluating the dangers that exist in particular countries, regions and venues; and a structured and considered system for informing members about those dangers.
2. Contingency planning – A well-considered set of policy guidelines covering the major components of security and crisis management;[7] and, an organizational commitment to the development and maintenance (updating) of security contingency plans (for example, evacuation procedures).
3. Training – Based on the evaluation of risks and dangers faced within the organization, providing appropriate training to members.

One component of this preparation is the issue of emotional trauma. Fawcett proposes a model that includes both pre-employment and in-field occupational stress-management components. His pre-employment model includes:

---

[7] Crisis Management Teams (or other organizational response plan); Ransom/Extortion; Negotiations in Kidnapping Cases; Evacuations; Information Management and Media; and, Relocation and Care of Families.

1. Providing applicants with accurate information regarding the program, country, political, cultural and current events.
2. Providing general information regarding stress, stress management education, critical event and critical incident intervention.
3. Providing new staff with specific, up-to-date country and security profiles (Fawcett 2000:117).

His in-field model includes parallels to the overall security management recommendations:

1. Each office having a comprehensive security management plan.
2. Each office having clear policies regarding stress management.
3. Each office providing access to appropriate stress management and trauma recovery resources (local and international).
4. Each employee receives a thorough briefing immediately upon arrival in the country with specific references to security issues.
5. Senior or experienced staff are responsible for on-site orientations of new staff.
6. With (organizational) assistance and on-going support, new employees are encouraged to develop and initiate (and maintain) his or her own stress-management program (Fawcett 2000:117-118).

It is also critically important that the organization communicate to its staff that it does value them, and that it is both aware of the potential impact of emotional trauma and is ready and able to assist the member in dealing with that trauma. The organization's commitment to this must be both visible and real. "Such programs should not be confined to phrases in corporate mission statements but need to be clearly measurable components of a complete human resource management structure" (Fawcett 2000:120). The author is aware of a missionary organization that is training some members in the recovery process known as the Critical Incident Stress Debriefing (primarily a method of intervention following trauma), but which has recently closed out its psychological services department and professional staff. One cannot help but wonder what kind of mixed message this may appear to be to members of that organization.

Indeed, the literature suggests that the individual member's appreciation of the commitment and competence of the organization's leadership is a large factor in the prevention and mitigation of emotional trauma. Jonathan Shay says, "The most effective way of preventing stress injury is the all-around excellence of leadership — leadership that strengthens staff in this way also creates trust, mutual respect and positive enjoyment of the field community."[8] In his book *Failure to Scream*, Robert Hicks says

> Trauma brings to the surface all the dissatisfaction in our lives. Since one of our major identity roles is found in our jobs and careers, if this area is producing a generous amount of satisfaction, then work can become a place of therapy for the traumatized. If, on the other hand, it is a place of dissatisfaction, then the dissatisfaction turns to total

---

[8] Jonathan Shay, Workshop Presentation, International Society for Trauma Stress Studies, San Francisco, CA (1997).

disillusionment. In response, the individual, often within the year of the tragedy, leaves the job or career.[9]

Just knowing that someone understands, cares and is willing to help in these traumatic situations is a key to emotional health and recovery. Jerome Cook and Leonard Bickman studied 96 people who were victims of a major flood in Virginia at one-week, six-week and six-month intervals. They concluded that the mere perception and knowledge that financial assistance and social agency support were available were critical in lowering initial traumatic symptoms.[10]

A Response Protocol

It is inevitable that despite best efforts at staff screening, risk assessment, contingency planning and training, some events will occur that will result in traumatic emotional injury to missionary staff. The first step in responding is the understanding by the organization of the need for policies in this area. The author has a professional background in law enforcement, and there are clear parallels between missions and law enforcement regarding the "stigma" attached to emotional and mental trauma, and especially the seeking of professional assistance to deal with that trauma. In law enforcement, experience in years past was that far too many police officers, after being involved in shootings or similar highly emotional events in the line of duty, became dysfunctional, left the profession, and even committed suicide. The profession's initial efforts to deal with this involved

---

[9] Robert Hicks, *Failure to Scream* (Oliver-Nelson Books, 1993), pps. 203-204.

[10] Jerome C. Cook and Leonard Bickman, "Social Support and Psychological Symptomatology Following a Natural Disaster," *Journal of Traumatic Stress*, 3 (1990).

providing access for police officers to qualified mental health professionals following such events. But that didn't work, primarily because the organizational culture was a strong disincentive for the officer to take advantage of this resource. The stigma was just too strong. Only after law enforcement recognized this, and dealt with it by creating policy mandates requiring officers to meet with mental health professionals after such events, was a turnaround detected. The author has seen many of the same reactions to seeking professional mental health assistance from missionaries as he did from police officers.

In its training for missionary organizations, Crisis Consulting International (the author's organization) recommends that the organization have a policy mandating immediate intervention, and follow-up as indicated, following traumatic events. Dr. Karen Carr, recognized as a leader in this field in the missionary community, offers similar but more in-depth recommendations:

> If we can equip missionary administrators to recognize early symptoms so that they can make appropriate referrals and compassionate interventions, then we can go a long way in reducing the numbers of casualties on the mission field.
>
> There are three very important goals that each mission board should have in response to traumatic events:
>
> Goal #1 – Response and Prevention: Any missionary who experiences any type of trauma should receive an immediate response which is designed to enhance his or her coping resources and to prevent the development of stress related illnesses.

Goal #2 – Early Recognition: Each mission center should have the training and capability to recognize early signs of stress or mental illness so that early intervention can be provided.

Goal #3 – Referral for Treatment: Each mission center should have representatives who have received training that provides them with the capability to refer missionaries who are experiencing multiple and prolonged symptoms of stress related disorders to a mental health professional. (Carr 1993)

The concept of peer support should also be a major component of the organization's response plan. Peer support has both proactive (preventative) and reactive (post-event) value. Law enforcement and other public safety agencies that deal with highly traumatic events on a regular basis are increasingly embracing the concept of formal peer-counselor programs, training police officers, firefighters and paramedics in this area. In his research regarding combat during the Vietnam War, Shay concluded that there is a direct relationship between a soldier's ability to withstand the emotional trauma of combat and violence and the strength of his relationship with fellow soldiers (his peers).[11] Especially when dealing with violence, danger, moral depravity or any of the other "blacker" areas of human behavior, there is a very unique quality that a co-worker, who has shared the same (or similar) experiences can bring to the individual struggling to cope with what he or she has seen or experienced. The author's wife (a 28-year veteran police officer) has been a peer counselor with her police department for many years and

---

[11] Jonathan Shay, Achilles in Vietnam: Combat Trauma and the Undoing of Character (Atheneum, 1994).

can attest to the fact that fellow officers will contact and confide in a trusted co-worker long before they would do the same with a superior officer, a mental health professional, and in many cases even a spouse.

It is important, however, that co-workers who might fill this role have a good understanding of both appropriate and inappropriate means of support, and also have a solid appreciation of boundaries and limitations in their own competence. Dr. Farley provides valuable guidelines:

1. Model Christ's love by being supportive and non-judgmental. The survivor is usually his/her own harshest judge.
2. Maintain strict confidentiality. Do not violate the survivor's trust.
3. Be available to what may be a full and oftentimes contradictory range of emotional expression. Even if the feelings are unfair or uncalled for, remember that to be supportive means to be receptive to the complete range of the survivor's expressions. Speak the truth in love and not as a dictator. Tolerate their feelings and behaviors within the confines of good judgment.
4. Sometimes just being there for fellowship, to cry or pray together, or simply for a time to be quiet together is what the survivor needs most.
5. Remind the survivor that it is normal to experience conflicting emotions simultaneously. The horror of recounting specific events, joy over surviving, grief for those who may not have been so fortunate, and guilt over not having performed up to one's expectations – all are normal emotions.

Caring for Those in Crisis 135

6. Be a liaison for the survivor to friends, family and the organization.
7. Assist the survivor with planning for the immediate future. Dealing with issues such as needed time off from work and other responsibilities or coordinating medical care are all important. Be careful of the survivor's premature desire to "get back in the saddle."
8. If involved closely with the survivor or the event, take care of yourself, too. Burnout can be a very real problem. Be sure your own support system is intact.
9. Be ready to admit it if you find yourself "in over your head" with the survivor's issues. Requesting help from a qualified professional may be essential (Farley 1992:151-152).

The Critical Incident Stress Debriefing (C.I.S.D.) is an intervention process developed by Dr. Jeffrey Mitchell and Dr. George Everly. Although originally intended for use in the public safety sector, experience has shown that it can be used in almost any setting. Dr. Carr specifically recommends C.I.S.D: "I believe one of the best models which is designed to prevent the development of PTSD is the Critical Incident Stress Debriefing developed by Jeffrey Mitchell…In my experience this model has a much broader applicability than just emergency services personnel (Carr 1993:9-10).

Greatly summarized, the C.I.S.D. is a "group meeting or discussion about a distressing critical incident. Based upon core principles of education and crisis intervention, the CISD is designed to mitigate the impact of a critical incident and to assist the personnel in recovering as quickly as possible from the stress associated with the event. The CISD is run by a specially trained team which includes a mental health professional and peer support personnel from the organization" (Mitchell and Everly 1997:8).

The general principles of the C.I.S.D. include

1. CISD is not psychotherapy.
2. CISD is not a substitute for psychotherapy.
3. CISD should only be applied by those who have been specifically trained in its uses.
4. CISD is a group process.
5. CISD is a group meeting or discussion designed to reduce stress and enhance recovery from stress. It is based upon principles of crisis intervention and education, not psychotherapy per se.
6. A CISD is a team approach. A CISD team is comprised of a mental health professional and several peer support personnel.
7. A CISD will not solve all of the problems presented during the brief time frame available to work with distressed personnel, but it may mitigate those that persist.
8. Sometimes it will be necessary to refer individuals for follow up assessment and/or treatment after a debriefing.
9. It is not necessary for everyone in the group to speak during a debriefing process for the process to be beneficial.
10. Generally it is best to have a voluntary debriefing, but there are times when it is better for the good of the group to require the attendance of all involved personnel.
11. Following most well-defined and delineated acute traumatic events, the ideal time for a debriefing is after the first twenty-four hours and before seventy-two hours.

12. CISD is primarily a prevention program but it can be used to mitigate post-traumatic stress as well.
13. Although CISD is a technique which was developed specifically for emergency personnel, it has been applied, with great success, to many types of non-emergency workers.
14. CISD accelerates the rate of 'normal recovery, in normal people, who are having normal reactions to abnormal events.'
15. CISD should be considered as only one helpful technique under the general heading of Critical Incident Stress Management (CISM), an integrated system of interventions which are designed to prevent and/or mitigate the adverse psychological reactions that so often accompany emergency services, public safety and disaster response functions. CISM interventions are especially directed towards the mitigation of post-traumatic stress reactions.
16. A CISD is best provided by those who are not well known to those who need it.
17. CISD is a crisis intervention process designed to stabilize cognitive and affective processes and to further mitigate the impact of a traumatic event. It is NOT an operational critique of a crisis situation or traumatic event (Mitchell and Everly 1997:8).

Conclusion

Researchers, private sector employers and even government agencies recognize the potentially destructive effect post-traumatic-event emotional trauma can have on staff members. There is also increasing recognition that in addition to the damage this trauma causes to individual employees, there is a corresponding negative impact on the organization. These factors apply in the Christian environment, including the missionary environment, just as they do elsewhere. However, there can be an added destructive dimension for Christian victims who mistake normal human reactions to horrific events with unspiritual, or even sinful behavior. Coupled with a certain stigma against psychology and professional mental health intervention that exists among the Christian community, the result is the real potential for higher-than-necessary casualties of emotional trauma amongst the harvest force of missionaries.

Perhaps the most challenging step for a missionary agency that seeks to address this entire area will be dealing with that stigma. Facing the issue head-on, recognizing the partnership between human endeavor and God's sovereignty that Captain Testrake described, and appreciating that the Biblical concepts of stewardship must certainly apply at least as much to people as they do to replaceable assets such as money, will help dispel the stigma.

Any organization that seeks to address the broader issue of fully caring for its members in a challenging security environment will develop a comprehensive program:

1. First, the organization will maintain a competent overall security and crisis management program that includes risk assessment, policy setting and contingency planning, and training.
2. Second, the organization will incorporate the principles outlined herein throughout its personnel management and human resource management systems.
3. Third, the organization will develop policies that both delineate and mandate appropriate intervention for its

members following traumatic events, and will demonstrate both the importance of these programs and the value it places on the emotional health of its members in all appropriate ways.
4. Finally, the organization will implement programs such as peer support and a C.I.S.D., so it provides early intervention and support in cases of both singular traumatic events, and cases of lower-level but constant (or increasing) danger and stress.

Contexts of Care Giving

Chapter 7

Caring for Partnerships

Jehu Hanciles

When the partnership model came to the fore of the global missionary agenda over half a century ago — if we date its official pronouncement to Whitby (1947) with the theme: "Partnership in Obedience" — it marked a momentous shift in missionary thinking. By then it was becoming evident that erstwhile "mission fields" (particularly in the southern continents) were rapidly transforming into centers of vibrant Christianity; a trend that discredited the "territorial" distinctions underpinning the western missionary enterprise and cast a shadow over the pattern of one-directional (often denominational) relationships.

The new framework thus involved an affirmation that mission was no longer a western colonial monopoly and privilege, but that the whole church had a missionary responsibility towards the whole world. It conceived every (local) church as a sending and receiving church and anticipated a sharing of material and spiritual resources within relationships of mutual commitment to mission that would reflect greater interdependence and make the most use of the widely diverse resources of the worldwide church. Here, then, was the weapon that could conceivably slay the dragon of oppressive western paternalism in global missions and transform crippling patterns of dependency between north and south into relationships of mutuality and solidarity. But, as became increasingly manifest, the new paradigm called for a degree of attitudinal reorientation and restructuring that made the ideal notoriously problematic.

The partnership model still presents the global Church with significant challenges today. Indeed, it has been in fashion for so long, and may have been the object of so much lip service, that the real danger lies in underestimating its demands or overlooking its cardinal nature. The main thesis of this paper is that over and above a clear Scriptural imperative, the rapidly evolving global context in which the Church finds itself at the dawn of this new millennium renders the partnership paradigm even more crucial than half a century ago.

Partnership: A General Appraisal

Scholarly appraisal of the partnership approach to mission is regrettably sparse, but there can be no doubt that it has so far proven to be an elusive ideal. The term itself is quite elastic and indeterminate, and a lack of fixed content makes the concept susceptible to manipulation, even to support contradictory agendas.[1] It also arguably means different things to different people (particularly along the north-south divide), which may be why William Taylor observed (tongue-in-cheek, surely) that "partnership is like the Holy Grail. Everyone is talking about it but no one has seen it."[2] A consultation on "Partnership in Mission — What Structures?" (Yaoundé 1991) questioned whether the term is "a euphemism to conceal unjust relationships;" it also noted that "the term is used less in the

---

[1] For a critique see Stanley H Skreslet, "The Empty Basket of Presbyterian Mission: Limits and Possibilities of Partnership," *International Bulletin of Missionary Research*, 19 (July 1995) 3, 98-104, 101.

[2] W Taylor, "Lessons of Partnership," *Evangelical Missions Quarterly* (October 1995), 406-415, 415.

south than in the north"![3] "Yes, *partnership* for you, but *obedience* for us!" was the memorable retort by an Indonesian pastor to a Dutch professor in response to the Whitby theme.[4] And as the partnership slogans multiplied — mutuality, interdependence, solidarity, co-operation, equal participation, etc — so apparently did the misconceptions.

To non-western Christians, by and large, "partnership" signifies liberation (from ecclesiastical domination and other oppressive Christian structures), an affirmation of self-determination, and a mechanism for tapping into the seemingly abundant material resources of the Church in the West. For western churches the term has the attraction of being inoffensive, negating the harsh images of missionary paternalism and colonial domination etched in the memory of the non-western Church. It also implies, in theory at least, an acceptance of the fact that non-western churches are not merely products or objects of missionary labor but self-acting agents of change and a major force for the worldwide propagation of the Gospel.

Expectations on both sides tend to generate more tension than synergy. The western sense of trustee obligations, of getting "more bang for buck," often dictates that provision of financial resources be linked to control, evoking the very notions of unilateral power that the spirit of "partnership" eschews. Equally, non-western sensibilities about self-determination and contextual integrity often sit uneasily with the desire for unrestricted aid; and it often comes as a surprise to many Christians in the south that "partnership" is not a self-equalizing construct.

---

[3] See the Consultation's Report in *International Review of Mission*, vol. 81 (July 1992), 467-471, 468.
[4] Cf. Bosch (1994), 466.

For a long time the ideal structure for partnership in mission was considered to be a virtual United Nations configured so as to enable co-operative decision-making and joint disposal of resources according to need.[5] Mission agencies would coalesce and pool collective resources to form one joint, complex, international agency. A notable example of this approach is the Council of World Mission (CWM) formed in 1977. Each of the 28 or so CWM churches is expected to give according to its ability and make requests according to its missionary needs. Within this co-operative structure churches from north and south "share resources multi-directionally, take decisions multilaterally and engage in common mission action."[6]

But while this arrangement circumvents the donor-recipient structure it neither abrogates the fact that "money carries with it notions of power, domination and paternalism" (which is to say that inequality and dependence are built into the relationships),[7] nor ensures that resources are utilized for identifiable or coherent mission objectives. So "partners" may well benefit from the same pool despite conflicting motives and priorities. Intentional (church-to-church) partnerships may also suffer as interaction is limited to periodic meetings between heads of ministries or churches: "It is not often," admits the 1995 CWM Report

---

[5] Cf. Peter Hamm, "Breaking the Power Habit: Imperatives for Multinational Mission," *Evangelical Missions Quarterly*, vol. 19 (July 1983), 180-189, 186ff.

[6] "Perceiving Frontiers, Crossing Boundaries," Report of the Partnership in Mission Consultation of the Council for World Mission, *International Review of Mission*, 85 (April 1996) 337, 291-298, 295.

[7] "Perceiving Frontiers, Crossing Boundaries," Report on the Partnership in Mission Consultation of the Council for World Mission, *International Review of Mission*, 85 (April 1996) 337, 291-298, 294.

ruefully, "that what CWM churches assent to at the council level finds expression at the local level."

There is something to be said for the CWM-brokered multi-directional flow of missionaries "from India, Samoa, Papua New Guinea and Hong Kong going into Africa, Great Britain and Holland, and missionaries from the European regions going into distant islands on the Pacific and the Atlantic."[8] Yet, even this globalized movement could end up being nothing more than self-satisfied ecumenism unless the aim of "partnership in mission" remains a central focus.

Other speed-bumps liable to impede this "United Nations" approach to partnership are readily identifiable:[9] (1) when demands outstrip supply discrimination and partiality may be inevitable; (2) negative past experiences in similar relationships and hidden rivalries can ferment mistrust and painful misunderstandings; and (3) differing perceptions of mission can seriously undermine the project. Too often also the partnership becomes an end in itself — the embodiment rather than an instrument of mission — which, as Stanley Skreslet warns, "might well cause us to lose light of the core concerns of the gospel message."[10]

Clearly there is no shortage of obstacles and dilemmas to be surmounted and resolved in implementing the partnership model. And, the search for meaningful structures and forms of partnership is likely to continue. Questions abound about the

---

[8] Daisy G Ratnam, "Partnership in Practice: The Council for World Mission after Four Years," *International Review of Mission*, 76 (October 1987), 489-492, 490.

[9] Cf. J Andrew Kirk, *What is Mission? Theological Explorations* (London: Darton, Longman and Todd Ltd), 1999, pp. 192f.

[10] See Stanley Skreslet's criticism of the mission agenda within the Presbyterian Church (USA) — (1995: 101, 103).

mechanisms of change: Who should partner with whom? At which level (parish, denomination, ecumenical/international conferences, etc)? For what purpose? Parachurch or voluntary organizations, which often combine social engagement with mission objectives, often work closely with secular aid agencies. They tend to regard the traditional structures of the church as a hindrance to meaningful partnership, and in need of assessment.

But if the practice is so palpably problematic, what makes it such a good idea or an ideal? Andrew Kirk argues that partnership, like mission, "is not so much what the church *does* as what it *is*"; that "however diverse may be patterns of worship, methods of evangelism, styles of leadership, involvement in society and ways of expressing faith, there is 'one body and one spirit…one hope…one Lord, one faith, one baptism, one God and Father of all' (Eph 4:4-5)."[11] Partnership, in essence therefore, "is the expression of one, indivisible, common life in Jesus Christ." He further identifies four aspects of partnership modeled in the New Testament and embodied in the term "sharing" (or *koinonia*): namely, sharing in a common project (Phil 1:5; 4:3, 15); sharing of gifts (1 Cor 12:7; Eph 4:11-13); sharing in suffering (2 Cor 1:7; 1 Cor 12:26; Phil 3:10); and sharing of material resources (Rom 16:24-29; 2 Cor 8:1-15, 9:1-5).[12]

Since unequal material resources and uneven economic relationships tend to be at the center of much of the debate and confusion surrounding the partnership paradigm, we shall return to the last of these four New Testament patterns later in the paper. It is necessary first of all to set the rest of our discussion firmly within the current global context.

---

[11] Kirk (1999:187).
[12] *Ibid.*, 189-191.

The World as Context

Larry Pate has observed that "it is only when churches are committed to each other as much as they are to the message that the Gospel can carry the moral authority and power the world is searching for."[13] It cannot be emphasized too strongly that the exigencies of the new global context make the partnership paradigm imperative for an effective global witness. This need appears even more compelling when we consider the demographic shifts within global Christianity itself and the seemingly inexorable forces of globalization.

Global Christianity

The history of World Christianity is marked by episodes of massive accessions and dramatic recessions that periodically produce shifts in its geographic and demographic center of gravity, relocating the "center" to the "periphery." The latest of these momentous shifts took place in the course of the last ten decades as progressive de-Christianization in Western Europe and North America, the most considerable recession in the history of Christianity since significant losses to emergent Islam, combined with explosive Christian growth in the southern continents (Africa, Latin America, and the Pacific). So extensive was this process of transformation that Christianity has emerged as a non-western religion. The third millennium Church will be largely defined and influenced by developments within Third-world Christianity.

The case of Africa is particularly striking. In the course of a century the continent transformed from a "mission field" which, in 1900, boasted the smallest number of Christians of any

---

[13] Pate (1991), 60.

continent (with the exception of Oceania),[14] into an area arguably "experiencing the fastest church growth of any region" in the world.[15] "Black Africa," as Adrian Hastings has observed, "is inconceivable today apart from the presence of Christianity."[16] Admittedly, African Christianity is not the unmitigated success that a purely head count or statistical approach often makes it out to be. Much of West Africa, for instance, is still *not Christian*, in the face of a vibrant Islam[17] but its progress has consistently embarrassed the skeptics.[18] The dawn of the new millennium sees the Church as one of Africa's most powerful institutions, a modernizing and missionizing force with a burgeoning membership drawn from among all classes of society, notably upwardly mobile social groups. And if current prognostications turn out to be accurate its present numbers will almost double in the next quarter of a century, making it, with the possible

---

[14] Cf. D B Barrett, 1999, "Annual Statistical Table on Global Mission" in *International Bulletin of Missionary Research* 23 (January 1999), 24-25.

[15] Cf. J A Siewert and E G Valdez (eds), *Mission Handbook* (California: MARC Publications), 1997, p. 34.

[16] Quoted in Gifford (1998:22).

[17] For an assessment, see J Hanciles, "Conversion and Social Change: A Review of the Unfinished Task in West Africa," paper presented at the Currents in World Christianity Consultation, Oxford (July 1999); also O Kalu, "Jesus Christ, Where are You?: Themes in West African Church Historiography at the Edge of the 21st Century," paper presented at the Global Historiography Consultation, Fuller Theological Seminary (April 1998).

[18] Paul Gifford remarks, for instance, that it was commonly thought during the era of independence that Christianity in Africa would become less significant "because it was associated so closely with colonialism and depended so strongly on its school systems which would be taken over by governments" (1998:21).

exception of Latin America, the continent with the most Christians in the world.[19]

Other regional shifts are equally momentous. Korea is now touted as the greatest missionary nation. By the 1990s, there were indications that the non-western missionary force would soon account for well over 50% of all Protestant missionaries.[20] The missionary presence and impact of countless numbers of Christians from the southern continents who have migrated to the industrial centers of the West is also significant, and we shall turn to this below.

For all this, the Church in the West still has a long way to go in divesting itself of chronic paternalism which manifests itself not only in a tacit assumption that the global mission initiative is a western privilege (by virtue of wealth, education and expertise), but also "in the surprise expressed at the vitality, spiritual maturity and intellectual strength of the Church elsewhere."[21] For many Christians in the north, the south is still the mission field. Some countries, however, like Brazil, send out as many missionaries as they receive.[22] But in the African experience, the number of full-time North American Protestant missionaries steadily increased throughout the 1990s, mainly in connection with the New Pentecostal wave.[23] This flooding of missionaries into Africa, contends Paul Gifford, has had an effect

---

[19] Cf. D B Barrett, 2000, "Annual Statistical Table on Global Mission" in *International Bulletin of Missionary Research* 24 (January 2000), 24-25.

[20] Larry Pate, "The Changing Balance in Global Mission," *International Bulletin of Missionary Research* 15 (April 1991) 2, 56-61, 59.

[21] Kirk (1999:194).

[22] Mark Hutchinson provides a succinct appraisal of the new crosscurrents of global missionary movement in his "It's a Small Church after all," *Christianity Today* 42 (November 1998) 13, 46-49.

[23] Cf. Paul Gifford, *African Christianity: Its Public Role* (Indianapolis: Indiana University Press), 1998, 44-47.

on the Christian landscape that is "just as substantial as that of the non-governmental organizations [NGOs]." What gives this comparison sharpened significance is the fact that NGOs now dominate critical spheres of public service, often wielding more power and influence in the socio-political terrain than weakened African governments. Indeed, an article titled "Sins of Secular Missionaries" (which appeared in *The Economist* of all places!) argued forcefully that some Western NGOs "are used to propagate western values" in much the same way that "Christian missionaries did in the 19th century."[24]

In a sharp and candid critique of modern missionary structures, Engel and Dyrness observe that "the door is slowly but steadily swinging shut on North Americans who are reluctant to recognize that the Two-Thirds World churches now lie at the very center of world missions influence and initiative. The need now is to come alongside in a spirit of *partnership and submission*, participating where possible in an enabling and facilitating manner to help increase the impact of all that God is doing in this era [italics added]."[25]

This observation usefully highlights the need for north-south partnerships. Local-local partnerships have immense value; but in the current global context, creative partnerships cross the

---

[24] "Sins of the Secular Missionaries," *The Economist* (29 January 2000), 25-27, 27. The article maintains that, relying solely on outside resources NGOs often promote western-defined solutions which cause social disruption on the ground and, like earlier western missionaries, are prone to become "self-perpetuating:" refusing to disband or depart when the job is done. For further treatment see Julie Hearn, "The NGO-isation of Kenyan Society: USAID & the Restructuring of Health Care," *Review of African Political Economy*, 25 (March 1998) 75, 89-100.

[25] J F Engel & W A Dyrness, *Changing the Mind of Missions: Where have We Gone Wrong?* (Ill: InterVarsity Press), 2000, p. 21.

north-south divide that recognize and utilize the different kinds of resources available in both are increasingly crucial. A few international agencies have invested a great deal of effort in creating this kind of mutuality and interdependence; but of how many such agencies can it be said that Third World missionaries/partners are incorporated on equal footing at all levels? This is where the real challenge lies. A western program, dominated by a western board, and directed from headquarters located in the West, can only proclaim partnership as a public relations gimmick, no matter how many non-western missionary personnel it funds. It is noteworthy that as late as 1990 only 3% of Third World missionaries served with a western agency.[26]

Deliberate internationalization of structures, leadership and ministries geared towards a global mission movement is needed. It is time to reflect on which models or strategies Third World missionaries will/should adopt as they become the largest segment of the Protestant missionary force. There is much to learn from the earlier western missionary enterprise; but, crucially, this non-western movement boasts neither the educational, economic and technological advantages of the former nor the protection of strong economic and military powers that the former enjoyed. In sharp contrast to the western missionary movement it comes not from the *centers* of political power and economic wealth but from the *periphery*. Its models and strategies must be radically different, more akin to the biblical model.[27] It is arguably more church-based; and some suggest it may be modeled on "the kenotic Christ," the "Jesus who carried on his mission from a position of powerlessness," or

---

[26] Pate (1991), 58.
[27] Engel and Dyrness are suggestive (2000:40-43).

on the Apostle Peter who proclaimed, "Silver and gold have I none; but such as I have give I thee" (Acts: 3:6).

It is too early to say how this movement will evolve, but one dimension stands out — migration. This element, as Escobar notes, has been a functional element in Christian expansion throughout the centuries, even though "it seldom gets to the records of formal institutional missionary activity."[28] Countless nameless Christians are included in the huge migrant populations that daily flow into the rich industrial centers of the north. This movement in itself owes its emergence to the forces of globalization which, to paraphrase Bruce Scott, is transforming the world less into a global village than a "gated community" (as the industrialized nations erect higher barriers against immigration).[29] Among the hordes who pass through the gates are many non-Western Christians who, through active participation in various western Christian communities, become agents of new spiritual vitality and help initiate effective forms of outreach to multicultural neighborhoods.[30] Describing the London situation, Andrew P. Davey notes:

> The presence of members from minority ethnic communities in the congregations of the established denominations has

---

[28] Samuel Escobar, "The Global Scenario at the Turn of the Century," W Taylor (ed), *Global Missiology for the 21st Century: The Iguassu Dialogue* (Michigan: Baker Academic), 2000, 23-46, 34.

[29] Bruce Scott, "The Great Divide in the Global Village," *Foreign Affairs* 80 (Jan/Feb 2001) 1, 160-177, 160.

[30] For helpful comment, see Andrew P. Davey, "Globalization as Challenge and Opportunity in Urban Mission," *International Review of Mission* 88 (October 1999) 351, 381-389; Samuel Escobar, "Global Scenario at the Conclusion of a Century," paper presented at the World Evangelical Fellowship International Missiological Consultation, Iguazu, Brazil, October 1999.

influenced styles of worship and witness...[and] has renewed many inner city congregations. A diversity of cultures within a congregation often leads to fresh understandings of the role of narrative and the practice of community as personal stories of migration and pilgrimage are retold against the backdrop of the biblical narrative. Personal links with churches in other countries offer a sharper understanding for whole congregations of issues previously considered remote.[31]

This testimony can surely be multiplied in other major cities in the West. In many US cities, for instance, Korean churches are among the most dynamic; in many multicultural neighborhoods also, Africans and Latin American migrant Christians often act as agents of new spiritual vitality and help initiate effective forms of outreach. If nothing else this reality suggests that the contours of global missionary outreach are more fluid and complex than mere statistical data (mainly compiled and analyzed in the West) makes its out to be.[32]

The Forces of Globalization

The impact, scope and pervasiveness of globalization stretch the imagination. Its immensely complex dimensions are the focus of burgeoning literature that portends a new order, a new international system. Some authorities regard this as the natural successor to the "Cold-War" era — the one defined by division

---

[31] A P Davey, "Globalization as Challenge and Opportunity in Urban Mission," *International Review of Mission* (October 1999) [5].

[32] Pentecostalism, even in the northern hemisphere, continues to gain new ground. See, for instance, "Jesus at 2000," *Macleans* (29 November 1999), 60-66, 64.

and partition, the other by integration and interconnection.[33] It can be described as the process whereby the world's people are becoming increasingly connected in all facets of their lives, through the integration of markets, finance and technologies.[34] In its economic aspects, globalization is essentially a western project, a product of the culture of capitalism — building on the foundations of European colonialism — and "principally driven by international trade and investment through the actions of some 300 giant multinational companies." Simultaneously, developments in mass media and information technology are dissolving conventional boundaries of language, time and distance, creating a global "consumer" culture.

The dizzying ramifications of globalization can hardly be discussed here, but it is important to bear in mind that the process is fraught with paradoxes: convergence and integration accompanied by conflict and social (as well as political) disintegration. Interconnectedness and the shrinking global space creates a sense of the globe as "one place" while at the same time heightening cultural and religious diversity. Similarly, in cases where the activities of multinational companies boost the economies of developing countries the process often exacerbates income inequalities within the same countries. The increased production created by economic integration is often at the expense of the environment.

---

[33] Probably the chief proponent of this view is Thomas L Friedman: see *The Lexus and the Olive Tree: Understanding Globalization* (NY: Farrar, Straus & Giroux), 1999, 5-14, 25ff.

[34] This statement combines definitions from two authorities: George Lodge, *Managing Globalization in the Age of Interdependence* (San Diego: Pfeiffer & Co.), 1995, p. 1 and Thomas Friedman and Ignacio Ramone, "Dueling Globalizations," *Foreign Policy*, 116 (Fall 1999), 110-127, 110.

That this new global order has far-reaching implications for the mission and witness of the Church is unquestionable, though there is space here only to highlight one or two notable aspects. It is important to note that globalization increases the economic hegemony of the already dominant group (the industrial north) while further impoverishing and marginalizing most of the southern continents.[35] Not surprisingly, many Third World observers see globalization as a dark force that "contributes to greed, the desire for control, materialism, consumerism and the promotion of a global culture or lifestyle that destroys values, customs and traditions in local communities."[36] A 1998 meeting attended by thirty-seven church leaders from India, Pakistan and Sri Lanka concluded that the open market system and multinational corporations have increased the misery of the poor in developing Asian nations, and it called on churches "to fight globalization."[37] The plight of sub-Saharan Africa, where 25 of

---

[35] Using a "core-periphery" analysis Ankie Hoogvelt advances the thought-provoking argument that under the impact of globalization, the relationship between the developed nations (the "core") and Third World countries has declined since the colonial era from structural exploitation to structural irrelevance — A Hoogvelt, *Globalization and the Postcolonial World: The New Political Economy of Development* (MaryLand: John Hopkins University Press), 1997, chapter 4.

[36] Cf. D Mukarji, "Gospel and the Search for Identity and Community." *International Review of Mission*, 25 (January 1996) 336, 25-34, p. 26; Martin Khor, "Global Economy and the Third World," in J Mander & E Goldsmith (eds) *The Case Against the Global Economy and for a Turn towards the Local* (San Francisco: Sierra Book Clubs), 1996, 47-59.

[37] The meeting was organized by the Association of Christian Institutes for Social Concern in Asia and the Urban Rural Mission of the National Council of Churches in Asia — Teresa Malcolm, "Meeting Deplores Globalization," *National Catholic Reporter*, 34 (April 1998) 24, 9.

the 30 least developed countries in the world are located, is even more stark.[38]

These menacing economic inequalities are also reflected within the global Christian church in so far as the average income of Christians in the northern hemisphere far exceeds that of their brethren in the southern continents. Thus, almost invariably, discussions on partnership focus on the acute economic disparities in the worldwide church and need for a sharing of resources. Such an expectation, as stated earlier, has Scriptural support. Paul's writings reveal a clear expectation that the needs of one part of the body should be met by the resources of the other parts. And of particular relevance is his relief initiative for the impoverished Church in Jerusalem (Rom 15:25-27; also 2 Cor 8:1-15; 9:1-5), from which at least four lessons for partnership can be gleaned:[39]

- the sharing of resources is described as "a ministry to the saints" (NRSV), with the implication that such material considerations are not to be distinguished from other forms of Christian service or commitment,

- the "financial" drive succeeded despite cultural barriers and evidence of resistance and resentment among the donors (though it is worthy of note that Paul was not averse to adopting 'arm-twisting' methods — 1 Cor 9:1-3),

- the scheme was rooted in mutuality and reciprocity: Paul's principle argument was that Gentile Christians who had

---

[38] See J S Saul and C Leys, "Sub-Saharan Africa in Global Capitalism," *Monthly Review*, 51 (July/August 1999) 3, 13-30.

[39] I am indebted to Samuel Escobar for most of these insights.

benefited from the spiritual blessings of the Jews could now return the favor by sharing material things with them, and

- Paul insists that there must be "a fair balance" between *abundance* and *need* in the Church.

It is, of course, necessary to point out that however helpful these guidelines are, their application to our contemporary historical context is not without significant limitations: (a) in Paul's missionary practice, the sending church did not presume to exercise authority over the new born communities — thus there was no historical legacy of dependency or missionary paternalism to be overcome between the Gentile and Jewish churches; (b) the *older* church, not the struggling *younger* "offspring," was the recipient in the relief transaction, which rather presents a different dynamic with regard to paternalism, for instance; (c) the relief in question appears to have been a one-time collection for a specific situation of need, not a strategy for long-term aid; and (d) even though Paul invested the transaction with profound theological significance, it was geared less towards a mechanism of interdependence *for mission* than towards the practice of Christian unity (even though these two are inseparable).

But, even with these qualifications, the principles enshrined in this test case provide a useful construct for assessing our assumptions about partnership for mission and testing our commitment to its demands. Those demands are greater now than ever. For one thing, even if it translates into credible action, sharing material resources is not enough. Much of the misery of the Third world is self-inflicted, yet so many of its problems are traceable to western policies and programs. As the western church partakes in the redemptive stream of God's mission it must reflect on the fact that it is called by a God who wants to liberate humanity from every form of oppression, injustice and alienation. The missionary agenda of the church in the new global age cannot be true to the gospel and remain silent about the poverty and exploitation of the majority of the world's population.[40] This calls for a renewed affirmation of the declaration of the 1974 Lausanne Congress that argued that both evangelism and social responsibility are "necessary expressions" of the Church's mandate.

Further still, the dilemma confronting a global mission in the area of financial resources is more complicated that a focus on the north-south divide allows. Many experts detect a gradual shift in economic power generally speaking from the Atlantic (Europe and North America) to the Pacific (Japan, Singapore, Hong Kong, and the Arab oil states). In the new millennium, the bulk of the world's wealth may well lie in *non-Christian* hands for the first time since the sixteenth century with clear implications for mission.[41] Robert Schreiter argues that not only would Asian domination of the global economy intensify the poverty of the south (where 70% of the world's Christians live) it would also transform the evangelical encounter with other religions. However, since the West will still retain much of the economic resources that can be used for Christian mission, the need for partnership and interdependence will become more acute, not less.

The West clearly cannot afford to ignore the vigor and vitality of non-western Christianity, and genuine

---

[40] David Bosch is suggestive: *Believing in the Future: Towards a Missiology of Western Culture* (Pennsylvania: Trinity Press International), 1995, 35-40.
[41] See Robert J Schreiter, "Mission into the Third Millennium." *Missiology*, 28 (January 1990), 1, 3-12.

interdependence calls for an emphasis on both the material and spiritual resources of the Church. Robert Ramseyer argues correctly that "only when we value these spiritual resources in just as concrete and practical a way as we do the resources valued by modern industrial society will we be able to move towards real interdependence...able to understand that our perception of the 'unequal partnership' is a result of our failure to perceive the full range of resources which God makes available to his church."[42]

It should be an even greater missiological concern that the Church displays the most explosive growth and increasing missionary vitality in the most destitute and poverty-stricken regions of the world (South Korea excepted). This signifies that in this millennium, unlike the last, the new heartlands of Christianity lack the resources for global missionary enterprise.

The relationship between the situations of harsh economic hardship, rapid social change and massive urban crises that exist in the south and the spiritual vitality and numeric growth of Christianity in that part of the world is liable to be romanticized. But, for all their vibrancy, the churches and Christian communities in the south are hardly immune to the debilitating constraints of their harsh economic environment. Often, they form links with churches in the north out of desperation and a need to avoid homelessness within the "global village." While this draws much needed resources, it also makes them vulnerable to structures of dependency and can work against the genuine partnership that is needed for a truly global missionary movement.

---

[42] R L Ramseyer, "Partnership and Interdependence," *International Review of Mission*, 69 (January 1980), 32-39, 34.

It also makes them susceptible to subtle forms of exploitation. One of the most inimical aspects of globalization is the drain of resources from south to north. Intellectual property rights are a case in point. The global entertainment industry stands accused of systematically "uprooting the music of indigenous peoples from its native soil and treating it as a free commodity;"[43] it is also claimed that "80% of patents granted in developing countries now go to the residents of industrial countries while new patents ignore the accumulated knowledge of indigenous peoples."[44] These secular trends have parallels within the global church. As Andrew Kirk acknowledges with laudable candor, the mission insights of Third World scholars are often not credited as such in the West. The same may also be said of forms of music and worship.[45]

By and large, relationships between older mainline denominations across the north-south divide have come further along the road of partnership than the new evangelical and Pentecostal networks. One thinks, for instance, of the unity and mutual accountability that allowed African bishops to take a stand at the 1998 Lambeth Conference on critical issues they considered inimical to the spiritual wellbeing of the Anglican Communion. By contrast, the strong links forged with North American Pentecostal groups by many of the "new breed" churches in the south tend to be heavily one-directional. The latter's commitment to modernization and extensive use of media production as a tool of evangelism make them wholesale conduits for the dissemination of American Pentecostal models

---

[43] Khor (in 1996:76).
[44] Guy Arnold, "What are we Globalizing?," *New Africa* 379 (November 1999), p. 38.
[45] Kirk (1999:193).

and media production. Self-support and autonomy may not be lost, but self-theologizing often becomes a casualty. In the Latin American context, the spread of the American-inspired "Prosperity Gospel" has been sharply criticized for espousing the same logic that drives "neo-liberal capitalism." It is also said to ignore the local realities and to foster a consumer-oriented Christianity.[46]

This criticism allows us to point out the quite obvious fact that the paradoxes of the globalization process are increasingly reflected within the global church. While technological developments and burgeoning communications infrastructure provide the tools that could facilitate new forms of global partnerships for mission, they also infinitely increase the potential for tension and friction as local Christian identities come under strain. Missionaries may now criss-cross the globe with greater ease, but many in the field can now spend more time on the internet, interacting with kith and kin back home, than they do with the communities they actually live among. The Australian scholar, Mark Hutchinson, observes that the "globalization of evangelicalism means that the traditional locus of power, the First World, no longer has the ability to control the conversation;" yet, at the same time, email access and satellite conferences mean that ideological divisions and other forms of disunity are no longer restricted by space, time or geographical network.

In the new global context most problems confronting the world are increasingly of a global nature and only yield to global

---

[46] Claudio de Oliveira Ribeiro, "Has Liberation Theology died? Reflections on the Relationship between Community Life and the Globalization of the Economic System," *The Ecumenical Review*, 51 (July 1999) 3, 304-314. He also draws a contrast between the vision of the "prosperity theology" and "liberation theology."

solutions involving multilateral action, vigorous networking, use of new communications technologies, local-local relations, and long-term international strategies. When asked how she managed to build an international coalition in favor of a landmine ban without much government help and in the face of opposition from the major powers, Jody Williams (who won the Nobel Peace Prize in 1997 for her contribution to the International Campaign to Ban Landmines) gave a simple reply: "E-mail."

The term "global mission" may sound "loaded" and presumptuous, but it points to the enormous challenges and opportunities that the worldwide church faces at the dawn of this millennium. It signifies a call for the partnership model to be the focus as we grapple with "a global way[s] of being church." It further indicates that the witness of the Church would be entirely inadequate unless it is understood within a global context. Interdependence is a fact and factor of globalization, and it would make for bitter irony if one of the most deliberately globalizing movements the world has known should falter in its mission for want of interdependent structures. Similarly, if partnership is a "holy grail," a rapidly evolving global context, not to mention a clear biblical mandate, demands that we pursue it to the ends of the earth.

Chapter 8

Caring for Indigenous Harvesters

Sue Russell

The changing global mission context is creating a new harvest force that needs support, training, and care. Keyes (1999:745) projected that this year there will be approximately 164,000 non-Western missionaries working crossculturally, compared to 132,000 Western missionaries. This number is expected to increase. Butler (1999:757) notes that the missionary growth rate in the West is about 3% whereas the growth rate in non-Western countries is over 13%. However, many more non-Western missionaries could join the mission endeavor with the training and support that partnerships could offer.

Technological developments have created an environment where this training and support can occur. New software programs and the development of distance education networks make it possible to share technology, train and care for this increasing harvest force. The rapidly developing communication technology is also creating unprecedented opportunities for partnership development and information sharing at a global level. However, we need to develop new strategies for teamwork, training, missionary care, and mutual support for the harvest force of the 21st century.

This paper focuses on one sector of the new mission force, the indigenous harvest, those Christians already on-site. I propose that one of the most effective ways to care for the indigenous harvest force is through partnerships that "come alongside with a desire to facilitate and enable all that those on-site are trying to accomplish (Engel and Dyrness 2000:97). In this paper I present the theological foundation and a missiological framework for developing partnerships that would provide the support, training and care to enable the indigenous harvest force to effectively participate in missions. I then discuss mission strategies and new technology that promote partnership and care of the indigenous harvest force. Finally, I examine training needed for the expatriate to work in partnership.

Theological Foundations for Partnerships and Training

Working in partnerships in global missions is not a new idea. As early as 1974, the Lausanne Covenant noted that because of the diminishing role of the Western church and the growing significance of the role of non-Western church's in world missions, churches and mission agencies must continually reevaluate their role in missions and in partnerships. Lausanne II of 1989 also continued to explore the role of partnership in world missions. Several mission strategists, from both the North and South have written on the need for churches to form partnerships to fulfill the Great Commission (Bush and Lutz 1990; K.P Yohannan 1991; Kraakevik and Welliver 1991; Mc Alister 1995; Taylor 1994; Steffen 1999; Keyes 1999; Butler 1999). But how we define partnerships and our theological foundation for partnership affects the kind of partnerships we form and the strategies we implement. To create partnerships based on relationships, rather than programs, we need to begin with a sound biblical foundation.

The theological foundations for partnerships can be derived from the metaphor of the body of Christ. There are three important truths that are imperative for partnership in global missions. The first concept is unity. Believers in Christ are all members of one body. It is important to note that it is always individuals who are defined as members in one body, not a church. The local church is only the particularization of members in one location (Saucy 1972:25). Partnerships are formed between members of different local assemblies who are in the same body of Christ. Although there is local autonomy of leadership, local churches have no claim on the gifts, talents and resources of their members for exclusive use of their local assembly. These gifts and resources are given for the building up of the whole body of Christ.

The second concept is diversity. As members of one body in different local assemblies, we have access to different resources that we can contribute to the program of the church in the world. In missions, strategies for partnerships are based on the fact that members have diverse gifts and training. Technology now allows us to share those gifts on a global level with members of the body in distant and remote locations.

The third concept is mutuality. According to Saucy this implies that members are interdependent upon one another. Each member is concerned about the other and there is a mutual sharing. In missions, partnerships must be formed on this same sense of mutuality. Each partner contributes something to the partnership to accomplish the goal and vision that they share. As Engel and Dyrness (2000:96) note, there must be mutual submission and interdependency in a true partnership. Each partner is heard and each partner learns from the other.

Partnerships that facilitate and enable are based on these three concepts. Both partners recognize their membership in the same body of Christ and desire to mutually share their diverse gifts, talents, and resources, to accomplish the task that God has given them. Partnerships are not built upon strategies, plans or goals, but upon relationships. It is only as we first develop relationships based on our mutual membership in the body of Christ that we can develop strategies and training that reflect the unity, diversity and mutuality of the body of Christ.

Missiological Framework for Partnerships and Training

Working in partnerships requires assessment of the strengths and weakness of each partner in order to mutually share in the task of translating the gospel into another culture. A framework is needed that assesses (1) how to best utilize the resources of each partner, (2) what each partner lacks, and (3) when the task is complete.

Over the years different models have been developed to discuss the concept of translation of the gospel into another cultural context. They have been expressed as the translation of the message (Sanneh 1989, 1990), the indiginization of the gospel (Kraft and Wisley 1979; Smalley 1979; Taber 1979); receptor-oriented communication (Kraft 1991b), inculturation (Arbuckle 1990; Shorter 1988), dynamic-equivalence (Nida 1990; Kraft 1991a), transculturation (Shaw 1988), and more recently contextualization (Hesselgrave and Rommen 1989; Hayward 1995; Hesselgrave 1995; Shaw 1995; Davis 1993).

"Contextualization" has been used as a general term to encompass the whole task of translating Christianity into another culture. Hesselgrave and Rommen (1989:200) define it this way:

> ...Christian contextualization can be thought of as the attempt to communicate the message of the person, works, word and will of God in a way that is faithful to God's revelation, especially as it is put forth in the teachings of the Holy Scripture, and that is meaningful to respondents in their respective cultural and existential contexts. Contextualization

is both verbal and nonverbal and has to do with theologizing, Bible translation, interpretation and application, incarnational lifestyle, evangelism, Christian instruction, church planting and growth, church organization, worship style-indeed with *all of those activities involved in carrying out the Great Commission.* (Italics mine)

This definition identifies several of the tasks involved in contextualization, from evangelism to theologizing. Others have listed similar tasks in the process of contextualization (Hayward 1995; Kraft 1979). All of these writers emphasize that the process of contextualization must include all of the tasks involved in Great Commission. The tasks involved in contextualization can be grouped into three stages in the process of contextualization: (1) introduction of the gospel, (2) establishment of the gospel, and (3) maturing of the gospel (Russell 1999). (See: Table 1.)

As Hesselgrave and Rommen note, all of these activities correspond to the carrying out of the Great Commission. Each of the stages corresponds to one of the participles in Matthew 28:18-20 that are the means of making disciples. The first stage of contextualization, the communication of the gospel, reflects the "go" participle. Going to all nations often involves cross-cultural communication of the gospel. At this stage the missionary seeks to live an incarnational lifestyle, seeking to communicate the gospel in the most appropriate way for a particular culture.

The second stage of this framework, the establishment of the gospel, corresponds to the "baptizing" stage. In this stage believers are incorporated into a local church. It involves building up the growing body of believers into a mature church. It is at this stage that many missionary strategies begin to

Table 1: Three stages of contextualization

Stage	Tasks
Introduction of the gospel 'going' *Crosscultural Communication*	• Receptor-oriented communication • Incarnational life style • Use of non-biblical imagery to communicate Scriptural concepts • Use of culturally appropriate forms of communication
Establishment of the gospel 'baptizing' *Church planting and growth*	• Christian instruction/ education • Culturally appropriate church organization and leadership • Culturally appropriate hymns and worship styles • Use of culturally appropriate forms of communication • Culturally appropriate art forms
Maturing of the Gospel 'teaching' *Discipleship, theology and missions*	• Emergence of culturally appropriate ethics and values • Cross-cultural missions • Incorporation and integration of church and faith with society • Contextual theologizing • Life application in cultural context • Communication and participation in the global church

phase-out (Steffen 1997) of the area as local members take leadership of the growing churches.

However, there is a third stage in the contextualization process that is often not a part of our mission strategies. The third stage, maturing of the gospel, corresponds to "teaching them to obey all things." Wilkins (2000) notes that this stage is often the "great omission" in discipleship programs. As a result, many of the potential harvest force are not equipped to participate in global missions.

Wilkins (1999) suggests that the themes of the five discourses in Matthew are an outline of what is to be included in "teaching them to obey all things." Table 2 below shows five themes that correspond to what missiologists have suggested as signs of the contextualised church. Caring for the indigenous harvest force must include providing the tools so that they can complete the contextualization process in their own community. They need all the tools necessary for effective discipleship, including tools to be able to do biblical theology, crosscultural missions and develop biblical ethics.

Framework for Training

The contextualization framework provides a guide for the kinds of training that both partners require to effectively carry out the Great Commission. Baba (1991) notes that one of the greatest needs for enabling missions in Africa is practical crosscultural training. Even though members of the indigenous

Table 2: Matthew's five discourses and contextualization

Discourse themes	Contextualization outcome
Kingdom life (Mt 5-7)	Emergence of culturally appropriate ethics and values
Missionary disciples (Mt 10)	Crosscultural missions
Presence of the Kingdom (Mt 13)	Incorporation and integration of church and faith with society
Community Life (Mt 18)	Contextual theologizing Life application in cultural context
Jesus' Return (Mt 24-25)	Communication and participation in the global church

harvest force are from a culturally close group, there are still differences in culture and language, not to mention differences between their culture and those found in the Bible.

There is also a necessity for training in biblical languages for Bible translation. Training in literacy and literacy development may also be appropriate along with fundamental accounting and business skills for community development projects. Increasingly there is also a need to train personnel in communication and computer technology to reach out to the world-wide Church.

Framework for Partnership

Using the framework of contextualization we can also develop mission strategies in which partners mutually share their diverse gifts. First, we can access where each partner is in the contextualization process to mutually build up one another in weaker areas. Second, we can use this framework to consider how both partners can most effectively use their resources at each stage of the process in planting and growing churches among an unreached group. For instance, we may find that the indigenous harvest force is more effective than expatriates in carrying out the first two stages of contextualization. Or, they need to train expatriate personnel to effectively participate in these stages. Several reasons for this come to mind.

First, they do not need visas to be in their own country. Even counties that are closed to traditional missionaries, such as Indonesia, India, and China, have a body of Christians within the political boundaries that can effectively reach people groups in their own country. In countries where no local bodies exist near the unreached people groups, there are Christians in neighboring countries near the group. These Christians often have far easier access than expatriate missionaries. In many cases, people do not need visas to enter neighboring countries.

Second, Christians on-site already speak the language of wider communication of the country. This allows them to initiate contact with an unreached people group. For instance, many people in Kalimantan are bilingual in the Malay trade language and their own mother tongue. In contrast, personnel from outside the country must begin their term by learning the national language before traveling to an unreached group.

Third, Christians on-site often speak a related language to the unreached people group's language. For instance, in many countries, the majority of the unreached people groups often speak languages from the same language family as the indigenous harvest force. Although people from the indigenous harvest force may need to learn a different language, it is often structurally similar to their own. Additionally, unlike many Americans who are monolingual, many of the indigenous harvest force are multilingual. Learning another language is a natural part of learning to communicate. They do not have the psychological barrier to language learning that many Americans possess.

Fourth, Christians on-site are able to live an incarnational lifestyle that reflects the culture in which they work. For most Western missionaries, living in a remote village requires major lifestyle adjustments. However the indigenous harvest force have lived in similar situations all of their life. They are often able to participate more fully in the lifestyle. For instance, when I began working in the village I went out with people to their fields and helped with clearing, planting, and harvesting. I think the people were amused that I tried to help, but I didn't really contribute to the work of the day. However, when an indigenous Christian was planting a church in the same area, he received permission to start his own field. He went out each day with the villagers and worked with them. At the end of the harvest time not only did he harvest his rice, but he also harvested a group of new believers.

Fifth, Christians on-site often understand the worldview of the unreached people groups because they have similar worldviews. One of the greatest adjustments many expatriates must make is how the spirit world affects people. Often because we do not understand it, and have no experience dealing with it in our own countries, we do not know how to address it. I was made aware of my inadequate training in spiritual issues the first time I went to help clear a field with one of my new indigenous friends. When she came back from a neighbor's field and told me that her friend had just seen an evil spirit in her field I had no idea what to do. I did not know that if someone saw an evil spirit in their field they had to stop clearing the field and start somewhere else. Later I had an opportunity to ask a local evangelist what he would have done. He said that he would have prayed over the field and told them that the power of Christ is greater than that of any spirit.

As demonstrated in the example above, the indigenous personnel had expertise in an area that the expatriate personnel lacked. However, in other areas the expatriate personnel may have resources that the indigenous personnel lacks. For instance, in the third stage of contextualization there is a need for training in theology, crosscultural missions, and communication technology. An expatriate church may have personnel who are experts in these areas and could share their gifts with the indigenous harvest force, enabling them not only to build up the church, but also participate in missions. The contextualization framework provides a tool to evaluate each partner's contributions, and the type of training required. It also provides a framework for mission strategies that includes the selection, care, support and training of both partner's personnel.

Mission Strategies for Partnership and Training

The theological foundations and contextualization framework provide the guidelines for partnerships and training. I suggest that an effective way to support and train the indigenous harvest force is through mission strategies that are based on partnership. There are numerous examples of partnerships that have worked, both between mission agencies, and between churches (Bush 1991; Moats 1991; Cummings 1994; Pate 1991; Srinivasagam 1994). However, the foci of the strategies I develop below concentrates on the training and enablement of the indigenous harvest force to carry out the Great Commission.

Unreached people Groups

The first strategy focuses on the unreached people group movement. Since its inception at Lausanne 1974, along with the influence of MARC and others, the unreached people group movement has grown in prominence as an effective strategy for finishing the task of world evangelism. Robb (1994:29) proposes three stages in effective ministry to unreached people groups: (1) research, (2) strategy, and (3) ministry. Many of the people groups that remain are in countries where there is an indigenous harvest force that could effectively reach these groups if partnerships and training were a part of each of these stages.

Research Stage

To develop a partnership the initial research could be focused on discovering who is the potential indigenous harvest force. Questions could include: What are the nearest local churches?

At what stage are they in the contextualization process? Are there people we can contact to form a partnership? Another effective research option would be to find which local churches have geographical and social proximately to the greatest number of unreached people groups.

After finding the potential harvest force, both partners could share in further research of the unreached group, mutually sharing the information necessary for strategic planning (Baba 1991). Local churches have numerous resources they can contribute to the assessment of unreached people groups in their country. For example, when I made an assessment of translation need in languages related to one of the local languages, I asked the chairman of the local translation committee and some of its members to accompany me on a research trip. I discovered that this joint trip mutually benefited all involved. Their contribution to data gathering allowed for greater efficiency and depth than if I had gone alone. They made all the contacts for housing and transportation during the trip, introducing me to the village headmen and explaining the intention of our visit. In a few cases where there were only monolingual speakers, they learned enough language in our short stay to effectively communicate with those speakers. Only then could I apply my technical expertise to gather the needed data. In the process they gained a vision for reaching people in these related groups and now had pertinent data to begin planning a church-planting strategy.

Strategy Stage

In the strategy stage both partners could work together to plan an appropriate strategy. Each partner assesses what resources their members can contribute to reaching the unreached people group. If they find they are lacking resources to accomplish the task, they may need to find additional partners with the needed resources.

At this stage a multi-year plan could be worked out that is mutually agreed on by each partner. The resources and personnel each partner will contribute should be written out in detail as well as a detailed plan for the training and care of personnel. For instance, an expatriate church may have personnel who could train the indigenous harvest force in communication technology, or business. The local partner could provide personnel to teach language to expatriate personnel. The expatriate church may provide financial support of the team. The local church may be responsible for the care and supervision of the outreach team. No matter how the details are eventually worked out, for it to be a true partnership, all partners must mutually share their resources.

Ministry Stage

At the ministry stage both partners work together to send out teams. Some teams may include expatriate personnel with specific skills, for instance in development or medicine. The church on-site may provide evangelists and church planters. Each team may provide Bible translation personnel or literacy teachers. Since each partner shares in the ministry, each partner shares fully in the blessing of the results.

An example of an outreach partnership developed between my expatriate church and the Tagal translation committee. My sending church decided to partner with the Tagal translation committee to reach a group of villages that had been resistant to the gospel. As the representative from my church, I worked with the Tagal committee to develop a ministry plan to reach this area. My church provided the boat, engine and the cost of fuel for two years. The committee provided the personnel for evangelism, care and maintenance of the boat, and care, training and supervision of the evangelists. At the end of two years, churches were planted in seven of the fourteen villages. During this time I worked with the committee to produce reports and keep its partner informed of the progress of the work. At the end of the two years, my church sent two couples from its mission board to meet with the committee and assess further opportunities for partnership.

Bible Translation

Another ministry that could be enhanced through partnership is a Bible translation project. Most translations projects today are not done in unreached people groups but where churches are already planted (Dye 1986). Because of this, a partnership is possible from the very beginning of the translation project. Bible translators could be sent to work with a church that is in an area with a number of unreached groups. The end goal of the translation project would not be just to translate Scripture for the church's use, but to equip the church on-site to effectively carry out contextualization of the gospel in the related languages, including Bible translation.

This kind of partnership strategy affects the goals and assignment of a Bible translation team. Rather than assigning one team per language, the traditional approach, teams, including members from the indigenous harvest force, would be assigned to the translation task for a cluster of related languages. The focus of the expatriate team is training the indigenous harvest force so that they can start the same ministries in neighboring languages. Training would include language analysis, Bible translation principles, biblical background, and Bible languages. If literacy is needed, the indigenous harvest force is given training in literacy development, teacher training, and desktop publishing. All of this training can take place within the context of the translation program for the on-site church.

While the strategies I developed have different foci, both are based on the biblical principle of multiplication and discipleship. The focus of the expatriate partner is not just to accomplish a particular task but to equip the indigenous partner to carry out the Great Commission in other areas. Both of these strategies focus on maximizing the resources of both partners to reach several unreached people groups.

Technology for Partnerships and Training

New technology provides additional options for developing partnerships and training the indigenous harvest force. A training center with a computer could be set up to provide training and resources for the indigenous harvest force. Although many remote areas do not have access to electricity, often there is a nearby town where a training center could be established near the ministry outreach. If the country is inaccessible, a training center could be made available in a neighboring country.

In this center, computers and resource materials could be made available on CD ROM or other media. Smith (1995) reports that the Decision Making Empowerment Project is creating a CD ROM library that will give scholars in remote locations access to books, articles, dissertations, and other documents that would otherwise be impossible to obtain. Other projects are needed to provide the indigenous harvest force tools to do translation, theology, and crosscultural missions.

Not only can resource material be placed on CD, so can 'live' training courses. One of the barriers to computer and on-line training has been the expense of producing and delivering material (Elliston 1999:265). However, the latest upgrade to

PowerPoint®[1] enables the recording with audio on a CD. Training courses for crosscultural missions, Bible translations, Bible languages, and theological training could be produced very inexpensively on CD in a variety of languages with only minimal computer hardware necessary for playing it. Smith (1995:149) believes that this type of delivery system overcomes local and systemic restrictions for equipping local members with resources for personnel development as well as strategic planning.

Another technological development that has tremendous potential for training personnel is Distance Education which is rapidly increasing. Michael Chasen, co-founder and president of one of the largest Distance Education providers, reports that in 1999 over 500 new colleges began using the online resources of their site and 200-300 new courses are added each day. He contends that Distance Education has now shifted from the early adapter stage to the mainstream educational process.

On-line courses are increasingly becoming a viable option for training personnel in remote locations. The same PowerPoint lectures that are recorded on CD can also be delivered on-line with audio. Although the creation and serving of the courses requires special hardware, the only requirements for the person taking the course is a computer with Microsoft Explorer® and an internet connection.

One advantage of on-line courses is that a variety of courses could be placed on a Web site so people could individualize their own training. If a church wanted an additional course they could make their request on the Web site. Internet also allows for interaction with others and with an instructor. Additional resources, such as live links, can be incorporated to the on-line version of the course. Additionally, on-line interaction provides

---

[1] Available in Microsoft office 2000.

the indigenous harvest forces a means to gain support and encouragement from the global Christian community. They also can gain a more global perspective of Christianity.

Expatriate Personnel: Training for Partnerships

If we are going to effectively care for the indigenous harvest force through partnerships and training, the role of the expatriate missionary is going to radically change in the 21st century. In many cases, new strategies mean that the expatriate will no longer be the doer, but enablers, facilitators, and partners. They may be involved in crosscultural training, business training, theological training, etc., but will do so under the leadership of local partners.

However, this will not be achieved unless we prepare expatriate missionaries for partnerships. Our training of expatriate workers must prepare them to work within the leadership structure of the national church. Internships and short-term missions can prepare students to work under national leadership. Instead of teaming students up with expatriate missionaries we could team them up with indigenous missionaries. Students or short-term workers would then work under the leadership of the indigenous church, contributing their skills and training to the programs. Far too often short-term teams go with their own agenda, rather than seeking out the agenda of the indigenous church.

It will be a challenge for expatriates to work under indigenous leadership. It requires them to let go of their way of doing things, listen and learn. But the trade off is that both parties learn and change from the experience. I had an intern join me as I worked under the leadership of a local church in S. E. Asia. After acquiring language skills, she and the leaders of the local church discussed how she could best use her skills to contribute to the needs of the church. They decided that what they needed was more training in desktop publishing. So she used her computer skills to train their secretary and develop a desktop publishing manual. The committee used this manual to train people to format literature for use in the church. Her short six-month stay made an incredible impact on the mission of the church. Her internship also left an incredible impact on her because she got to participate in an effective national ministry.

Conclusion

In the 21st century a growing number of people from the indigenous harvest force will desire to become involved in the world-wide mission movement. If we deliberately seek to establish partnerships founded on relationships, we can help equip, support, and care for this growing harvest force, enabling them to also participate in fulfilling the Great Commission. Partnering with the indigenous harvest force is not only an effective strategy, it also enables every congregation to participate in the world-wide outreach (Shenk 1994: 152). Like those who wrote the Great Commission manifesto, we must "dare to pray and dream of what might happen if appropriate autonomy of churches and ministries could be balanced with significant partnership." Today more than ever we have the resources and technology to care, train, and enable the indigenous harvest force through partnerships. The question is, will we?

Chapter 9

Caring for Hungarians

Joi Van Deventer

During the past ten years of freedom, most states in Central and Eastern Europe have graciously received volumes of literature and 'how-to' programs from many Western Christian brothers and sisters. Compared to the time of Brother Andrew, the transport of Western curriculum and books across boarders is now essentially hassle-free. Since few obstacles remain — an infrequent request for taxes — the task of translating and getting materials into readers' hands has been exponentially expedited.

During these ten years, while living in Budapest, Hungary, I have been involved in designing training materials for a variety of ministry efforts. Five years ago I helped start an organization, now run by Hungarians, that aims to assist churches in their Christian educational efforts by equipping leaders and teachers, by publishing curricula, and by offering a journal publication for children's workers of all denominations. I also aim to help Hungarians network and learn from each other; this is beginning to happen.

Specifically, as Director of Leadership Development, my task is to build up and expand the current structure, content, and the overall educational processes, which is called "Total Leadership Development Process." In the teacher-training curricula I plan to incorporate many American ideas, using a blend of critical thinking (Noddings 1997) and experiential learning (Kolb 1984) to equip adult learners for the Christian education classroom. Since the typical learning environment in

Hungary does not employ methods from these philosophies, I assume that the adult learners do not have the needed background knowledge to learn the new concepts.

The Challenge: Looking Behind the Cultural Curtain

When I was initially assigned this task, I considered my experience with curriculum development in the States to serve as an adequate beginning base. Yet unknown difficulties soon appeared and challenged this assumption. Two evaluative measures quickly opened up my eyes to the reality that curriculum design included more than translation and contextualization of materials: results from assessing my first attempts at creating and using training materials and critiques by trusted Hungarians — who understood American minds, their own traditional educational approach, along with insight into the differences. On-going discussions began in hopes of discovering remedies to the disparity I saw in learners' eyes.

Though I was ignorant of the cultural issues that inhibited learning, I knew that factors existed behind the Hungarian cultural curtain that could inform my efforts and thus aid my pursuit. I asked: "What needs to be adjusted?" "How much extra experience do the adult learners need in their own training context to 'catch up' to my assumed knowledge base?" "What would be appropriate structures and methods for the equipping process? When adults go through the training process, do they only acquire new knowledge, or does the training also develop Christian character and skills for ministry? I aim to equip them to not only teach God's word to children and youth but to incorporate these new methods in their classrooms to create experiential learning environments.

The obvious need for a new approach in curriculum design compelled me to investigate tenets of cross-cultural education. This led me to examine the complex relationship between educational materials and the entire educational process, which can be said to 'contain' the "hidden curriculum" — the methods, models, roles, expectations, values, content, and context — of the setting. Without intervention I realized that these components would remain American and unknown to the Hungarian learners.

Proposal: An Approach from Educational Anthropology

After some initial examination, I believe instruction from educational anthropology can provide a framework to help answer these questions. As a guide into the depths of the educational processes, this theory provides tools for evaluating and revising the explicit and hidden curricula. I propose that an appropriate approach for designing curriculum could be based on the tenets of educational anthropology.

I summarize here the propositions of educational anthropology as four main tenets.

Learning is a Process of Cultivating Minds

Educational anthropology examines the nature of the mind and the nature of culture in human educational activities. In these activities, it examines the transmitter and learner as well as the content and method of transmission to discover what and how learning happens (La Belle 1976). It believes that educational encounters should result in understandings, not focus on performance or outcomes (Bruner 1996). Erickson adequately sums up: the center of attention in this process would be

> a focus on the pedagogical encounter itself, on the sequential organization of interaction between the individual learner (and teacher) and the *materia paedagogica* present in the immediate environment, on charges in the character of that interaction across real time, and on the meanings to the actors of the action that takes place. (Erickson 1982:174)

Educators aim to understand the learning process, what the learner brings to the educational environment, and what the learner does to adapt to certain environments and to learn new knowledge (Mercer 1993).

Educational Processes Cannot be Extracted from the Social and Cognitive Context

Educators cannot understand mental activity (learning and thinking) unless they take into account "the cultural setting and its resources, the very things that give mind its shape and scope. Learning, remembering, talking, imagining: all of them are made possible by participating in a culture" (Bruner 1996:x-xi). This significant context contains or influences the "hidden curriculum": the arrangement of the physical environment, the expectations of the teacher-learner relationship, the rules and style for the instructional process, expected outcomes or competence, and expected behaviors and tacit understandings.

Learning is not solo or unassisted; all learning is situated. An individual often relies on others to furnish the instruction and judgment that leads to achieving competence. "Mental life is lived with others, is shaped to be communicated, and unfolds with the aid of cultural codes, traditions, and the like" (Bruner 1996:xi). Likewise, learning occurs as a communicative, cumulative, constructive process, one which takes place in situations where past learning is embodied in present learning activity, and in which participants draw selectively on any information which is available to make sense of what they are doing (Mercer 1993:44).

This process extends beyond school settings to all social domains: the church, the family, the friendship circle. Thus, education does not only occur in classrooms, but in conversation around the dinner table and during ordinary daily tasks.

Bruner's (1996) culturalist view looks at the culture as a system of values, rights, exchanges, obligations, opportunities, and power. Thus, the systems of culture can actually impose external and internal constraints on the process of education. I assume that the underlying structure of a learning and teaching task involves patterns in the arrangement of social relations — the intersocial interaction in an individual's many subcommunities.

The social context also entails the wider environment of interaction up and out to the level of society as a whole — the variety of influences and institutional qualities of socio-political contexts. These influences often determine how participants in the learning environment are allowed to interact with each other (Lingenfelter 1998). How education is situated in the culture reflects the distribution of power, resources, status, and other benefits. The educational system could function to preserve the elite or to guard equality for all citizens. Education then takes on institutional qualities, which often carry and maintain cultural agendas. In societies where educational systems are changing, new institutions powerfully sculpt social classes. Even in the church community, cultural factors govern the role of the educator, leader, teacher-in-training, and non-titled. All these must be considered in developing curricula.

Furthermore, culture also provides the toolkit and the institutional structure for both traditional and school learning

(Bruner 1996, Jacobs 1997). The materials necessary for the learning process come from both the material and immaterial realms. 'Space' has a history and culturally shared meaning and use. The deliberate arrangement of the aspects of the social and physical environment carry intentions of stimulating and assisting the learning of individuals (Erickson 1982). The physical context is actually united with the social within the thought process. Thus, cognition is typically "situated in a social and physical context and is rarely, if ever, decontextualized" (Butterworth 1993:6).

Outside the family, religious involvement and school classrooms are the main contexts that play a crucial role in the shaping of self (Bruner 1996). "Learning in the classroom is culturally saturated in both its content and structure and accomplished through dialogue which is heavily dependent on an implicit context constructed by participants from current and past shared experience" (Mercer 1993:43). Classrooms of all kinds have their own body of cultural knowledge, and their own ways of communicating and legitimizing knowledge.

In many cases though the development of personal knowledge can take place without explicit tutelage; knowledge simply emerges from cognitive structuring. However, this always occurs in some type of context, not *in vacuo*. Cultural psychology argues that reality can only be known by the properties of the mind and the available symbol systems on which the mind relies (Bruner 1996).

The Aim or Outcome of Education is to Impart Cultural Knowledge

Cultural knowledge is learned as a result of several methods: from calculated intervention — cultural transmission — and from learning by an individualized process — cultural acquisition. Educational anthropology aims to discover the cultural knowledge that people hold in their minds, how it is acquired and how it is employed in social interaction (Spindler 1997, Wolcott 1987). Human beings are enculturated through involvement with their symbol systems and through the implementation of the systems in cultural tasks. Individuals' experiences, their frames of reference, and their means of sense making would not be possible without the integration of their specific intellectual computational capacities with human symbolic activity (Gardner 1983).

In general, individuals acquire knowledge either through the development of innate potentials or from external sources, or from a combination of both. This acquired knowledge is being continually stored in a manner that makes it relatively easily accessible when necessary (Gardner 1983). Forms of personal knowledge are seen as being encoded in public symbol systems (D'Andrade 1984). 'Reality' then is represented by a symbol system shared by members of a cultural community in which a technical-social way of life is both organized and construed in terms of that symbolism. They construct these "realities" and meanings to adapt them to the system; they even institutionalize these beliefs as common sense or as 'proper' systems for education. They do so though at a personal cost. Their way of structuring knowledge limits their way of objectively conceiving of "foreign" matters outside their defined cognitive world (Bruner 1996).

However, individuals are also active agents (Jacob 1997) with self-generated intentions. Their contextually based symbol system domains do not completely restrict them from the ability to choose what will influence them.

When I study how the adult learner receives knowledge, I intend to examine how the demands of a cultural system affect those who must operate within it. I will also consider how knowledge is structured and organized. The underlying structure of a learning and teaching task involves patterns in the sequencing of the cognitive operations and manipulation of materials necessary to complete the task. It has been pointed out to me many times that Hungarians organize and sequence different from Westerners. This is especially obvious when someone is translating from English to Hungarian. Thus, I cannot simply translate my curricula from English to Hungarian without considering how knowledge is structured.

Finally, while working with Europeans, it is crucial to address history and philosophy when considering educational efforts. Their world view and values have developed from their view of history and philosophy (Olsen 1996), so I need to understand their view of history, philosophy, and phenomenon, and how these affect their identity and the learning environment.

A Theory of Educational Anthropology Suggests that Educators Learn to Evaluate and Adjust the Structure of Educational Processes

Transmitters, educators, also naturally bring content and expectations to the educational environment including how they expect participants to learn and behave. Even though learning is seen as a process, educators still need to be cognizant of their expected outcomes for which they are preparing the learners, even when the "outcomes" may be a series of stages toward competence. They need to learn to adjust these to fit the cultural setting.

Educators need to understand the explicit and tacit components (the hidden curriculum) of the educational process. They must learn to recognize and accept cultural differences without creating disadvantageous separation or segregation, whether self-imposed or imposed from the dominant group (Spindler 1997). They need to learn to evaluate and correct this process so that new approaches holistically facilitate learning.

Strategy: Implementing a New Approach in the Hungarian Context

As I now consider the Hungarian setting, I intend to adjust my curriculum design strategy so that the adult learners in their context, with their learning styles and conceptual and cultural bias, may learn without needing to jump cognitive-cultural hurdles. In my aim to implement a new approach to learning, I must learn about the adult learners' cultural knowledge — their tacit understandings of the hidden curriculum.

In the near future, along with a multi-cultural team, I will be creating more curricula as well as teaching what I design. I intend to employ the framework of educational anthropology to better analyze this endeavor. While training educators in the church, I intend to not only give them necessary content for teaching children but also a new methodology for teaching children. This means I need to address what could inhibit the reception of the new methodology. Previous cultural values of education, what has traditionally been done in the church, will most likely become an arena for dissonance.

I realize that the adult learners' bring their culture with them to their classroom, which includes prior knowledge and expectations of Christian education and knowledge that is attached to the context. They also bring expectations to the training environment. They actually desire new information and gladly sign up for training because they believe they need additional knowledge. However, I want the process to be more than an arrangement or accumulation of knowledge. Rather, I expect them to grow in character, skills, and knowledge.

When examining my aims and expectations in the curriculum, I recognize that I will be introducing new cultural knowledge through using another model of teaching, "experiential learning" (Kolb 1984). This new methodology carries new standards of competence. It will probably induce some disparity in the adults' learning since "experiential learning" promotes different values from those found in traditional Hungarian educational environments. It actually resembles the teaching method suggested in Deuteronomy 6. Here Moses instructs adults to *impress* God's commands on their children; to *talk* about them when they *sit at home* and when they *walk along the road*, when they *lie down* and when they *get up*; to *tie them as symbols on their hands and bind them on their foreheads*; and to *write* the commands on the doorframes of their houses and on their gates (Deuteronomy 6:4-9).

If I am essentially suggesting a change in values, I need to learn what arenas and interventions best facilitate cognitive shifts. As I instruct them to use this new methodology in their educational efforts, I need to consider their expectations of learning in the environments of church and Christian education. Additions or alterations to their expectations of learning in these arenas may cause disparity. I intend to evaluate where disparity could occur and how to help the learners understand the new approach and move through any obstacles.

Individuals will more readily incorporate a new methodology when matching values have been internalized. Without acceptance of new values, new techniques may be tentatively implemented, but with less longevity (Goulard 1996). Consequently, along with a new approach for curriculum design,

I intend to understand how I can successfully help learners adjust their value systems.

Over the past ten years I have observed a decade-long value change in Hungary. Specifically, I cite here a value shuffle in their education system. Prior to 1989, Hungarians were required to study Russian and discouraged from studying English and German. The young were prepared for jobs which supported a communist state. Today, the opposite has not only been implemented but also is working quite well. English is the most popular language to learn; German is now second. The young are still prepared for jobs to support the Hungarian state, but many new jobs have been created in information technology and business. Fortunately, Hungarians have responded positively to this new system of public education. The older generations have gladly embraced this change.

Despite the disruption of traditional cultural transmission, citizens agree that this change is necessary for the country to reach their goal — participation in the European Union. Education is currently considered the highest priority for attaining success in all vocations. Families sacrifice so their young can receive over-and-above instruction. Interestingly, many Hungarians have not completely discarded their folk narratives with the entrance of this new era; rather, it is quite popular among the university educated to hold onto traditional customs while embracing the new. This example shows how individuals can accept new frameworks and values. Under the right conditions and for the right reasons, people adjust.

When individuals embrace new values, usually their identity also changes. Naturally, this process creates dissonance. If the struggle with new values occurs in the right context, the dissonance results in positive adjustment toward acceptance of new values and a new identity. Participants may even adopt the adjusted or new system as their own and recruit members to this new sub-culture. When new values and methodology are seen as improving the social order, e.g., the quality of education for their children and real Christian growth, participants will more likely own this new cultural knowledge.

After briefly examining the components of the "hidden curriculum" — methods, models, roles, expectations, values, content, and context, I propose a set of questions to aid in adapting and designing cross-cultural curriculum.

Proposed Questions for Evaluation

1. Is the educational setting relevant to the present life situation of the adult learners and their communities?
2. Is the curriculum relevant to the present life situation of the adult learners and their communities?
3. Does the hidden curriculum promote values that are incompatible with those held in the society?
4. Does the curriculum and teaching method incorporate appropriate motivational strategies?
5. Does the system make use of traditionally accepted modes of communication?
6. If new values are introduced, does the curriculum help process the adult learners?
7. Do the teaching methods give recognition to relevant cognitive styles among learners?
8. Does the role of the teacher include an adequate blend of the teacher's culture and the traditional expectations?
9. Is there adequate and appropriate teacher-student interaction and relatedness in the setting?
10. What are strategies used for feedback and evaluation?
11. Who are the real owners of this education system?[1]

---

[1] Adapted from Baer, Christel. 1989 *The Development of a Contextualized Indigenous Education System.* Ed.D. Dissertation, Biola University.

Proposed Interventions for the Hungarian Context

As I consider what process, structures and methods I could employ as intentional intervention to get adult learners involved in various types of corporate and self-learning, I want to focus on four specific vehicles: narrative, modeling, mentoring, and promoting community in the classroom. I intend to develop a consistent new cultural system to preserve genuine learning in the training context.

Using Narrative to Create Identity and Adjust Values

"Within a culture, ideas are exchanged and modified and belief systems developed and appropriated through conversation and narratives, so these must be promoted, not inhibited" (Brown, Collins, and Duguid 1989:40). Conversation and narratives are essential components of social interaction and learning. They provide access to much of the distributed knowledge and elaborate social structure. As participants contribute to the collective wisdom of the training environment greater internal consistency is possible.

Human beings typically organize and mange their knowledge of the world in two broad ways: (1) a system for treating of physical "things" using logical-scientific thinking; (2) another for treating of people and their lives, using narrative thinking. Myths, histories, and folktales frame and nourish learners' identity. A system of education that introduces a new system or culture must help the learners find an identity within that culture. It is only in the narrative mode that learners can construct an identity and find a place in their culture (Bruner 1996).

"If narrative is to be made an instrument of mind on behalf of meaning making, it requires work on our part — reading it, making it, analyzing it, understanding its craft, sensing it uses, discussing it" (Bruner 1996:41). Narrative turns dialogue from being a mode of thought to a vehicle of meaning making. Using imagination through fiction, proverbs, songs, or poetry also opens up new possibilities. The success of the process of teaching and learning depends on teachers and learners using discussion and discourse to build a shared contextual framework which will support future joint educational enterprises" (Mercer 1993). Thus, narrative will influence the development of a corporate identity and a new values system.

Hungarians naturally use narrative to construct their national identity; TV, school classrooms, theater, songs, and folk tales told by grandparents mold the Hungarian mind. I intend to examine the curriculum and build in more places for narrative. My learning environment must cultivate and nurture identity, and cease taking it for granted. I believe that through participating in a narrative context, the adult learners will implement this tool in their own learning contexts.

Implementing Community in the Classroom

The traditional one-way dialogue in instruction is the least successful. Thus, I need to create environments where learners interact in subcommunities. As they 'bootstrap' each other I, as the teacher, presume the role as orchestrator of the proceedings rather than ruler (Bruner 1996).

Valuable peripheral learning occurs in groups. "Peripheral participation", listening to discourse and not participating, is particularly important for people when entering a new culture or adjusting their value system. As adult learners listen and then contribute ideas, they "co-produce" situated knowledge, which develops their own unique classroom culture (Brown, Collins and Duguid 1989).

Like all social groups that intervene or interfere with learning (Wolcott 1987), churches prepare their young and old to be mature members of their groups. As an educator, I am part of this process of intervention. As a designer of curriculum, I aim to develop bridges between the traditional and new in the church setting.

The local gathering of believers represents a system with its own unique cultural knowledge and values. I need to be aware of the tacit understanding about this domain that cognitively incorporates participants for membership and for operations in it. Scripture presents a variety of descriptions of this domain to aid believers in their understanding of and participation in the body of Christ; (see the Epistle to the Ephesians for one example). Through the teaching about the body of Christ, I see that Christians are intended to work together — they are united together in Christ; they actually have no choice about being a member of this group. How people live out this relationship is affected by cultural expectations.

The model of groups working together for learning purposes is not foreign to Hungarians or to Christianity. Hungarians prefer to operate as members of a group. Thus, incorporating group in the training should produce a good and familiar atmosphere. As the orchestrator, I will need to intentionalize the learning activities to obtain the benefits of group learning.

Incorporating Modeling

Bandura (1963) suggests that people can learn almost everything vicariously by watching others — from their successes and failures. Learners "need to observe how practitioners at various levels behave and talk to get a sense of how expertise is manifest in conversation and other activities" (Brown, Collins and Duguid 1989). When an educator is watched for not only content, but also skill and character, more purposeful instruction occurs.

Along with traditional instruction, I propose to intentionalize modeling in the education process. I will not only talk about the experiential learning model, but I will use this model in the teacher-training process. This way the adult learners can see its form, consciously evaluate the model as they experience it and even anticipate how they may utilize it in their classrooms.

Incorporating Mentors

The activity of mentoring invades both the formal and informal aspects of the education process. Mentoring gives opportunity for personal and objective evaluation and correction. Mentors can guide learners in the practice of 'self-monitoring' to offer important feedback. Bandura (1963) suggests that through self-monitoring an individual can better retain new learned behaviors if they are based on internalized values or symbols. Thus, mentoring also facilitates the adjustment of a learner's value system.

In developing curriculum I intend to incorporate the mentor relationship between the transmitter and learner. I aim to encourage learners to internalize God's truth and live these principles out in the classroom. A mentoring relationship will only enhance this process. Perhaps participants may learn more from me than from my instruction. That is a scary thought.

Mentoring has already been considered a worthy method of instruction for new teachers in Hungary (Falus 1996). Furthermore, this form of instruction is not entirely foreign to Hungarian society, in which "masters" and "apprentices" operated in most professions. Finally, the word for "apprentice" has successfully been incorporated into other leadership development curriculum.² Therefore, I believe that it can also be used in my educational plan.

In both mentoring and modeling, I will need to examine how I view relationships. My expectations of power and status in and out of the church are significant in terms of how I communicate and interact with others. Americans often teach as facilitators even though the local educators teach in an authoritarian or egalitarian way. The Hungarian church is an interesting place in this regard: except for interaction with the minister, Christians often embrace an egalitarian structure; and ministers often operate in an authoritarian way even though the congregation has ultimate power in church polity. Similarly, the role of teacher is a highly regarded position because of its place in society; thus, teachers are expected to fulfill a certain role. I aim to build on the local church egalitarian model by emphasizing a community of learners (Giroux 1997) while maintaining the traditional expectations of teacher as the conductor of the training.

Concluding Thoughts

Human beings are moldable, complex whole beings. They develop and learn in both cognitive and spiritual realms. Two dominant features of learning for human beings are the human mind — with its multiple intelligences and rational and non-rational expressions of thought — and, the human heart — with its wide range of desires, will, and emotional responses that constitute the intuitive and irrational in human life and

---

² In 1995 I helped design curriculum for training small group leaders in local churches. We used the word *inas* "apprentice" for someone in training. In the curriculum design process, we worked with Hungarians to assure cultural receptivity. This word was well received and has remained in the curriculum and training materials.

experience (Lingenfelter 1991). If curriculum is molded according to a relevant framework, individuals can learn new methods of education. They can even successfully navigate through a cross-cultural training plan that aims to stimulate change in their cognitive and spiritual understandings.

When faced with this enormous endeavor of developing curriculum for the Total Leadership Development Process, I initially feel overwhelmed, especially after reviewing the task through this paper. I am comforted when I realize that along with the theory of educational anthropology, the Holy Spirit directs my design process and the learning of the participants. The theory and my Counselor provide parameters and expose potential points of failure.

In this paper, I have presented an initial evaluation on how the four tenets can inform my curriculum design efforts. They reveal many of the hidden relationships concealed in the educational process. Applying insights from educational anthropology helps form a new approach to cross-cultural curriculum development. Since it draws upon a broad spectrum of educational theories, it needs to be carefully tested for cross-cultural application in real contexts. It holds great promise for further activity in designing cross-cultural curriculum. As I examine additional elements of the training arena, I believe that even more insight will emerge about adult learning contexts in Hungary. Amazingly, through God's power and wisdom, I am able to participate in His transformation process in the Central European context.

Chapter 10

Caring for Members

Brent Lindquist

I come to the Evangelical Missiological Society as an outsider. My field of study is Psychology, and therefore I am naturally concerned with the membercare environment as it exists in Missions today, as well as its hoped for future. I therefore elected to take a personal, reflective journey through the current state of affairs in membercare, and some personal reflections for the future.

As we stand on the threshold of the new millennium and look at the future of membercare, what do we see? Depending on our perspective, we can see great promise, some promise, some peril, or great peril.

Those who see great promise probably comprise the largest group. We most often are the mental health professionals, and the "survivors" of the missionary enterprise. It is undeniable that membercare was instigated and is driven by the intrusion of psychological concepts (Christian, biblical, or otherwise) into the missionary life and organization. For too long, we say, relationships, and emotions have been disregarded in running the missionary enterprise. The survivors join in, singing praises for ministry approaches that may not damage others as they were themselves damaged.

Those who see only some promise may perhaps excuse our more illustrious colleagues for their excess. We know that the missionary enterprise can probably be better by incorporating a balanced approach drawing from the wisdom of multiple disciplines.

Those who see some peril are feeling discomfort. We do not know what is happening, only that "stuff" is happening, and it has the potential to draw us from our true calling.

Finally, those who see great peril or see the evil psychology, as well as the other disciplines not mentioned by name in Scriptures, as indeed drawing us away from the purity of the Great Commission. Our missionary endeavor is being diluted. We may not say, but may very much feel: "Why all this fuss? We have a mandate to tell the story. Doing anything else, even caring for each other, takes away from that mandate!"

So what is the correct approach? I find myself vacillating between all four perspectives. There is no easy answer. Each perspective has its strengths, but more importantly, its faults. How do we make sense out of all of this? What should our priorities be? What should "drive" the missionary endeavor? What could the future be like? We will together review some perspectives from which we could gain a better understanding. Bear with me...

A Few Caveats

I have come to the missionary endeavor on a rather circuitous route. I grew up in a Christian home, and was present when the dream of Link Care became a reality almost 36 years ago. I grew up hearing stories about how missionaries had struggles and how they got helped by the practice of psychology. When I made Psychology my profession, and entered the real world, I was mentored by a linguist/anthropologist who helped me see the larger picture of ministry in a cross-cultural context. I have been in a top administrative position in ministry for 17 years, and this has informed me on the realities of balancing the many competing parts of organizational life. In this reality, sometimes we have to make forced choices, and the final choice may be an add-on in one arena, and a take-away in another. This has given me a sensitive appreciation of leadership and decision making.

For the last 10 years I have been involved in leading a behavioral health management service organization. Through that, I have come to a greater understanding of the financing of medical and mental health services, the captivation of benefits, and how actuarial tables and processes are developed and managed. Through this company, we have designed an insurance-policy-through-treatment-delivery-system for about 25-30% of the state of California. This has given me good experience for investigating alternative financing packages for missionary membercare. Finally, I have been consulting in an industrial-organizational psychological arena, as well as human resources, in both ministry and business contexts. Coming at emotional needs from these organizational frameworks has again sensitized me to the bigger world outside of the clinic.

For 17 years I helped develop and run a prefield orientation program, as well as its overseas component for newcomers, helping them and their missions get off to the right start in language and culture development. Through this process I have had to balance language, culture, emotional, and social learning needs to provide a motivational environment for adult learning.

These experiences initially produced a sense of rootlessness and identity crisis. I spent a lot of time becoming a Licensed Psychologist (in California), and then it seems my life experience has been relieving me of its ethnocentric bias. I can only thank God for that, because the process has moved me to keep looking for the cores of what this is all about. It does make for some lonely times, though.

The caveat for the reader is to beware of my foundations. I bring together a wide variety of nontraditional dimensions to this missionary endeavor, without apology. It is my hope that we can see bigger pictures and relationships through these other perspectives that will help us on our path.

Of necessity, the following observations will not be fully developed, but will hopefully present the big idea, offer some cogent forecasts, and provide some questions to drive your own further investigation.

The Missionary Endeavor from the Perspective of Effectiveness

Over the years, Don Larson[1] and I helped many missions evaluate their organization along the lines of "effectiveness." We worked with almost 100 organizations, with many different theological and doctrinal differences. Hence we tried to stay out of the way there, helping them evaluate within their own contexts. I think we were pretty successful. An outcome of this stance has been a criticism of me as being weak in theological formulations (which I am!). Some organizations have used that critique to dismiss this approach rather than investigate. It has always been my perspective that I need to tread carefully in the core theological and spiritual values of my mission clients. Time will tell if this approach is valuable.

We have focused on the concept of effectiveness as the central organizing principle around which the missionary endeavor is built. In so many words, what we have been trying to

---

[1] Don Larson was a Linguist who directed the Toronto Institute of Linguistics for over 20 years, and was the Senior Consultant in Crosscultural Living and Learning at Link Care Center for 20 years.

get at is the idea that all behavior has meaning, and is intentional, and purposive. We need to provide all our resources to the missionary endeavor in ways that continue the development of effectiveness. Is this a moot point? I do not believe it to be of little consequence. Look at the explosion of membercare in our missionary world. There are numerous agencies, ministries, and individuals scurrying around providing a myriad of services. Most are quite admirable efforts, and some have even produced tangible results. However, when I ask how these services and activities have furthered the development of effectiveness in the missionary, I am not very happy with the answers.

Often the answers indicate an assumption that any effort to "help" missionaries is good, and should not be questioned. But I see too much effort and expense going to fix broken things, rather than understanding the relationships around the issue of why something broke in the first place. For most of my professional life in missions, Link Care has been seen as the place to send broken missionaries. I am pleased we can help, but we should be paying more attention to the causes, not the effects.

A similar issue is the "directionality" of helping, and the idea of what I call intentional incarnation. I do not believe I am called to fix missionaries. I believe I am called to help missionaries discover, or rediscover, the issues that led to their being hurt, and help them figure out how to manage, adjust, plan for, and in some small cases, overcome them. I believe the overarching goal of membercare is not helping alone, but helping people to become effective, moving them in an intentional direction, which is making them more effective in the context in which they are called to serve, becoming "closer" to the people they are called to serve. If membercare does not take this as a given, then I see little to separate it from standard clinical approaches to care used in the home country. These standard approaches are not wrong, but I do not believe they should be paramount, guiding principles for the Great Commission ecosphere.

Questions to consider:

1. How have our models of membercare taken into account the issues of effectiveness and incarnational ministry?
2. What difference would it make if membercare models started from the presumption of effectiveness?

Language Learning: Is English Enough?

Don Larson was incredibly brilliant in terms of reducing language to its mostly irreducible state. Building from the premise that there is inherent order in language, even after the Tower of Babel, he looked at the basic building blocks of language, within its perspective as a holistic communicative event. Don was one of the premier champions of community-based language learning (as opposed to classroom-based language learning). He believed in both the community and the classroom, but he was particularly concerned about the need of missionaries to learn while they lived. He put together a series of 200 situations which a person could work through over three years, or so, to become truly crossculturally communicatively competent. That still was not enough, so he focused on the first 20 situations, and came up with a model for a person to reach the "critical point" in only 20 days of fulltime language learning. The critical point is the point at which the missionary has enough language to continue to learn the language from ordinary people in the surrounding community. This model has been used by thousands of new language learners and we have in process at

Caring for Members 205

least 15 manuals for specific languages. More needs to be done with this.

Don Larson was very concerned about the trends in missions in the last few years (it never really went away) to focus on "English is enough." A recent issue of *Atlantic Monthly* (Wallraff, 2000) bears out his concerns. I include it here, because membercare is largely an English only process, at least at its leading edges. This is not to say that non-English speakers are not setting up membercare programs, but that English speakers' models are frequently adopted too easily into non-English (language and culture) contexts.

In an article entitled "What Global Language," Barbara Walraff makes some very interesting points. I see a trend of mission activities resorting to English only, inspite of the following information. It is the impression of many knowledgeable forecasters, that English (Standard American English) will not be the global juggernaut we expect it to be. There are three times as many speakers of Chinese as English today. By 2050, English will be third behind Chinese and Hindi/Urdu, and just ahead of Spanish and Arabic. Among 15-24 year olds, English will be fourth behind Chinese, Hindi/Urdu, Arabic, and just ahead of Spanish.

Why would not English continue to ascend? A number of reasons are postulated. Among them: the rise of regional trading blocks that may exclude US Americans (Asia, Arab World, Latin America), or may include us tangentially. World changing technological innovations arising out of nations where English is little spoken. A backlash against our culture and values, leading to desires to create in no-English contexts. In addition to this, mission activities are operating out of the mistaken assumption that there are no varieties of English. Sure, we joke about accents, and creoles, but only because we have not tried to communicate or influence in a Creole dominated context. Even where people are assumed to speak English, their reality is very much like those of us who felt we never learned language in High School. Perceived versus actual skills worldwide in English are very discouraging.

I gave a presentation to the Second International Congress on Missionary Language Learning a couple of years ago (Lindquist 1998) during which I put forth the idea that counseling-influenced membercare programs were going to steal the thunder from the importance of language and culture learning. This is largely coming to pass. Most membercare gatherings spend little time looking at the language component inherent in effectiveness. Wycliffe people seem to have grasped this, but I'm afraid I do not see a lot of movement or recognition elsewhere.

The increasing tendency of local churches to send people out directly without regard to the linguistic issues in communication is another arena where English is perceived as "enough." Mission organizations are doing much better at language than the church at large. I still see a trend of sacrificing language and culture learning if the timeframe does not permit depth. Time takes precedence over relationships! This is not incarnational ministry.

Questions to Consider:

1. Should not we include the linguistic component intentionally in this membercare equation?
2. How have you communicated in your own arenas, and research, about language and culture, or indeed, this multi-perspectivality?

Diversity: Multiple Dimensions in a Postmodern World

Dave Broucek wrote a perceptive article, dialoguing about diversity in missions (Broucek 2000). He points out that by 2050, US America will be only 53% white, compared with 87% in 1950. Yet, our North American mission organizations remain very white/European. He points out that the business world, *only* driven by profit and legal action (vis-a-vis our divine calling) is way ahead of us of making diversity work. Yet we overcame some of our tribal boundaries in the 50s, especially in his mission, and mine. (In 1950 the Swedes and the Norwegians/Danes merged their two "Free" denominations into the EFC of America, paving the way for Swedes and Norwegians to marry without other than normal consequence, as in my case!) I do not mean to trivialize the incredible racial and cultural divide by this example, but would it not be great to see the same kind of diversity develop in missions over the next 50 years? We have a divine calling to be a people of God. Small steps are being made, but more emphasis needs to go here.

I see another diversity issue to manage, and that could be summed up in our definitions of dysfunctionality. More and more people are coming into missions from "dysfunctional" backgrounds. We typically, thanks to our clinical perspective of membercare, see this as a bad thing. I think it is a reality that is not going away. Therefore, we could relabel dysfunctional as an issue to manage through appropriate membercare strategies, rather than exclude these people. In much the same way that the recent Consultation on Language and Metaphors sought to reframe the military-oriented language of missions with other words, perhaps we need new metaphors around which to communicate about dysfunctionality.

Questions to Consider:

1. What are some ways or situations in your context that signify important shifts with regards to diversity?
2. How can we provide health-oriented services to targeted populations which destigmatizes such services and conditions?
3. How do we keep balance in helping the missionary, without undue emphasis on becoming a clinic, or hospital?

Inclusivity vs. Exclusivity in our Christian World View

Every few years over the last decades I have noticed the ebb and flow of anti-psychology in the Christian world. I have tended to come to see these periods of questioning and rejection as an overall hopeful process. I think we always need to examine ourselves and our perspectives (Search me! Oh God!), and asking ourselves whether we are still being true to our original calling. Unfortunately, there are always the extremes, which seem to delight in stating their respective positions with such force that reasonable dialogue space is lost.

I would hope that we can avoid this extremism as we try to develop the new order of membercare. We talk of contextualizing the gospel, so that it can be heard without the static of our frame of reference. I hope we can contextualize and harmonize the various social sciences in a way that allows the Great Commission to shine through all we do. However, great care should be exercised when bringing membercare to bear in the missionary context. We must not forget what the main purpose of missionary work is, and we must not allow our "treatments" to become iatrogenic (physician caused illness) in terms of the tasks we are called to fulfill.

What would that look like? (Fools rush in where angels fear to tread comes to mind here!) Let's imagine the foundation of the Great Commission community (or ecosphere) as the seat of a three-legged stool. Each leg is integrally connected to the other, but each serves the central organizing principle of holding the church up, allowing it to grow to its full purpose.

The first leg would be the biblical principles underlying the missionary activity. These would be applied by the missiological principles as researched and discovered. These principles would be the bridges between the biblical and other legs. The second leg would be the community of the missionary. This would include the realms of the social sciences as they interact with the personal, interpersonal, emotional and spiritual arenas. The third leg would include the arenas of the targeted activities and communities. The steps/bridges between the legs would be bi-directional, in that information and input would go back and forth. There would be checks and balances to ensure compliance with biblical principles. The final evaluation points would be the growth of the Great-Commission Community, built on the three legs.

The above is too brief and probably a poor metaphor. More thought needs to go into it. However, it does begin to illustrate the interactive principles necessary for further progress. I like it so far, because it is directional, that is, the purpose of the legs is to hold up the stool. The purpose of our "work" is to build the "community."

Best Practice, Standards of Care, and Continuum of Care Issues

As the membercare field continues to develop, there are signs of maturity in the understanding of what to do (Best Practice, Standards of Care) and when to do it (Continuum of Care).

What to do deals with the problem of diagnosis. Careful diagnosis will enable us to understand the existing condition, and develop the appropriate treatment, to use a clinical perspective. I am concerned that most of us who work on the "what" problem, are not talking together enough, or are not talking outside of our own disciplines. For example, this meeting should have many more people like me here. We need to understand your perspective. We are by and large disconnected. Another arena is the Language Learning congress. I have been at all of them, mostly by my psychological self. I leave here tomorrow to go to a "Mental Health and Missions" conference in Indiana. It will be great, but will over emphasize the mental health perspective.

Continuum of care looks at the perspective of doing what, when, and by who. In my work in managed care, we have looked at this in detail. What sorts of problems pop up in the population and when, and who may be best suited to work on them? In that business, the bottom line can be a primary decision point in who does what, but I hope it does not become so in missions. I do see numerous mission organizations embracing a managed care perspective, but I see that as healthy overall. While used mainly in the medical or clinical professions, continuum of care models could be extremely useful for missions, if they truly became multiperspectival. Let's look at this in more detail…

Membercare in the Service of Missions: Model Building

In this new order, we need to determine who are the "players." At the least, in designing a membercare strategy, we need to include the theologians, missiologists, psychologists, anthropologists, linguists, sociologists, but what else? I do not claim to know. (I want to make plain that I am talking people, here, not just ideas. It is within the community of the people of the disciplines that true synergy takes over.) What about "disciplines" that do not fit well here? I am thinking about the topic of spiritual formation. Who takes responsibility for that? Of course, let's not forget the perspective of the non-North American. If we leave that out, all is in vain. Then we would need to decide on the overall purpose of the task. This may already be understood, but I doubt it. Once we have identified the task, and key concepts, then we could develop "treatment strategies." I do not like the word treatment, though, because of its "illness" metaphor. I prefer a Human Resources context where we are training, coaching, and evaluating toward the central organizing principles.

I have stated elsewhere that I believe effectiveness and incarnation are two of the central points we need to build around. What else? I need your help.

How can we help each other?

1. *Commitment to connection.* The various disciplines each have their own spheres of influence. We all go to different events during the year, and there is little opportunity for dialogue. It would be good to identify what events are worth attending, and assign staff to various events outside of their typical arena.

2. *Bring in outside consultants to speak on your problems from their perspective.* Having a problem with attrition? Do not just bring in the shrink. Bring in the HR specialist to review your evaluation forms. What are you evaluating for? Or, should you be coaching for targeted behaviors? See what I mean?
3. *Ask yourselves the following question: If we did not exist, would we go to the trouble of creating ourselves just this way?* During my tenure on the EFMA Board, we have asked this question when it came to what to do about EMIS, ACMC, and ourselves. It has made for some interesting changes. Ask others to answer this question about you as well.
4. *Listen.*
5. *Actively seek input across the disciplines to discover what should be contributing to the core of the mission.* Each discipline ideally should connect to our core values about what we are all about. If effectiveness is a core value, then all the departments in an organization should be able to explain how they help further the ministry to achieve effectiveness.
6. *True effectiveness lies within the relational community.* It begins with our relation to our creator, then to each other as members of the larger family, then to our relationships as specialists in a community.

Chapter 11

Caring for GenXers

Tom Steffen

In this chapter, I would like to reflect on two GenXer preferences, highlighted in three short case stories, which should impact mission strategies in the new millennium. Rather than refer to the term GenXer as a consumer category I will use it in this paper to reflect a generation that shares a common social and historical location that determines range of relevant experience and action (Mannheim 1952:291-292). I will discuss the incoming personnel's (primarily American youth) commitment to short-term ministries (in contrast to long-term), the desire for connectedness, and possible ministry implications: piece-meal participation and partnerships.

Case Stories

Case Story 1: At Biola University every undergraduate is required to take the Acts class. Professors, particularly Dr. Harold Dollar, author of *St. Luke's Missiology,* designed the course to provide students with an overview of the victorious first-century Christian movement. Students are also encouraged to identify possible short-term ministry opportunities so that they can immediately participate along side those in full-time service, or support them at a distance through prayer, finances, e-mail, and so forth. A few students each year will go into full-time ministry as a direct result of this class. After one class a student talked to me about going on a summer short-term trip abroad.

She expressed one major concern: "Six weeks away from home is like a lifetime!"

Case Story 2: This summer in a consultant session I listened to a young GenX missionary tell his story about how the mission agency had let the couple down. They sent them off to a far country, and then contact ceased. How could leadership send them off in such great fanfare, then pull the plug? The couple felt betrayed, abandoned, forsaken, deserted. Their agency left them unconnected. Seeing the founder of Frontiers in the audience (representing a prior generation), Greg Livingston, I asked him how he would have responded. Greg related their own experience: "We wanted to go to India. The Mission leadership said, 'Good, it's east, and a big country, you can't miss it.' My own boomer reaction? Great, I have some autonomy and more time to focus on 'real' ministry rather than bureaucracy." Possible reaction by the Builder generation, dutifully send in those monthly reports even if the other end remains silent.

Case Story 3: In light of Baker's desire to update Herbert Kane's classics *The Making of A Missionary* (1975) and *Life and Work on the Mission Field* (1980) with a new text I reread through the two volumes. After 480 pages of straight print (no pictures or graphs), I felt I had entered another planet, certainly not the e-world. The myths regarding mission, the definition of a missionary, the call, hang-ups and obstacles, qualifications, trends, support raising, training, language learning (which seemed to assume culture learning), and a host of other topics, definitely seemed for a previous era. And then I learned that these books still find their way to the missions classroom!

Personnel

Stereotyping any generation is certainly dangerous. The comments that follow recognize that exceptions certainly exit in any generation, and that behavioral characteristics dominant in one generation do not necessarily stop within a particular age group. While much has been written on the various generations, I will focus on two related dominant characteristics associated with GenXers, followed by two possible implications for the future of missions. These related characteristics include the need to feel connected and the fear of long-term commitments. [1]

As the first case story vividly pointed out, new missionaries leaving the shores of America require connection. In this case, the young couple did not feel the connection between themselves and mission leadership extended overseas, resulting in friction and frustration.

But the need for connection does not stop with mission leadership. In talking with a veteran missionary responsible for the member care of personnel from a number of mission agencies in Asia, I asked, "What are some of the major reoccurring issues that you're finding?" Here's my summarized overview of his response.

I see two major challenges, particularly for the younger generation, but not necessarily limited to it. The first has to do with people's time on the computer. Rather than getting out with

---

[1] Let's not forget the generation that proceeded these 80 million born between 1961 and 1981. Almost half of GenXers grew up in single-parent homes. That means the remaining spouse most likely worked, creating a new term: "latchkey kids." Who else did they have to connect and commit to ("hang out" with) but themselves? (See Flory and Miller, eds., *Gen X Religion*, 2000).

the nationals, many missionaries spend an inordinate number of hours per day on the computer. Its like they no longer have to really separate from family and friends back home; they check in daily on e-mail to find out what's happening. Long and short transmissions race back and forth between the missionary's computer with those on the other side of the pond, not to mention all other parts of the globe. Beside keeping up to date on "happenings" I see a lot of missionaries involved in computer projects that consume most of their time, again time that separates them from the people they came to reach with the gospel. The computer age has opened the door for missionaries to stay connected, but not necessarily with nationals.

The second area I see, which may be connected to the first, is that many young missionaries have no idea what they should be doing. Ministry strategy seems lacking, if not totally absent. By the time furlough rolls around, these folks can point to few fulfilled ministry goals. This impacts not only their self-esteem, but also post-furlough vocational goals.

While the above may seem to highlight the negative, I would rather consider it more the reality of our times, and ponder possible ways not only to challenge it, but also redirect it. The need for connection is definitely there. Closely associated with connection is commitment. When connections are suspect, unknown, or even known, commitment tends to wane. Commitment to a crosscultural ministry for an extended period of time, or even six weeks, is difficult for many. Case Story 3 demonstrates it is certainly a different era of missions. Present mission trainers must not overlook or minimize these realities. The advertisement for a car manufacturer rings just as true for mission managers: "This is not your father's Oldsmobile."

The command for Kingdom-based ministry that establishes new communities of faith and renews those faltering, as evidenced in Acts (1:3,6; 8:12; 14:22; 19:8; 20:25; 28:23,31), never changes, even though the terminology may (Church Growth, Kingdom Growth, Church Health, Church Planting, Church Multiplication, Kingdom-based Church Multiplication, Church-Planting Movements). Jesus gave his followers the command to make obedient disciples of all peoples. But how this will be accomplished will differ from generation to generation. I will now consider two implications related for a generation of missionaries who require connection (yet have difficulty with personal relationship), and do not like to commit to long-term relationships.

Piece-meal Participation

Effective crosscultural ministry tends to take time, much more than the present generation seems willing to invest. In that Christianity is a way of life, missions must therefore deal with much more than the spiritual needs of people; it must also address physical and social needs. Missions is much more than starting a church; it also includes the development of indigenous leaders and relevant challenging curricula. Missions is more than developing indigenous leadership and relevant curricula; it is also the facilitation of an ongoing movement that impacts society, including holistic mission training (Steffen 1997). Such comprehensive ministry goes far beyond evangelism to congregating a new community of faith in such a way that Scripture becomes central to the movement, and the Holy Spirit the source of power as it reaches out locally, regionally, nationally, and globally. Will expatriate short-termers, even if they know the local language and culture, see such a legitimate movement completed within six weeks?

To gain a better perspective on the time element for such ministry it is helpful to look at Pauline teams. Overall approximate timeframes for some of the on-again, off-again ministries look like this: Antioch (4 years), Corinth (approximately three visits over 4 years), Ephesus (several visits over 3 years), Caesarea (2-3 years), Rome (2-3 years). Paul personally spent approximately 15 of his 25 ministry years in five different centers! *Leavings preceded leaving.*

What should be noted about these timeframes is the type of ministries conducted under them. Looking at it missiologically, the majority of missions[2] (M) conducted by Pauline teams in Acts were in Jerusalem (M1) and Judea/Samaria (M2) where linguistic and cultural differences remained minimal due to broad Greek and Roman influence. On at least three occasions one can find Paul involved in M3 ("ends of the earth"[3]) where linguistic and cultural differences were distant: Lystra (13), Athens (17), Malta (28). Two of the M3 were serendipitous, and major cultural misunderstandings occurred in Lystra. M1 and M2 were predominant in Acts, requiring less linguistic and cultural sophistication of the Christian worker. The more complex M3 was rare. This raises a pertinent question: If it took Paul and his

---

[2] Holistic ministry that consisted of "word and deed," is evident in Luke's first volume through the ministries of Jesus and his disciples, and continues in the second, Acts. Evangelism and signs and wonders are often found together. But when one's theology does not allow for the use of such signs and wonders, other types of social ministries should be administered so that the whole person and community receive attention.

[3] Paul (and Luke) most likely would define "end of the earth" as anything beyond Palestine. Rather than view M3 primarily as linguistic / cultural barriers, as I'm doing, they would probably prefer to view M3 as geographical, theological, emotional, and psychological.

teams this long to conduct M1 and M2, what makes many feel today they can complete M3 in less time than it took first-century apostles? This leads to my first strategy change that addresses the connection and commitment issues that concern many Christian workers today.

Strategy Implications

Some may argue that because this generation prefers to participate in short-term ministries they should be encouraged to do so. Why challenge the status quo? Some would advocate for short-term ministry globe trotters that use translators or English. But what about building relationships with the recipients? Should this be sacrificed for cultural comfort? Are deep relationships (see Acts 21:1) and modeling no longer important in ministry, especially when founding and facilitating a holistic church-planting movement?

Here's another option, one that provides this audience with a doable goal, does not minimize the complexity of M2 and M3, responds to the felt needs of connection and commitment, and provides challenges from Scripture for frontline involvement (Steffen 1996). This strategy calls for four levels of action to draw the sometimes reluctant, yet spiritually gifted and skilled, off the sidelines to reach one unreached people group in their lifetime. It contains a comprehensive ministry strategy that leads to an ongoing, biblical-centered, indigenous movement; task commitment levels for team members; connection provisions assured by the assembly or agency; and, the ongoing challenge to participate as long as it takes to complete the task. This strategy recognizes that the promised Paraclete is always present (see Table 1). Should these components be in place, *the challenge to reach one unreached people group in their lifetime will seem feasible.*

The comprehensive level calls for mission leadership in the assemblies, agencies, and academics to provide a ministry model that creates indigenous Christian movements. This selection demonstrates to all that they know what must be done and intend to do whatever is necessary to fulfill the Great Commission and the Great Commandment.

The above model begins with language and culture acquisition as a means to earn the right to be heard. It recognizes that building relationships through this vital ministry is fundamental to long-term church-planting movements. *Relationships determine results.* It recognizes that team members cannot assume that all people groups are so alike (universality) that time spent learning language and culture is no longer necessary. Nor does it assume that every group is so different (particular) that fragmentation is inevitable.

Table 1: Action Strategy to Reach One Unreached People Group

Comprehensive:	*Preevangelism*	*Evangelism*	*Postevangelism*	*Phase-out*
Commitment:	Short-term 1			
	Short-term 2			
		Short-term 3		
		Short-term 4		
			Short-term 5	
			Short-term 6	
Connection:	Provision	Provision	Provision	Provision
Challenge:	Discipleship & Development	Discipleship & Development	Discipleship & Development	Discipleship & Development

Figure 1 shows that when universality (we are all alike) is too highly privileged by the ministry team, cultural blindness tends to prevail, leading team members to impose cultural dominance, often unintentionally, thereby minimizing the opportunity for true unity (in contrast to uniformity) and inclusiveness. Figure 2 shows that when the ministry team privileges particularly, differences tend to predominate, thereby maximizing fragmentation and individual particularities. This tends to minimize reception and the possibility for critical contextualization.

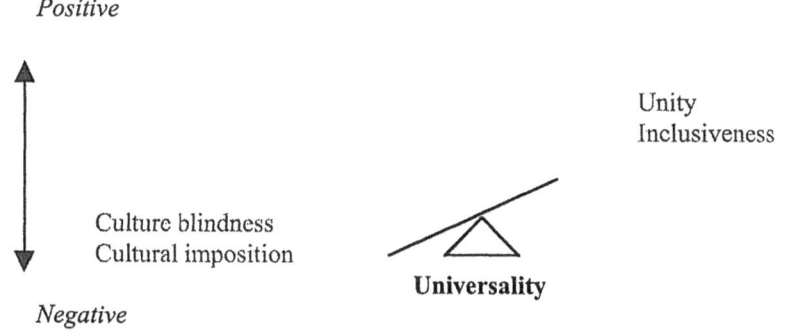

Figure 1: Bringing balance to universality

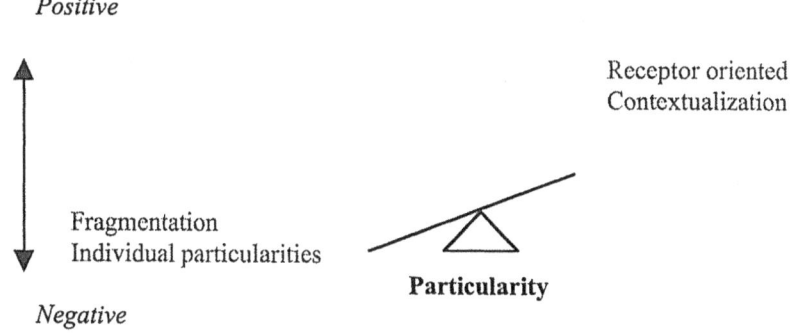

Figure 2: Bringing balance to particularity

The strategy also calls for mission leadership to provide ongoing connections at all pertinent levels. This would include leadership on the local, national, and international levels in areas such as member care, ministry strategy, and life-long learning through formal and non-formal means. Those who participate in any short-term ministry will find themselves assured that connections in multiple areas are available when needed, whether offered directly through the sending institution or through strategic partnerships.

Not only does mission leadership commit to a comprehensive ministry model, and provide continual connections, so must those who experience God's call to participate. These participants must also make a time commitment, even if viewed by many as far too short. To encourage long-term participation, mission leadership will provide numerous means to challenge short-termers to move beyond their present commitment and connection comfort zones in discipleship and development.

To keep from overwhelming those who have a difficult time making a long-term commitment, wise mission leadership will present this audience a *comprehensive plan with a shared goal in mind* delivered in *piece-meal fashion*. They will ask for commitment to only a small, yet significant segment of the total plan. Once completed, they will ask participants to make another commitment to another piece of the plan. Future commitments to the total plan should not prove that difficult if these short-termers experienced genuine connections and challenges. This model allows participants to begin in their comfort zone, yet grow and expand beyond it. It emphasizes process and pilgrimage over program; it recognizes that a comprehensive ministry plan driven by authentic connections and challenges can lead to multiple short-term commitments that lead to long-term commitment. They discover over time that *they can reach one unreached people group in their lifetime.*

Two churches doing a superb job in this piece-meal approach to long-term commitment are Wasilla Bible Church (800 attendance) in Alaska and the Willingdon Church in British Columbia (3000 attendance). Wasilla offers high schoolers short-term trips from their Freshman through Senior years. All participants must go as a team. The Freshman trip involves no crosscultual element. During their Sophomore year participants go to Mexico with YUGO. Outward Bound is offered in their Junior year while the Senior year is a trip to a sister church in Siberia.

Willingdon starts short-term trips in Jr. High, continuing through high school and college, and like Wasilla, all participants must go as a team. Jr. Highers stay in British Columbia learning and practicing ministry skills in the mornings with afternoons as fun times. All participants must qualify (which includes ministry experience) to go on this trip, and succeeding ones. Not all applicants are accepted. None of the trips include building projects. One of these two-week trips is to Mexico, lead by team members from the church who know Spanish. During college years, students are encouraged to take 8-10 months to go to a field of choice for crosscultural ministry. The church will provide 50% of their support. Willingdon uses this trip to recruit for full-time ministry. Both churches prepare participants for long-term, quality crosscultural ministry through teams. The smaller church accomplishes this through partnerships with other institutions; the larger church accomplishes this with its own international personnel. Either way, each church will intimately know the gifts and skills of those they chose to send forth and support, whether short-term or long-term.

Partnerships

Because GenXers like to connect, genuine international partnerships become a strong possibility. This generation has the potential to take missions to a higher level in strategic partnerships than possibly any previous mission generation. In this section I would like to discuss how GenXers may respond to partnerships, possible challenges they will face, and a present model that may see various versions in the future. I recognize I walk on thin ice when trying to speak for another generation, and welcome all corrections. I will now look at definition, theory, theology, and structure, raising many more questions than answers.

Definition

Bush and Lutz define partnerships as: "an association of two or more Christian autonomous bodies who have formed a trusting relationship and fulfill agreed upon expectations by sharing complementary strengths and resources to reach their mutual goal" (1990:46). GenXers may challenge Bush and Lutz' definition of partnership, and similar ones. How will they respond to "autonomous bodies" in the above definition? Will they tend to shy away from the legal, contractual boardroom term, "partnership," preferring to substitute something more personal, such as fellowship? Will they look for new metaphors, such as "connection.com?" What metaphors outside the business world will they prefer? Will they prefer a definition that focuses on goal fulfillment? Task completions? Or relationships? Some combination of both, such as "shared goals" or "shared tasks?" Will they favor Rickett's definition: "A partnership is a complementary relationship driven by a common purpose and sustained by a willingness to learn and grow together in obedience to God" (2000:1). What aspects of partnerships will GenXers cause present mission leadership to rethink?

Theory

The call for the moratorium of all foreign mission agencies issued by the Presbyterian leader John Gatu from Kenya in 1974 has grown silent, yet residue of this view can still be heard in a few corners of the world. In their place new voices call for other church-mission relationship options: (1) departure, (2) subordination, (3) parallelism, and (4) partnership.

<u>Theory 1: Departure</u>. Once the national church reaches maturity, the expatriates depart physically, although they may continue to send funds. Henry Venn (1796-1873) and Rufus Anderson (1796-1880) must be credited for this unrivaled mission theory of the nineteenth, and first half of the twentieth century: the three-selfs (self-propagating, self-supporting, self-governing) that can produce an "indigenes church." John Nevius (1828-1893), sensing the practicality of the three-selfs, instituted them first in China, and more effectively in Korea. Nevius' *The Planting and Developing of Missionary Churches* remains a classic. Roland Allen (1869-1947) continued to echo Venn and Anderson's theory in the twentieth century, arguing that the three-selfs work not just because they are practical, but because they are biblical; they are Pauline. Allen makes this argument in his classic *Missionary Methods: St. Paul's or Ours?* (Hesselgrave's (2000) "Pauline Cycle" continues Allen's emphasis on the centrality of Scripture.) Failure of the "three selfs" to address the more global questions, among other things, would eventually date this theory.

Theory 2: Subordination. Once the national church reaches maturity, expatriates work under national leaders while providing their own support. This unilateral theory transfers complete control to the national church. Some view this theory as ecumenicalism at its best; others see it as distorted partnership, while still others think this should be the ultimate goal.

Theory 3: Parallelism. Since the national church is mature, each party develops complementary, yet separate agendas while maintaining individual organizational structures, personnel and budgets. This theory respects the unity, diversity and autonomy of all players. Proponents see the international body of Christ in action, utilizing the different parts to fulfill unified goals. Opponents believe it stifles the Great Commission within the national church, leaving evangelism and missions to outsiders.

Theory 4: Partnerships. This theory advocates institutions work not *apart* from each other (Theory 1), or *under* each other (Theory 2), or *unified* but *separate* (Theory 3), but as *equal* partners. Proponents argue this multilateral theory protects both the commission of the national church and expatriates. Opponents argue the complexity of ethnic relationships, diversity of economic levels, and so forth, make this theory extremely difficult to accomplish.

Will GenXers vote for the fourth theory? Or, will they prefer smaller networks of connections that may allow for identify retention and more autonomy? Whether through partnerships or networks, most would probably agree that inclusion, interdependence and role changes should replace isolation, independence or departure.

Theology

At the American Society of Missiology this summer, Chuck Van Engen presented a superb paper entitled "Toward a

Theology of Mission Partnerships." In that paper he argued that Christology should serve as the basis for partnerships. While this view rang true for part of the audience, others did not feel as comfortable. Some would have preferred that bibliology, rather than Christology, serve as the basis for partnerships. This change, they believe, would allow for tighter boundaries. Which theology will drive the GenXers' perspective of partnerships? How would an overall grasp of God's sacred Storybook influence an understanding of partnerships? Going beyond the scope of this paper, how will GenXers' theology of unity and diversity impact partnerships? Ecclesiology? The gospel? What will GenXers do to prevent post-modernism from influencing their interpretation of Scripture? These are a few challenges that face GenXers theologically, having major implications for the future of missions.

Structure

If structure determines strategy, then the partnership model, however defined, will play a significant role in the new millennium. What models might surface? I will now present a basic overview of Pioneers' current model, one that hits hard on commitment and connection.

Ted Fletcher, former national sales manager for the Wall Street Journal, and founder of Pioneers, had the idea of partnerships from its conception. The Mission Statement reads: "Pioneers mobilizes teams to glorify God among unreached peoples, by initiating church-planting movements in partnership with local churches." This ethos has resulted in a recent model — Internationalization. Pioneers views the model not as a multinational corporation, but as a "fellowship." The model calls for autonomy and accountability. Each of the six mobilization bases (countries) is responsible to grow its own organization quantitatively and qualitatively, and reach out contextually, all funded by its own budget. Differences are celebrated rather than feared. Participating members must commit to the agency's doctrinal statement and core values. "Pioneers" remains the brand name with the country added—Pioneers <u>Country</u>.

The International Council (IC) added another dimension to Pioneers' organizational chart, impacting the existing structure. To assure a field-focused agenda and minimize "pockets of power," leadership of the IC is comprised of an International Director, Founder of the organization, Area Directors, and Mobilization Base Directors. The International Leadership Team (ILT), around 12 people, gathers every 18-24 months to develop relationships (connect), keep their eyes on the global goal to plant reproducing churches in unreached areas through teams, discuss common challenges, address policy, accountability, and legal issues. They do not meet to manage the business of other countries.

One change that Internationalization brought about was that of the U.S. Board's governance. Once responsible for the agency on the international level, the board now found itself responsible only for the USA. To their credit, they gladly gave up their collective power to empower others. "Structured flexibility" defines Pioneers, as evident in the U.S. Board's decision. This brief overview of the Pioneers Internationalization model certainly does not do justice to years of work, prayer, debate, organizational charts, and numerous changes that this bold adventure required of the agency.

Strategy Implications

Pioneers' Internationalization model addresses both GenXer concerns for commitment and connection. Another feature this generation may appreciate is the organizational flattening of the agency. It is a center-less partnership (or fellowship) rather than a multinational corporation model franchised around the world. Out are lone rangers, one color of skin, turf wars, positions of power (education, money, computer savvy, buildings, and so forth); in are organizational chaos, searching for help horizontally, fluidity, flexibility, focus, diversity of ideas, multinational agencies, community, connectedness.

The model also seeks to balance power. It empowers new leaders so that rightful representation is assured. At the same time, it asks those in positions of power to modify it. It's a new day. Leadership is shared. Vision is shared. Ideas are shared. People are shared. Finances are shared. Why? Because power is shared.

The role of the International Director is not the management of multiple mobilization agencies, rather it becomes the management of multiple crosscultural relationships. Qualifications for this leadership role would include at least the following: systems thinker, information flow expert, intercultural competencies, facilitator, life-long learner. Pioneers set out to design "A model which is serviceable and provides responsibility, accountability, authority, and leadership at every level." This model begins to address all these areas. But expect future modifications. That's the reality of our fast-changing times, and Pioneers' penchant to keep pace.

Conclusion

Mission leaders must learn to think long-term ministry through short-term assignments because GenXers, like the Acts class student, tend to think short-term. Rather than discredit an upcoming generation for lack of commitment and the need for strong connection, mission leaders must learn to skillfully guide them along to real, productive solutions. This will require, among other things, a comprehensive long-term ministry plan (remember those who lack ministry strategy) and a call to commitment and genuine connections (remember those spending all their time on computers and the couple who wanted connection with the home agency). These GenX factors should be carefully challenged continually. This must be done with patience and understanding since we should always remember the role the former generation played in producing this generation.

As Jesus expected his disciples' ministry to expand far beyond his own, so our generations should expect the same of GenXers. Challenged connections and levels of commitment may produce a generation that will take our ideas of partnership to a much higher level. This may require new metaphors for those who despise autonomous isolates. One such possibility may be "connection." When and where implemented, people will know we are truly Christ's disciples.

Chapter 12

Caring for the Children

Paul Cochrane

The topic of this paper was selected at the 1999 International Missionary Kid Educational Conference meetings as an important need for us to consider. It is hoped that the thoughts herein might stimulate us to concrete action. Our subject would be a challenging one for any intermission forum. Traditionally, intermission cooperation was not a practice of most mission agencies. Perhaps the one area they have found common ground most often has been MK education.

Recent world trends, however, are challenging the long-standing traditions of independence. Discussions on "partnership" are now common. Because our times have changed, our mission leaders are calling for more cooperation. It seems the climate is ready for new cooperation on a broader scale than ever previously seen. This in turn can provide the right atmosphere for increased and strategic collaboration in MK education.

We begin by looking at the realities of the current status of MK education. Then we will explore the pros and cons of collaboration. Lastly we will consider suggestions for deeper and more intentional working together in the light of indicators on the future of missions.

Looking at Some Facts

Obtaining data on MK Education is not easy. Mission agencies do not generally keep or publish the statistics on the number of MKs, their grade level, or their schooling location. Research is lacking to help us analyze the facts as we would prefer. Thus, if this paper resorts to generalizations, and approximate data, the reader will understand.

Using the Profile of Overseas Christian schools published by ACSI, the MARC Mission Handbook 1998-2000, and the EMQ MK School Directory, the following statistics are complied to give us a working overview of missions and their MK education facilities.

- 138 Schools, or 128 according to the EMQ MK School Directory.
- 25,574 students enrolled. If approximately 60% are MKs then 15,344 are MKs in those schools.
- 36,035 North American missionaries with 21,621 statistically estimated MKs.
- Approximately 5,000 MKs are not using ACSI listed schools.
- 839 agencies send personnel from North America.
- 36 mission agencies run most MK schools according to the EMQ MK School Directory.
- Outside of C&MA, Southern Baptist, Assemblies of God and the Evangelical Free Church, few denominations are listed as involved in MK education.
- 37 schools of the 138 are run jointly.

Thinking About Current Realities

The ACSI related schools, are primarily sponsored by faith-mission agencies and serve 60% of N. American MKs. Of the 138 schools listed, only 37 are jointly sponsored or 26% of the total. Perhaps the most shocking statistic is that of the 839 missions counted in the MARC handbook, only 36 are taking responsibility for their MKs by involvement in running a school. In addition, by estimation, there is still a considerable number of students outside the grid of the ACSI profiled institutions, approximately 5,000.

Among the schools listed, only 49 or 36% had ACSI and/or secular accreditation. At the high school level (9-12), only 45 schools can be thought of as "viable" choices for an accredited education overseas. Viable means sufficient students to create a healthy social atmosphere coupled with good academic services such as science labs, music and athletic programs.

Missions have not neglected MK education. Personnel, time and money to provide for this need is evidenced. However, the quality of these educational programs is, at least, not well assessed. The lack of accreditation does not necessarily mean that the schools are educating poorly. It simply means we are not measuring their quality. The fact that only 26% of the schools are jointly sponsored supposes another possible problem, that of duplication.

Lastly, where are the "other" 803 missions? If only 36 missions are operating schools we know the "other 803's" children must be in "our" schools! Is this a good thing? Certainly this statistic alone gives us reason to discuss our subject. Can there not be much more working together to meet the needs of the missionary force around the world?

The one fact that is ignored by these statistics is the rising need for non-North American MKs for an overseas education in English. Jim Engel and William Dyrness in their recent book *Changing the Mind of Missions - Where have we Gone Wrong?* speak of the majority missionary force as now being from non-North American countries. To ignore the critical need for these missionary children is to close one's eyes at what God is doing.

Why Work Together for MK Education?

In reflecting on this question, I have turned primarily to material available on mission partnership. It is because this question is foremost an administrative one. Thus, speaking more missiologically, here are some weighty reasons for working collaboratively.

Fairness

At present, 36 missions are the front line defense for all remaining 803 agencies. Statistically, this appears to be an "unfair burden" on those missions who actively assume responsibility for their missionary families. On the basis of fairness, it seems undeniable that we need to share the load more evenly. Having said this, it is true that many more missions enter into the picture than statistics show. But, we do not have a picture how "fair" their participation might be.

Kingdom Purposes

God seeks children from among all nations and the New Testament church reflects this kind of multi-ethnic composition. Beyond the Bible, a multi-ethnic community is also much more in line with "real" life. Creating and maintaining cloistered enclaves of children from one background is not a healthy way to teach our children God's love for the world. The problem of our MK education schools becoming a "little America" is real. While some champion such ethnocentrism, it can arguably be seen as a liability both in helping our children become future missionaries and enabling them to integrate into an increasingly diverse culture back home. Joining with other missions in providing education is a way of satisfying this needed cultural perspective. There are many pluses for a school established with multi-ethnic participation.

Stewardship

We must manage well our human and material resources. Proper accountability to our supporting constituency demands this in a day of limited resources. Few businesses or churches have the luxury to employ a person full-time to service the needs of only a few customers. Likewise, expecting a school to fill a classroom so that each teacher carries a full student load makes sense. *Proper* stewardship of our human resources requires collaboration.

Why Don't We Work Together?

Naturally, there are reasons why missions have not worked together. Collaboration is not easy. Some of the challenges of working jointly are common to all joint ventures.

Unity

Achieving unity is never easy. But everyone recognizes it is harder with a diverse group. Agreement on the philosophy and purpose of a school is fundamental to its success. The more groups represented in a collaborative effort, the more everyone has to work to achieve unity. Many find this too hard.

Control

Group ownership means that no one entity has full control. This loss of authority is an obstacle for some missions. However, the gift of collaboration is the wisdom of many counselors. Proper cooperation should not really mean a loss of essential areas of control because these principles can be built into the fundamental documents.

Responsibility

Taking ownership means each mission fulfills its responsibility toward the school. Getting each partner to share its full weight of responsibility is harder when you have a group. Participation in a joint school does not mean less responsibility. The tendency to let others do the work is one of the reasons members quit groups.

Money

Collaboration takes time and money. It is a false expectation that collaboration will make it cheaper. It can be harder to "sell" a jointly sponsored effort to your organization. This is true especially if your organization is facing a financial crunch. Sometimes missionary parents view the little "self-run" school as cheaper. This might be true on the level of personal finances when a mission provides a teacher. However, we know that actual costs are not less than running a larger school.

Caring for the Children 237

What Can We Existing Models of Collaboration Teach Us?

BFA, Faith Academy, Morrison Academy are good well-established models of collaboration. Each of these schools provides different perspectives on what collaboration can accomplish. One thing we know for certain. They are giving a good education. The positive reputation of these institutions has increased enrollment to the degree they often have long waiting lists for admission. Let's consider reasons why they are such good models:

1. Collaboration has produced academically excellent and socially attractive institutions. Working together can be positive and successful.
2. Commitment to commonly agreed organizational policies (Constitution, By-Laws, Board Policy) is a key to sustaining cooperation through the good and the bad days.
3. High organizational commitment to MK Education from the leadership of the mission is essential. Most missions that join others in creating schools accept MK education as a "calling." MK educators are not "second class" citizens among the ranks of their missionaries.
4. Competent and professional people are essential. High standards for board members, administrators, teachers and other staff characterize these schools. Any school board in the USA would be happy to have their personnel.
5. Solid financial commitment on the part of participating missions can be counted on. Spending for the missionary child's welfare receives a level of strategic importance in the mission so that raising large sums of money for this purpose is acceptable.

6. The establishment of balanced policies and practices that strike a middle ground between different values represented by Christian traditions. Because of this balance the school appeals to a wide range of missions and missionary families.
7. Existence in a strategic location. Clearly, location is one of the key factors to a successful school. Parents and mission administrators look for safety, good and relatively easy access (transportation), good communication, up to date facilities, a cosmopolitan culture, and extra services such as health care, shopping, and vacation possibilities.

Future Needs

Perhaps the greatest reason for working together is to enable future mission work to fulfill the Great Commission. It is unlikely that previous patterns of doing MK education will satisfy the rapidly changing mission scene. In reading new literature on this subject it seems future MK educational needs will push us to incorporate the following characteristics into our schools:

International Curriculum

An international curriculum that allows students access to a variety of universities around the world is long overdue. The missionary force is changing. Right now the majority of missionaries come from non-North American countries. This means the educational needs of the global missionary force will change. Fewer North Americans will be going overseas for long term service. More international personnel will be working with the emerging churches. While we can continue to think in terms of North American students, the evidence is strong that our future is not in servicing only that group.

Wholistic Education

There is a call for more a "wholistic approach" to education. It is not realistic to suppose all missionary children either want or are naturally qualified for a classical university preparatory curriculum. Technical/vocational education is lacking in most of our current institutions. We must expand our curriculums to prepare missionary children who graduate to the work force in their countries of origin. Teaching English as a second language and having special education professionals to meet remedial needs should become a standard operational procedure.

Urban Location

A location that meets the changing direction of missions from rural to urban settings will be more and more important. Cities are viewed as the place where the greatest missionary action should occur. We must provide schools in large urban centers so that there is easy access for day school purposes.

Internationalization of Leadership

Intentional multi-ethnic composition of board and faculty members will help reflect the unity in Christ of which we preach. This action will reinforce commitment toward to an international curriculum. The involvement of Christian leaders in education from the host nation should be an expected outcome of the expansion of national Christian education.

Formal Relationships with Nationals

There are two groups of nationals who might be concerned with jointly owned mission schools operating in their country. One is the host government. The second is the national evangelical churches.

We have at times ignored both of these groups. Many host governments already require legal statutes for private education. Where this is not the case, formalizing a relationship with the host government through the department of education or religion will be expected in the future. It is better to negotiate a clear relationship in this domain earlier rather than wait for a government decision to create the necessity. Secondly, relating to national churches and pastors is important. We should be helping local church leaders understand the cause for Christian education for their own people. Relating more closely to national believers will also help the school set standards which reflect a Christian view of life in accordance with practices of national evangelicals. The presence of a MK school must contribute positively to Christian witness in the country.

Structuring Cooperation

The challenge before us is how to bring mission leadership and MK educators together to proactively work on jointly sponsored schools. At the start of this paper it was noted that current intermission structures are not working on this subject. The question then is, are there other meetings where mission leaders are thinking and working together. The answer is "yes." Here are some forums that might become the future seedbed for cooperation.

Networking Groups

Today a number of networking consultations for reaching unreached people groups have provided an entire new wave of collaboration between missions. These groups have concentrated on cooperation in evangelism church planting, and discipleship. Providing Christian education for missionary children of workers for these strategic initiatives is important and could possibly find its place in the network. One of the main positive features of such consultations is that they are very international.

ACSI is a recognized international organization in the MK education field. Many missions rely heavily on ACSI to enable them to develop and run their schools. It is feasible that ACSI might have the ability to call for a meeting of mission leaders to discuss this need.

IMKEC could become an instrument in promoting school collaboration. We are not well known and this could be a liability especially if we wanted to "talk with leaders" from the non-sponsorship (803's) group of mission agencies. However, we are capable of publishing articles and disseminating information. We could encourage research and reporting of findings on strategic needs for MK education. We certainly could use some of our time at our yearly meeting to discuss initiatives and needs for new schools.

IFMA/EFMA has a triennial gathering that would be a splendid setting to get our message out. There was one attempt at getting the IFMA interested in what we were doing. It did not gain a hearing and we did not pursue it. Nevertheless, this grouping is still the largest gathering of mission leaders. We would most likely not get any platform time, but using this gathering with permission to distribute literature and/or recruit for involvement with an IMKEC sponsored meeting could hold some promise.

Conclusion

While much needs to be done, the track record of the 36 mission agencies doing MK education is remarkable. I am encouraged by the continuing progress of ACSI both with our

MK schools as well as the development of national Christian schools. This organization's potential in helping emerging missions and national Christians has only begun. The current activities in creating strategic partnerships in mission for church planting can only help us achieve greater collaboration for MK education. I believe the time is here for someone to take the initiative and set out a strategic plan for future MK education. The question is who will do this?

Bibliography

Allen, Roland
    1962   *Missionary Methods, St. Paul's or Ours?* Grand Rapids, MI: William B. Eerdmands Publishing Company.

Arbuckle, Gerald A.
    1990   *Earthing the Gospel: An Inculturation Handbook for the Pastoral Worker.* Maryknoll, NY: Orbis Books.

Baba, Panya
    1991   "A Two-Thirds World Perspective: A Case Study." In *Partners in the Gospel: the Strategic Role of Partnership in World Evangelism.* James H. Kraakevik and Dotsey Welliver, eds. pp. 109-116.

Baer, Christel
    1989   *The Development of a Contextualized Indigenous Education System.* Ed.D. Dissertation, Biola University.

Bandura, A. and R. H. Walters.
    1963   *Social Learning and Personality Development.* New York: Holt, Rinehart and Winston, Inc.

Barrett, D. B.
    1999   "Annual Statistical Table on Global Mission." in *International Bulletin of Missionary Research* 23 (January 1999), pp. 24-25.

Blomberg, Janet
    1995   "Directory of MK Schools," *Evangelical Missions Quarterly,* Volume 31 (April) (2): pp. 210-217.

Bosch, David
    1994   *Transforming Missions: Paradigm Shifts in Theology of Missions.* NY: Orbis Books.
    1995   *Believing in the Future: Towards a Missiology of Western Culture.* Pennsylvania: Trinity Press International.
    1997   Towards True Mutuality: Exchanging the Same Commodities or Supplementing Each Other's Needs. In *Supporting Indigenous Ministries.* Daniel Rickett and Dotsey Welliver, eds. pp. 52-64. Wheaton, IL: Billy Graham Center.

Broucek, David
    2000   "Perspectives: Thriving on Diversity." *Evangelical Missions Quarterly,* October, (36): 422-423.

Brown, John Seely, Allan Collins, and Paul Duguid
    1989   Situated Cognition and the Culture of Learning. *Educational Researcher.* 18: pp. 32-42.

Bruner, Jerome
    1996   *The Culture of Education.* Cambridge, MA: Harvard University Press.

Bush, Luis
    1991   In Pursuit of True Christian Partnership. In *Partners in the Gospel: The Strategic Role of Partnership in World Evangelism.* James H. Kraakevik and Dotsey Welliver, eds. Pp. 3-16.

Bush, Luisewis and Lutz, Lorry
    1990   *Partnering in Ministry: The Direction of World Evangelism.* Downers Grove, IL: InterVarsity Press.

Butler, Phillip
    1998   *The Power of Partnership,* Seattle, WA: InterDev.
    1999   "The Power of Partnership." In *Perspectives of the World Christian Movement.* Ralph Winter and Steven Hawthorne eds. 753-758. Pasadena: William Carey Library.

Butler, Trent C.
    1991   *Holman Bible Dictionary.* Nashville: Holman Bible Publishers.

Butterworth, George
    1993   "Context and Cognition in Models of Cognitive Growth." In *Context and Cognition: Ways of Learning and Knowing.* Paul Light and George Butterworth, eds. Hillsdale, NJ: Lawrence Erlbaum Associates, Publishers. Pp. 1-13.

Calvin, John
    1964   *Calvin's New Testament Commentary,* vol. X, trans by T.A. Smail. Grand Rapids: William B. Eerdmans Publishing Co., original English publication 1556.

Carr, Karen F.
    1993   Trauma and Post-Traumatic Stress Disorder: Recognition, Prevention, and Treatment for Missionaries, Presentation at the Mental Health and Missions Conference, Angola, IN (Nov. 20, 1993)

Chan, Polly
    1997-98   "Asian Children in MK Schools," Christian School Education, Volume 1, Issue 1.

Chasen, Michael
    2000   Keynote Panel Session. TechEd2000 Conference, Palm Springs, CA. March 9.

Cohen, Rosalie
    1969   "Conceptual Styles, Cultural Conflict, and Nonverbal Tests of Intelligence." *American Anthropologist* 71(5): 228-256.

Cole, Michael
    1992   "Culture in Development." *In Developmental Psychology: An Advanced Textbook,* Third Edition. Marc H. Bornstein and Michael E. Lamb, eds. Hillsdale, NJ: Lawrence Erlbaum Associates, Publishers, pp. 731-789.

Cole, Michael, John Gay, Joseph A. Glick, and Donald W. Sharp
    1971   *The Cultural Context of Learning and Thinking: An Exploration in Experimental Anthropology.* New York: Basic Books, Inc., Publishers.

Costas, Orlando
    1983   "Evangelical Theology in the Two Thirds World," in *Conflict and Context. Hermeneutics in the Americas.* A Report on the Context and Hermeneutics in Americas Conference Sponsored by Theological Students Fellowship and the Latin American Theological Fraternity, Tlayacapan, Mexico, November 24-29, Mark Lau Branson and C. René Padilla, eds. Grand Rapids: Eerdmans. 1986.

Cummings, David
    1994   "Some Aspects of Partnership in the Summer Institute of Linguistics and Wycliffe Bible Translators." In *Kingdom Partnership for Synergy in Mission,* Willliam D. Taylor. Pp. 205-208.

D'Andrade, Roy
    1984   "Cultural Meaning Systems." In *Culture Theory: Essays on Mind, Self, and Emotion.* Richard A. Shweder and Robert Alan LeVine. Cambridge, MA: Cambridge University Press.
    1995   *The Development of Cognitive Anthropology.* Cambridge, England: Cambridge University Press.

Davey, Andrew P.
    1999   "Globalization as Challenge and Opportunity in Urban Mission," *International Review of Mission* 88 (October) 351, pp. 381-389.

Davis, John R.
    1993   *Poles Apart: Contextualizing the Gospel*. Bangkok: Konok Bannasan. OMF Publishers.

Demorest, Gary W.
    1984   *The Communicator's Commentary: 1, 2 Thessalonians, 1, 2 Timothy, Titus*. Waco, TX: Word Publishers.

Dockery, David S.
    1992   *Holman Bible Handbook*. Nashville: Holman Bible Publishers.

Dodd, C. H.
    1936   The Present Task in New Testament Studies: An Inaugural Lecture Delivered in the Divinity School on June 2.

Dollar, Harold
    1996   *St. Luke's Missiology: A Cross-Cultural Challenge*. Pasadena, CA: William Carey Library.

Donohue, John W.
    1963   *Jesuit Education: An Essay on the Foundations of Its Idea*. New York: Fordham University Press.

Duraisingh, Christopher, ed.
    1996   "Perceiving Frontiers, Crossing Boundaries," Report of the Partnership in Mission Consultation of the Council of World Mission, *International Review of Mission*, 85 (April) 337, pp. 291-298, 295.

Dye, Wayne
    1986   "The View Ten Years Later." *Notes on Scripture in Use*. 86(11): 8-32.

Earle, Ralph
    1978   "1 Timothy," in *The Expositors Bible Commentary*, Frank E. Graebelein, Gen ed., vol. 11. Grand Rapids: Zondervan Publishing House.

Eddy, Elizabeth M.
    1997   "Theory, Research and Application in Educational Anthropology." In *Education and Cultural Process: Anthropological Approaches*. Third edition. George Dearborn Spindler. Prospect Heights, IL: Waveland Press, Inc. Pp. 5-25.

Elliston, Edgar
    1999   "Moving Forward in Missiological Education: Curricular Foundations." In *Teaching Them Obedience in All Things*. Edgar Elliston, ed. Pp. 240-278. Pasadena, CA: William Carey Library.

Engel, James F.
    2000   "Getting Beyond the Numbers Game." *Christianity Today* (August 7): 57.

Engel, James F. and Dyrness, William A.
    2000   *Changing the Mind of Missions-Where have We Gone Wrong?* Downers Grove: InterVarsity Press.

Erickson, Fredrick
    1982   "Taught Cognitive Learning in its Immediate Environments: A Neglected Topic in the Anthropology of Education." *Anthropology and Education Quarterly* 13(2):149-180.

Escobar, Samuel
    1999   "Global Scenario at the Conclusion of a Century," paper presented at the World Evangelical Fellowship International Missiological Consultation, Iguazu, Brazil, October 1999.

Falus, Iván
    1996   "Analysing Some Characteristics of Teaching Practice in Hungary." *European Journal of Teacher Education: Journal of the Association for Teacher Education in Europe* 19(3): 305-312.

Falwell, Jerry, ed.
    1983   *The Liberty Bible Commentary.* Nashville: Thomas Nelson Publishers.

Farley, Dr. Richard
    1992   "Post Traumatic Stress Disorder", *Contingency Preparation Seminar Manual.* Crisis Consulting International.

Fawcett, John
    2000   "Managing Stress and Trauma," *Complex Humanitarian Emergencies: Lessons from Practioners.* World Vision International.

Flory, Richard W. and Donald E Miller, eds.
    2000   *Gen X Religion.* N.Y: Routledge.

Ford, Rosalie
    1997   "Educational Anthropology: Early History and Educationist Contributors." In *Education and Cultural Process: Anthropological Approaches.* Third edition. Prospect Heights, IL: Waveland Press, Inc. Pp. 26-46.

Freire, Paulo
    1973   *Education for Critical Consciousness*. New York. The Continuum Publishing Company.

Friedman, Thomas L.
    1999   *The Lexus and the Olive Tree: Understanding Globalization*. NY: Farrar, Straus & Giroux.

Gardner, Howard
    1983   *Frames of Mind: The Theory of Multiple Intelligences*, Tenth-Anniversary Edition. New York: Basic Books.
    1984   "The Development of Competence in Culturally Defined Domains: A Preliminary Framework." In *Culture Theory: Essays on Mind, Self, and Emotion*. Richard A. Shweder and Robert A. LeVine, eds. Cambridge, UK: Cambridge University Press.

Gifford, P.
    1998   *African Christianity: Its Public Role*. Indianapolis: Indiana University Press, pp. 44-47.

Giroux, Henry A.
    1997   *Pedagogy and the Politics of Hope: Theory, Culture, and Schooling*. Boulder, CO: Westview Press.

Goulard, Elizabeth A.
    1996   Values, Assumptions, and Actions in an Administrative Team: a Symbolic Analysis of the Expression of Culture in One Community College Setting. October 11, 1999. Dissertation Abstracts Online; AAG9711830.

Gutek, Gerald L.
    1997   *Philosophical and Ideological Perspectives on Education*. Boston, MA: Allyn and Bacon.

Guthrie, Donald
    1957   *The Pastoral Epistles*. William B. Eerdmans Publishing Company.

    1970   *New Testament Introduction*. Downers Grove, IL.: InterVarsity Press.

Hamm, Peter
    1983   "Breaking the Power Habit: Imperatives for Multinational Mission," *Evangelical Missions Quarterly*, vol. 19 (3), 180-189.

Hanciles, J.
  1999   "Conversion and Social Change: A Review of the Unfinished Task in West Africa," paper presented at the Currents in World Christianity Consultation, Oxford (July).
Hansen, Judith Friedman
  1979   *Sociocultural Perspectives on Human Learning: An Introduction to Educational Anthropology.* Ingelwood Cliffs, NJ: Prentice Hall.
Hanson, A. T.
  1982   *New Century Bible Commentary: The Pastoral Epistles.* Grand Rapids: William B. Eerdmans Publishing Co.
Harland, Di
  1997-98   "Internationalizing the Curriculum: Geography," *Christian School Education,* Volume 1, Issue 2.
Hayward, Douglas
  1995   "Measuring Contextualization in Church and Mission." *International Journal of Frontier Missions.* 12(3): 135-138.
Hendrickson, William
  1979   *New Testament Commentary: Thessalonians, Timothy and Titus.* Grand Rapids: Baker Book House; originally published 1957.
Hesselgrave, David J.
  1995   Contextualization that is Authentic and Relevant. *International Journal of Frontier Missions.* 12(3): 115-119.
  2000   *Planting Churches Cross-Culturally: North America and Beyond.* Grand Rapids, MI: Baker Book House.
Hesselgrave, David J. and Edward Rommen
  1989   *Contextualization: Meanings, Methods, and Models.* Grand Rapids: Baker Book House.
Hinson, E. Glen.
  1971   "2 Timothy and Titus," in *The Broadman Bible Commentary,* vol. 11. Nashville: Broadman Press.
Hoogvelt, A.
  1997   *Globalization and the Postcolonial World: The New Political Economy of Development.* Maryland: John Hopkins University Press.
Hunter, Archibald M.
  1973   *Introduction to the New Testament.* Third revised edition. Philadelphia: The Westminster Press.

Huntington, S.
    1996   *The Clash of Civilizations and the Remaking of World Order.*
             NY: Simon & Schuster.

Hutchinson, Mark
    1998   "It's a Small Church after all," *Christianity Today* 42
             (November) 13, pp. 46-49.

Ignatieff, Michael
    1999   *The Warrior's Honour: Ethnic War and the Modern Conscience.*
             Toronto: Penguin Books.

Jacob, Evelyn
    1992   "Culture, Context, and Cognition." In *The Handbook of*
             Qualitative Research in Education. Margaret D. LeCompte,
             Wendy L. Millroy and Judith Preissle, eds. San Diego, CA:
             Academic Press, Inc.
    1997   "Context and Cognition: Implications for Educational Innovators
             and Anthropologists." *Anthropology and Education Quarterly*
             28(3): 3-21.

Kalu, O.
    1998   "Jesus Christ, Where are You?: Themes in West African Church
             Historiography at the Edge of the 21st Century," paper presented
             at the Global Historiography Consultation, Fuller Theological
             Seminary (April).

Kane, Herbert
    1976   *The Making of A Missionary.* Grand Rapids, MI: Baker Book
             House.
    1980   *Life and Work on the Mission Field.* Grand Rapids, MI: Baker
             Book House.

Kaplan, Robert
    1966   "Cultural Thought Patterns in Inter-Cultural Education",
             Language Learning 16/1, 4-14.
    1994   *Balkan Ghosts: A Journey Through History.*
    1995   *The Arabists: The Romance of an American Elite.*
    1997   *To the Ends of the Earth: From Togo to Turkmenistan, from Iran*
             to Cambodia, a Journey to the Frontiers of Anarchy.
    2001   *An Empire Wilderness: Travels into America's Future.*
    2001   *Eastward to Tartary: Travels in the Balkans, the Middle East,*
             and the Caucasus.

2001   *The Coming Anarchy: Shattering the Dreams of the Post Cold War.* New York, Random House.

Keyes, Larry
1999   "A Global Harvest Force." In *Perspectives of the World Christian Movement.* Ralph Winter and Steven Hawthorne eds. 744-747. Pasadena: William Carey Library.

Khor, M.
1996   "Global Economy and the Third World," in *The Case Against the Global Economy and for a Turn towards the Local.* J. Mander and E. Goldsmith, eds. San Francisco: Sierra Book Clubs, pp. 47-59.

Kirk, J. Andrew
1999   *What is Mission?: Theological Explorations* London: Darton, Longman and Todd Ltd.

Kolb, David A.
1984   *Experiential Learning: Experience as the Source of Learning and Development.* Englewood Cliffs, NJ: Prentice Hall PTR.

Kraakevik, James H., and Dotsey Welliver, eds.
1991   *Partners in the Gospel: the Strategic Role of Partnership in World Evangelism.* Wheaton, IL: Billy Graham Center, Wheaton College.

Kraft, Charles H.
1979   "Measuring Indigenity." In *Readings in Dynamic Indigenity.* Charles H. Kraft and Tom N Wisley eds. Pp. 118-152. Pasadena, CA: William Carey Library.
1991   *Christianity in Culture: A Study in Dynamic Biblical theologizing in Cross-Cultural Perspective.* Maryknoll, NY: Orbis Books.
1991   *Communication Theory for Christian Witness.* Maryknoll: Orbis Books.

Kraft, Charles H. and Tom N. Wisley
1979   *Readings in Dynamic Indigenity.* Pasadena, CA: William Carey Library.

La Belle, Thomas J.
1976   "An Anthropological Framework for Studying Education." In *Educational Patterns and Cultural Configurations: The Anthropology of Education.* Joan I. Roberts and Sherrie K.

Akinsanya, eds. New York: David McKay Company, Inc. Pp. 67-82.

Ladd, George
1974   *A Theology of the New Testament.* Grand Rapids: Eerdmans.

Lakoff, George
1987   *Women, Fire, and Dangerous Things. What Categories Reveal About the Mind.* Chicago: The University of Chicago Press.

Lea, Thomas D.
1992   *The New American Commentary: 1, 2 Timothy, Titus.* Vol. 34. Nashville: Broadman Press.

Lindquist, B.
1998   Language Learning and Membercare. Unpublished presentation, Second International Congress on Missionary Language Learning, October.

Lingenfelter, Judith
1999   A Model for Understanding the Roles that Teachers Play in the Classroom. Paper in Cross-cultural Curriculum and Teaching course, Biola University.

Lingenfelter, Sherwood
1991   "Mind, Emotion, Culture, and the Person: Perspectives from Cultural Anthropology and Scripture." In *Christian Perspectives on Being Human: A Multidisciplinary Approach to Integration.* J.P. Moreland and David M. Ciocchi, eds. Grand Rapids, MI: Baker Books. Pp. 117-143.
1998   *Transforming Culture: A Challenge for Christian Mission.* Grand Rapids, MI: Baker Book House.

Lodge, George
1995   *Managing Globalisation in the Age of Interdependence.* San Diego: Pfeiffer & Co.

Malcolm, T.
1998   "Meeting Deplores Globalization," *National Catholic Reporter,* 34 (April) 24, p. 9.

Mannheim, Karl
1952   *The Problem of Generations in Essays on the Sociology of Knowledge.* London: Routledge and Kegan Paul.

Maritain, Jacques
1962   *The Education of Man.* Notre Dame.

McAlister, Paul
    1995   "Teamwork to Finish the Task." In *Completing the Task Reaching the World for Christ.* Edgar J. Elliston and Stephen E. Burris, eds. Pp. 283-290. Joplin MS: College Press Publishing Company.
McCarthy, Bernice
    1980   *The 4MAT System: Teaching to Learning Styles with Right/Left Mode Techniques.* Barrington, IL: Excel, Inc.
    1986   *About Learning.* Barrington, IL: Excel, Inc.
Mercer, Neil
    1993   "Culture, Context and the Construction of Knowledge in the Classroom." In *Context and Cognition: Ways of Learning and Knowing.* Paul Light and George Butterworth, eds. Hillsdale, NJ: Lawrence Erlbaum Associates, Publishers. Pp. 28-46.
Merriam, Sharan B. and Rosemary S. Caffarella
    1991   *Learning in Adulthood: A Comprehensive Guide.* San Francisco: Jossey-Bass Publishers.
Mitchell, Jeffrey T. and George S. Everly
    1997   *Critical Incident Stress Debriefing* (2nd Edition Revised). Chevron Publishing Co.
Moats, James
    1991   "The Local Church as a Catalyst." In *Partners in the Gospel: The Strategic Role of Partnership in World Evangelism.* James Kraakevik and Dotsey Welliver, eds. Pp. 59-68.
Mukarji, D.
    1996   "Gospel and the Search for Identity and Community," *International Review of Mission*, 25 (January) 336, pp. 25-34.
Naisbett, John, ed.
    1991   *Megatrends 2000: Ten New Directions Transforming Our Lives.* NY: Warner Books.
Nevius, John
    1958   *Planting and Development of Missionary Churches.* Philadelphia: Reformed and Presbyterian Publishers.
Nida, Eugene
    1990   *Message and Mission.* Pasadena: William Carey Library.
Noddings, Nel
    1995   *Philosophy of Education.* Boulder, CO: Westview Press.

Olsen, Steve
    1996   *Czech Social Relations and Czech Academic Mentoring: With Implications for Christian Mentoring.* La Mirada, CA: Biola University.

Pate, Larry
    1991   "Partnerships: Path to the Future." In *Partners in the Gospel: The Strategic Role of Partnership in World Evangelism.* James H. Kraakevik and Dotsey Welliver, eds. Pp. 161-178.
    1991   "The Changing Balance in Global Mission," *International Bulletin of Missionary Research* 15 (April) 2, pp. 56-61.

Plummer, Alfred
    n.d.   "The Pastoral Epistles" in *The Expositor's Bible.* W. Robertson Nicoll, ed. Cincinnati: Jennings and Graham.

Ramseyer, R. L.
    1980   "Partnership and Interdependence," *International Review of Mission,* 69 (January), pp. 32-39.

Ratnam, Daisy G.
    1987   "Partnership in Practice: The Council for World Mission after Four Years," *International Review of Mission,* 76 (October), pp. 489-492.

Ribeiro, Claudio de Oliveira
    1999   "Has Liberation Theology died?: Reflections on the Relationship between Community Life and the Globalization of the Economic System," *The Ecumenical Review,* 51 (July) 3, pp. 304-314.

Richett, Daniel
    2000   *Building Strategic Relationships: A Practical Guide to Partnering with Non-Western Missions.* Pleasant Hill, CA: Klein Graphics for Partners International.

Riegel, Klaus F.
    1973   "Dialectic Operations: the Final Period of Cognitive Development." *Human Development* 16: 346-370.

Roazzi, Antonio and Peter Bryant
    1993   "Social Class, Context and Cognitive Development." In *Context and Cognition: Ways of Learning and Knowing.* Paul Light and George Butterworth, eds. Hillsdale, NJ: Lawrence Erlbaum Associates, Publishers. Pp. 14-27.

Robb, John D.
    1994   *Focus! The Power of People Group Thinking.* Monrovia, CA: MARC.

Robertson, A. T.
    1979   *Types of Preachers in the New Testament* (Paperback edition) Nashville: Broadman Press. Originally published 1922.

Russell, A. Sue
    1999   "Doing the Job Together: Integrating Bible Translation into the Framework of Contextualization." Paper present at Evangelical Mission Society Western Division Meetings. Biola University.

Rutherford, John
    1939   "Pastoral Epistles," *International Standard Bible Encyclopedia,* IV. Grand Rapids: William B. Eerdmans Publishing Co.

Sanneh, Lamin
    1989   *Translating the Message.* Maryknoll: Orbis Books.
    1990   "Gospel and Culture: Ramifying Effects of Scriptural Translation." In *Bible Translation and the Spread of the Church.* Philip C. Stine, ed. Pp. 1-23. Leiden: E.J. Brill.

Saucy, Robert
    1972   *The Church in God's Program.* Chicago: Moody Press.

Saul, J. S. and C. Leys
    1999   "Sub-Saharan Africa in Global Capitalism," *Monthly Review,* 51 (July/August) 3, pp. 13-30.

Schreiter, R. J.
    1990   "Mission into the Third Millennium," *Missiology,* 28 (1): 3-12.

Scott, Bruce
    2001   "The Great Divide in the Global Village," *Foreign Affairs* 80 (Jan/Feb) 1, pp. 160-177.

Shaw, Daniel R.
    1988   *Transculturation.* Pasadena: William Carey Library.
    1995   "Contextualizing the Glory." *International Journal of Frontier Missions.* 12(3): 155-160.

Shenk, David
    1994   *God's Call to Mission.* Scottdale: Herald Press.

Shenk, W.
    1993   "The Culture of Modernity as a Missionary Challenge," In *The Good News of the Kingdom: Theology for the Third Millennium.* Charles Van Engen, ed., NY: Orbis Books, pp. 192-199.

Shorter, Aylward
  1988   *Toward a Theology of Incarnation.* Maryknoll, NY: Orbis Books.
Shweder, Richard A.
  1991   *Thinking Through Cultures: Expeditions in Cultural Psychology.* Cambridge, MA: Harvard University Press.
Siewert, John A. and Valdez, Edna A., editors,
  1997   *Mission Handbook 1998-2000.* Monrovia, CA: MARC.
Skreslet, S.
  1995   "The Empty Basket of Presbyterian Mission: Limits and Possibilities of Partnership," *International Bulletin of Missionary Research,* 19 (July) 3, pp. 98-104.
  1999   "Impending Transformation: Mission Structures for a New Century," *International Bulletin of Missionary Research* 23 (January) 1, pp. 2-6.
Smalley, William
  1979   "Cultural implications of an Indigenous Church." In *Readings in Dynamic Indigenity.* Charles H. Kraft and Tom N. Wisley, eds. Pp. 31-51. Pasadena, CA: William Carey Library.
Smith, Christopher
  1995   "Mission Research and the Path to CD-ROM: Report on the Global Quest to Share Information." *International Bulletin of Missionary Research.* October 1995. Pp. 147-152.
Society of Jesus
  1954 *The Constitutions* IV, ch. 5, clarification E. Cited in George E. Ganss, *St. Ignatius' Idea of a Jesuit University.* Milwaukee: Marquette University Press.
Soós Pál
  1996   "University Adult Education in Hungary After the System Change in 1989." *International Congress of University Adult Education* 35(2): 77-87.
Spindler, George, D.
  1997   "The Transmission of Culture." In *Education and Cultural Process: Anthropological Approaches.* Third edition. George D. Spindler, ed. Prospect Heights, IL: Waveland Press, Inc., pp. 275-309.

Spindler, George, D. and Louise Spindler
- 1992 "Culture Process and Ethnology: An Anthropological Perspective." In *The Handbook of Qualitative Research in Education*. Margaret D. LeCompte, Wendy L. Millroy and Judith Preissle, eds. San Diego, CA: Academic Press, Inc., pp. 53-92.
- 1997 "Cultural Process and Ethnography." In *Education and Cultural Process: Anthropological Approaches*. Third edition. George, D. Spindler, ed. Prospect Heights, IL: Waveland Press, Inc., pp. 56-76.

Srinivasagam, R. Theidire
- 1994 Responding to Butler: Mission Partnership. In *Kingdom Partnership for Synergy in Mission,* William D. Taylor, pp. 31-42.

Steffen, Tom A.
- 1996 *Reconnecting God's Story to Ministry: Crosscultural Storytelling at Home and Abroad.* La Habra, CA: Center for Organizational & Ministry Development.
- 1997 *Passing the Baton: Church Planting that Empowers.* La Habra, CA: Center for Organizational & Ministry Development, Rev. ed.
- 1999 *Business as Usual in the Missions Enterprise.* La Habra, CA: Center for Organizational & Ministry Development.

Stott, John R.W.
- 1973 *The Message of 2 Timothy.* Downers Grove: InterVarsity Press.

Taber, Charles H.
- 1979 "The Limits of Indiginization in Theology." In *Readings in Dynamic Indigenity.* Charles H. Kraft and Tom N. Wisley eds. Pp. 372-399. Pasadena, CA: William Carey Library.

Taylor, William D.
- 1995 "Lessons of Partnership," *Evangelical Missions Quarterly.* 31(4): 406-415.

Taylor, William D., ed.
- 1994 *Kingdom Partnership for Synergy in Mission,* Pasadena, CA: William Carey Library.

Tennant, Mark and Philip Pogson
- 1995 *Learning and Change in Adult Years: A Developmental Perspective.* San Franciso: Jossey-Bass Publishers.

Toffler, Alvin
    1990   *The Third Wave.* New York: Bantam Books.

Tretham, Charles A.
    1959   *Studies in Timothy.* Nashville: Convention Press.

Vencer, Jun
    1994   "Control in Church/Mission Relationship and Partnership." In *Kingdom Partnership for Synergy in Mission,* William D. Taylor, pp. 101-118.

Vygotsky, L. S.
    1976   *Mind in Society: The Development of Higher Psychological Processes.* Cambridge, MA: Harvard University Press.

Wallraff, B.
    2000   "What Global Language?" *Atlantic Monthly,* November, pp. 52-66.

Walls, A. F.
    1996   "African Christianity in the History of Religions," in *Studies in World Christianity,* Vol 2, pp. 183-203.

Walvoord, John F. and Ray B. Zuck. eds.,
    1983   *The Bible Knowledge Commentary* (New Testament edition); Wheaton, IL: Victor Books.

Wilkins, Michael
    1999   "Teaching Them to Obey All Things: A View from the Matthean Account of the Great Commission." In *Teaching Them Obedience in All Things.* Edgar Elliston, ed. Pp. 32-66. Pasadena, CA: William Carey Library.
    2000   Personal communications.

Wolcott, Harry F.
    1987   "The Anthropology of Learning." In *Education and Cultural Process: Anthropological Approaches,* 2nd ed. George Spindler and Louise Spindler, eds. Prospect Heights, IL: Waveland Press, Inc., pp. 26-52.

Wright, George III.
    1992   *The New International Greek Testament Commentary: The Pastoral Epistles.* Grand Rapids: William B. Eerdmans Publishing Company.

Yohannan, K. P.
    1991   *Why the World Waits.* Lake Mary, FL: Creation House.

Appendix 1

Ken's "For Our Friends in Personnel" Electronic Newsletter
October 2000

Membercare FROM THE CRADLE TO THE GRAVE
Brent Lindquist, Ph.D., President, Link Care Center

One of my biggest frustrations over the current state of member and pastoral care, and U.S.-based missions in particular, of which I will direct my remarks, is the sense of a lot of things going on without a lot of coordinating efforts. I'm not suggesting that one agency become a super-agency and take over all of that. But I am suggesting that we need to look carefully at an integrated model, which may hopefully get at things in a more holistic and global fashion. I am talking about a continuum of care model for dealing with people's problems that runs the spectrum from life-adjustment issues to life-surviving issues.

The first stage of this continuous care model would look at the issue of membercare for the daily frustrations of normal life. I'm talking here about the frustration of managing your time, the frustration of dealing with little stressors as they come, of unforeseen issues, and of normal stuff that happens to us. Who should be the resources? I think ourselves, each other, and the people around us.

The next stage — there's no real mark where one stage stops and the next stage begins — is the issue of when problems become chronicized. That is, they don't go away quickly. In the first stage of daily life struggles, often just stopping doing that, doing something else, getting away for a couple of days, takes care of the problem. When problems become chronicized, they aren't really taken away or dealt with through denial, ignoring, or some quick and simple little strategy. When those kinds of things happen, I think the resources need to be a little bit more specific: focused readings, perhaps a contact with a pastoral care provider, maybe accessing some websites to look up some resources and actually setting up goals specifically to try to address those things. For example, in this stage would be somebody who finds they're feeling overly stressed out and the weekend away with the family didn't help things and they're really thinking they need to do something more. Taking some specific time out during their work week to do some stress-relieving activity, starting an exercise program, talking to the pastoral consultant or other nationals would be examples of treating this.

The next stage is where the problems haven't adapted to those kinds of issues, or a particularly thorny issue came up. For example, going through a heightened trauma or a crisis may necessitate doing a crisis-debriefing process. That needs to be done with the appropriate professionally trained and competent people. In addition, another issue is, for instance, feeling like you've done all the appropriate grief reading and talking, but you still can't get over the grief and it's impacting your daily functioning. At that point, I think some concerted efforts of seeing somebody and establishing some goals. An on-field counselor who is around may be able to do a short-term help, a pastoral care person who's around may be able to do some focus kind of helping in these areas, and probably up to this point many of these issues can be dealt with effectively on the field.

The next stage is where these problems are significantly impacting one's own and one's family's daily living. For example, a full blown depression may be impacting your ability to function and causing some serious questions. In addition, an overlooked issue in the desire to help people on the field is the impact of the person and their struggles on the larger missionary community. Sometimes we are so concerned about not removing people from the field that we end up causing pain and trouble beyond what we should be on the people around them. I think at this stage that people need to really look at what is in the best interest of the missionary family, the mission community and what resources are available. At this point often times a family should be removed, either at the beginning of furlough to allow closure, if a furlough is coming up soon; or if things are of such a crisis nature, as soon as possible, to a place like Link Care Center for off-site intensive consultation, care and treatment, and future planning.

Finally, the last stage — if there is a last stage — is where people are so debilitated that any sort of hope of dealing with things on the field or even in an out-patient setting are compromised because of the danger of the person to themselves and/or to others. In these cases, referral to a hospital program for stabilization and appropriate medications, etc.

A common component that is not necessarily out in front, but is often overlooked, is the whole issue of What is the purpose of all of this? It is my philosophy that the purpose of all of this — one of the basic purposes — is missionary effectiveness. Whatever we do needs to increase the effectiveness of that person, their surrounding teammates, and the missionary task as a whole. Certainly, in treating somebody for suicidal depression one isn't going to focus on how they can get through the daily chores. However, a treatment program that ignores how to apply the clinical learning in the cross-cultural setting is going to prevent that person from being truly ready to go back overseas.

One final thought on this is that any program needs to recognize the importance of incarnational ministry. I use the term *intentional incarnation* in that everything we do for a person, family or organization should help move people closer to the people whom they are called to serve. I think that's what sets membercare for missionaries and people in ministry apart from other membercare or generic counseling in that we need to have an over-arching purpose of moving people toward effectiveness and moving people closer to those they are called to serve. This includes taking into account during treatment the circumstances of the assignment and helping people to understand that there are probably a number of resources that can be met by nationals in their community. I'm not talking about intensive counseling, but I am talking about stress relievers, pastoral care, etc.

I'll stop here for now. Stay tuned.

www.ingramcontent.com/pod-product-compliance
Lightning Source LLC
Chambersburg PA
CBHW071232070526
44583CB00017B/2154